The most amazing stately homes in Britain

The most amazing stately homes in Britain

PUBLISHED BY
THE READER'S DIGEST ASSOCIATION, INC.
LONDON • NEW YORK • SYDNEY • MONTREAL

Contents

Introduction

Britain's stately homes are national treasures, each one with its own very special story. Explore their grounds, visit their gardens, walk their corridors and marvel at their glory with this amazing regional guide.

The 13th Duke of Bedford was a shy man. One imagines his apprehension, on opening day in 1955, as he watched the approach of two cars and a bicycle bringing the first visitors to Woburn Abbey. In 1953 he had inherited a neglected stately pile and a crippling burden of death duties. Was he to flatten the old place, as the Marquess of Lansdowne flattened the greater part of Bowood House in Wiltshire, or follow the lead of the Marquess of Bath at Longleat, welcoming the public and saving his estate for posterity? He chose the latter, and by the end of the first season had received 181,000 visitors, meanwhile coming into his own as a showman.

A 21st-century triumph

Britain's stately homes are one of the great success stories of the modern age. From the outbreak of the First World War the already declining country house way of life had become unsustainable. In a mood of deep gloom, in 1974, the V&A's 'Destruction of the Country House' exhibition named more than 600 properties demolished since 1870. Who would have imagined the thriving industry that stately home tourism would become in the 21st century, with National Trust visitor numbers rising by a million in 2011? Since Longleat and Woburn launched their safari parks, owners have found ever more novel ways to make their homes viable. They provide numerous diversions, but it is the houses themselves, above all, and their human stories, that speak to the imagination.

Abbreviations and websites

Many stately homes are owned or controlled by heritage organisations. The abbreviations listed below have been used throughout this book, at the end of the relevant entries.

- English Heritage (EH)
  www.english-heritage.org.uk
- The National Trust (NT)
  www.nationaltrust.org.uk
- Cadw (CADW)
  www.cadw.wales.gov.uk
- The National Trust for Scotland (NTS)
  www.nts.org.uk
- Historic Scotland (HS)
  www.historic-scotland.gov.uk

SCOTLAND
190-215

NORTHWEST
ENGLAND
142-155

NORTHEAST
ENGLAND
156-173

WALES
174-189

CENTRAL
ENGLAND
100-141

EAST
ANGLIA
86-99

LONDON
72-85

SOUTHWEST
ENGLAND
8-27

SOUTHERN ENGLAND
28-71

No country in the world has better access to so many fine residences. Hundreds are owned by English Heritage and the National Trust, but even cherished ancestral family homes are 'ours' insofar as they embody our shared culture, our history and heritage.

Today Britain is a nation enraptured with its past. We climb the stone stairs of medieval castles. We sigh over the architectural jewels of the Elizabethan age, gasp at gilded neoclassical mansions and looming Victorian Gothic edifices…. Through their great northern powerhouses we discover tales of the turbulent Nevilles, the Percys, the Howards. In these pages the reader is introduced to heroes and villains, hotheads, gamblers, traitors, lovers, losers, knights and knaves. Here can be found an obsessive collector who believed he was Bonnie Prince Charlie reincarnated, a decadent dancing earl whose car belched patchouli-scented exhaust, an irascible eccentric who invented a gun to shoot wasps….

Though ghost-hunting stately-home tourists may be disappointed of a glimpse of a lady in grey or a headless coachman, none can fail to sense the presence of the ancestors whose portraits line the walls of long galleries

and drawing rooms across the land. A day at a British stately home represents extraordinary value for money. These houses are repositories of art treasures and antiques. Their parks and gardens are matchless, their attractions thrillingly varied. They draw in the curious from all over the world, and are a source of national pride.

How to use this book

The map above shows the nine regions featured in this book. Each of them is sub-divided by county or, in the case of Scotland and Wales, by area. The numbers on each chapter map show the location of the stately homes and gardens.

Directions by road – or in the case of London by public transport – are listed at the end of each entry, together with the postcode for satnav users.

Almost all the featured houses are open to the public for part or all of the year: some are free to enter; others charge a fee. Check opening hours on websites or by phone before visiting as times of houses and gardens are subject to change according to year and season. In the case of privately-owned properties, always book ahead for tours.

Southwest England

Rolling hills and dramatic coasts are fitting locations for the Southwest's Tudor manors, Italianate palazzos and country mansions. In the mild climate, superlative subtropical gardens flourish.

Ilfracombe

A39

5

Barnstaple

Bideford

A386

A377

6

A39

DEVON
16-19

Bude

Okehampton

A30

A39

Launceston

A30

A386

9

Padstow

Bodmin Moor

Tavistock

Dartmoor National Park

4

1 Bodmin

Liskeard

Newquay

CORNWALL
10-13

2

A38

A30

A390

8

3

Plymouth

A38

St Austell

1

Truro

A390

6

St Ives

A3

5

Penzance

A394

Falmouth

7

Helston

Bristol

6

7

A38

A37

Bath

Weston-super-Mare

Mendip
Hills

Frome

A361

Minehead

2

A39

Somerset
Levels

A361

Exmoor
National
Park

Bridgwater

Glastonbury

A361

Taunton

3

M5

SOMERSET
24-27

A303

Shaftesbury

A396

1

A350

A354

8

4

A303

Tiverton

5

Yeovil

A30

2

7

7

Honiton

A303

6

Blandford
Forum

3

A31

Exeter

A30

9

A35

A37

DORSET
20-23

4

A348

A338

10

Lyme
Regis

A35

A35

Poole

Bournemouth

5

3

A35

Dorchester

4

Exmouth

Weymouth

Swanage

2

A38

A380

Torquay

A385

Dartmouth

alcombe

KEY

1 Main entry

County boundary

Motorway

Principal A road

CORNWALL

The old manors of Cornwall rise out of the landscape like natural features formed from the rock itself. Their gardens are a plant lovers delight, overflowing with rare and exotic flowering specimens.

❶ Pencarrow

In the 1850s the owner of Pencarrow was proud to show off to friends a rare specimen of the so-called 'Chile Pine', *Araucaria imbricata.* 'What a puzzle that would be for a monkey to climb,' remarked Charles Austin, a parliamentary lawyer. Thus it was here that the nickname 'monkey-puzzle tree' entered the language.

Pencarrow has been home to the Molesworth-St Aubyn family since John Molesworth was appointed auditor to the Duchy of Cornwall and Elizabeth I. The house of today is a model of Georgian elegance, a square, ochre, stuccoed Palladian mansion built around a predecessor, with 19th-century additions. There are guided tours of eleven rooms, filled with antiques and oriental porcelain, family photos and toys. They include the Library, and the Music Room, which has a rococo ceiling-painting of the four seasons. The collection of family pictures includes works by Reynolds, Raeburn, Scott and Birley.

The 20 ha (50 acres) of grounds include the Italian garden, rolling lawns, lake, woodland walks and an abundance of flowering plants and shrubs. Anyone approaching in spring by the mile-long carriage drive should prepare to be dazzled.
▶ *PL30 3AG. 4 miles NW of Bodmin off A389. Seasonal opening for guided tours.*

❷ Lanhydrock House

'Driving through an ancient gateway of dun-coloured stone, spanned by the high-shouldered Tudor arch, they found themselves in a spacious court, closed by a façade on each of three sides.' Thomas Hardy used Lanhydrock as his model for Endelstow in his novel *A Pair of Blue Eyes* (the original 'cliffhanger') in 1873. Seven years later, fire devastated the splendid 17th-century house, sparing only the north wing and its sensational 29m (95ft) Long Gallery with carved plasterwork ceiling. What visitors see today is a magnificent high-Victorian country house on land seized from an Augustinian priory in Henry VIII's Dissolution of the Monasteries in the 1530s.

Lanhydrock had been standing vacant, barely furnished, and had fallen into disrepair, when, in the mid 1800s, the 1st Baron Robartes of Lanhydrock and Truro engaged George Gilbert Scott to remodel and modernise it. When the building caught fire in 1881, he lost not just his home, but his wife, who succumbed to shock days later. Lord Robartes died the following year, and his son Thomas commissioned Richard Coad, who had worked under Scott, to rebuild the house once more, adding a Jacobean façade.

No sense of catastrophe is felt here, in one of the National Trust's most visited houses, where tours take in 50 rooms, above and below stairs. Manicured lawns, topiary and colourful plantings surround the house. The distinctive gatehouse described by Hardy, dating from the 18th century, survives. Vast acres of parkland extend down to the River Fowey.
▶ *PL30 5AD. 2 miles SE of Bodmin off B3268. NT. Seasonal opening of house; garden open all year.*

❸ Antony

This handsome 18th-century manor found unlikely fame in 2008 when it served as the background for the filming of the Mad Hatter's Tea Party in Disney's *Alice in Wonderland.* The estate of East Antony has been home to the Carew family for 600 years. Their most celebrated son, Richard Carew, was a child prodigy, sent to Oxford in 1566, aged just 14. In 1602 he published his Survey of Cornwall. His grandson, Alexander, 2nd Baronet, declared for Parliament in the Civil War but betrayed the cause. Off with his head! Alexander's half-brother, John, was a signatory to the death warrant of Charles I, for which he was hanged, drawn and quartered. The present house was built for Sir William Carew between 1711 and 1721 in parkland lapped by the estuaries of the Tamar and Lynher and the sea. A silvery-grey stone-faced central block is joined by colonnades to two brick wings. An imposing porch was added in the 19th century. The interior contains Dutch oak panelling, fine 18th-century furniture, and paintings, including work by Reynolds. There are portraits of Richard Carew, the ill-fated Alexander and Charles I. The grounds are partly the work of Humphry Repton, with topiary created by the Hon. Reginald Pole Carew, who redesigned the gardens in 1800.
▶ *PL11 2QA. 2 miles W of Torpoint on A374. NT. Seasonal opening of house and gardens.*

THE GATEHOUSE, LANHYDROCK HOUSE

❹ Cotehele

In the chapel of this lovely Tudor manor, the bell of the oldest turret clock in the UK strikes the hour – and yet time seems an illusion. The medieval manor of Cotehele came to the Edgcumbe family through marriage in 1353. It was rebuilt over the 30 years from 1490 by Sir Richard Edgcumbe and, after him, his son Piers, using local granite and slate. Within can be found old oak furniture, pewter, brass and suits of armour. Rooms are hung with astonishingly vivid tapestries, spared the bleaching glare of artificial light over the centuries. Terraced gardens step down to the Tamar. There are flower borders, a medieval stewpond and dovecote, ancient yew hedges and orchards planted with local apples and cherries. The estate corn mill has been restored to working order, and that venerable clock soldiers on as it has since 1489, without a face, and driven not by a pendulum but by weights.

▶ *PL12 6TA. 8 miles SW of Tavistock, off A390. NT. Seasonal opening of house; garden and estate open all year.*

❺ Caerhays Castle Gardens

The home of the Williams family is a Georgian fantasy, a 19th-century 'Norman' castle designed by John Nash, on a renowned shooting estate. In 1895 John Charles Williams of Caerhays quit a career in politics and contributed the equivalent of £300,000 towards the plant hunter George Forrest's forays. In return for his largesse Williams received seed from numerous plant species including Chinese rhododendrons,

THE WHITE ROOM, COTEHELE

magnolias, camellias and azaleas, beginning a programme of hybridisation that continues today. Caerhays is an important botanical research centre and at its most spectacular in spring. In 1970 it appeared as Manderley in the BBC's adaptation of Daphne du Maurier's Rebecca.
▶ *PL26 6LY. 10 miles SW of St Austell on minor roads. Close to Porthluney Cove, 1 mile E of Portholland. Seasonal opening.*

⑥ Trewithen House and Garden

The 'House of the Trees' has been home to the same family since 1715, when a lawyer, Philip Hawkins commissioned Thomas Edwards to rebuild it in the elegant 18th-century manner. Trewithen's walls are built of granite from the family's quarry, upon which a species of lichen produces a faint, becoming blush. Before the First World War, a descendant of Hawkins, George Johnstone, travelled in Australia, New Zealand and Japan, conceiving a passion for botany and determining to create a 'garden of excitement and discovery' within Trewithen's original landscape and woodlands. As a sponsor of great plant hunters he received many seeds from South-east Asia, Australasia, and North and South America, and set about creating an earthly paradise. Among the wonders are 24 champion trees, the tallest or widest of their species in the UK; the Magnolia Fountain, inspired by Trewithen's renowned blooms; the fabulous rose garden; a small museum of curios; and, in springtime, the Sycamore Avenue, awash with 3,000 varieties of daffodil, crocus and scilla.
▶ *TR2 4DD. On A390 11 miles SW of St Austell, 6 miles NE of Truro. Seasonal opening of house and gardens. Garden tours.*

⑦ Godolphin

The height of fashion in the 1600s, this once great house was long ago abandoned to fall into romantic ruin. The sweeping north range is distinguished by a colonnade of Doric columns and mullioned windows. Within are pieces of fine furniture and tapestries, some original to the house.

In the beamed dining room hangs a painting, by John Wooton, of the 2nd Earl's celebrated stallion Godolphin Arabian, a founder of today's Thoroughbred racing bloodstock. The garden, with its medieval layout, is of historic importance in Britain and in Europe.
▶ *TR13 9RE. 5 miles NW of Helston on minor roads, off B3302. NT. Seasonal opening of house and gardens; estate open all year.*

⑧ Port Eliot

In the Round Room at Port Eliot can be seen the intriguing 'Riddle Mural', painted by the late Robert Lenkiewicz, one of the most celebrated modern artists in the southwest. Some 12m (40ft) across, it was the work of nearly 30 years and is considered Lenkiewicz's masterpiece. How an Augustinian priory on the Tamar estuary, stripped and wrecked in the Dissolution of the Monasteries, passed into private hands is no riddle. It was begged from Henry VIII by John Champernowne, a Devon squire. In 1564 John Eliot bought the property from Champernowne's son and it has been in the family ever since.

The house that grew up here almost organically over centuries is home to Peregrine, the 10th Earl, and the Countess of St Germans. In the 18th century Port Eliot was extensively remodelled by Sir John Soane, and it underwent a further refit in the 1800s. With eleven staircases, 15 back doors, 82 chimneys and half-an-acre of roof, this is indeed a noble pile. Soane's conservatory annexe was part of the transformation of the Tudor ground floor. The drawing room was once the monastery refectory. The gardens, like the house, are full of surprises, including an 18th-century boathouse, orangery and secret maze. The Norman parish church beside the house was once the cathedral for Cornwall.
▶ *PL12 5ND. 8 miles W of Saltash on B3249, off A38. Limited seasonal opening of house and gardens.*

⑨ Prideaux Place

An Elizabethan manor of 81 rooms – 45 of them bedrooms, of which only six are habitable – has been in the same family for 14 generations. Begun by Nicholas Prideaux in the 16th century, and continued by Edmund Prideaux in the 18th century. The family were for Cromwell in the Civil War, but by great good fortune Edmund Prideaux's sister married Sir William Morice of Werrington, future secretary of state to Charles II, on the eve of the Restoration, securing a pardon for the family 'for crimes past, present and future'. Here, Elizabethan architecture meets Strawberry Hill Gothic to striking effect. Guided tours are offered of this lavishly furnished house, overlooking its deer park and Padstow harbour. The gardens, landscaped by Edmund Prideaux in the 1730s, are being restored with the help of Tom Petherick, who worked on the Lost Gardens of Heligan.
▶ *PL28 8RP. NW of Padstow town centre. Open all year for guided tours.*

From Elysian fields to an English country garden

The radical vision of the great landscape designers paved the way for future gardeners to indulge their own artistry.

Lancelot Brown (1716–83), had a singular gift for seeing 'great capabilities' in an estate. Nicknamed 'Capability Brown', he laid out more than 170 parks for wealthy aristocrats. One of the finest is at Petworth in Sussex, grazed by the oldest herd of fallow deer in England. Ralph Allen sought his advice in creating Prior Park near Bath. Brown's influence is pervasive. It is said he declined to work in Ireland because he had 'not finished England yet'.

Capability Brown was the greatest exponent but not the originator of the naturalistic English style. Charles Bridgeman (1690–1738) and William Kent (c.1685–1748) had already begun to conceive less formal designs, with garden buildings harking back to antiquity. Kent pioneered the classical Arcadian landscape inspired by the Grand Tour. Horace Walpole wrote about one of his creations in 1753: 'There is a scene of a small lake, with cascades falling down such a Parnassus! With a temple on the distant eminence; and there is such a fairy dale, with more cascades gushing out of the rocks! And there is a hermitage ... on the brow of a shady mountain, stealing peeps into the glorious world below!' Kent 'leaped the fence, and saw that all Nature was a garden'.

Bridgeman laid out the grounds at Rousham House in Oxfordshire, with meandering woodland walks and pools. Kent brought to it some of the glories of ancient Rome. Bridgeman, Kent and Brown all worked upon the landscape of Stowe in Buckinghamshire. It was probably Bridgeman who replaced garden walls with ditches here, so the eye might take in the wider prospect.

Satirical poet Alexander Pope laid down in verse the principles of English landscaping.

Consult the genius of the place in all;
That tells the waters or to rise, or fall;
Or helps th' ambitious hill the heav'n's to scale,
Or scoops in circling theatres the vale;
Calls in the country, catches opening glades,
Joins willing woods, and varies shades from shades,
Now breaks, or now directs th' intending line;
Paints as you plant, and, as you work, designs.

For the ambitious hill to scale the heavens, hundreds of tons of earth had to be moved. Brown created acres of rolling grassland with his signature snaking paths. Streams were dammed to fill serpentine lakes.

So closely did he emulate nature that some critics complained that the two were indistinguishable. At the same time John Constable declared: 'A gentleman's park is what I abhor. It is not beauty because it is not nature.'

Romance and ruins

After Brown's death, the Picturesque movement reflected another shift of mood with the surge of Romanticism. Landscapes were to be wilder, more dramatic, with enthralling ruins. Russell Page wrote in didactic verse of 'counterfeit neglect', 'art clandestine', and 'grace that springs from an unfetter'd mind'. He charged that Brown encouraged clients to 'tear out their splendid formal gardens and replace them with his facile compositions of grass, tree clumps and rather shapeless pools and lakes'.

Humphry Repton (1752–1818), Brown's most influential successor, reintroduced buildings to the landscape and made greater use of flowers. He worked extensively in Cornwall's Tamar Valley, notably at Antony and Port Eliot. The charming 'Red Books' he produced for his clients contained explanatory text, watercolours and overlays to show 'before' and 'after' views. His last book contained proposals for a variety of 'different kinds of garden' – anticipating the 'Mixed' or 'Gardenesque' style beloved of the Victorians.

The 19th century was a time of horticultural innovation. The first rock garden was established at Pencarrow, Cornwall – where the newly reintroduced Chile Pine acquired the nickname 'Monkey Puzzle'. Joseph Paxton created the Crystal Palace in 1851, and glasshouses and conservatories became must-haves. New species of rhododendrons were imported from the Himalayas.

The Edwardians craved a rural idyll, and a collaboration between Gertrude Jekyll and Sir Edwin Lutyens came to define the English garden. Their finest creation is at Hestercombe in Somerset, on the southern slopes of the Quantocks. Here the visitor sees not only their flower-filled formal garden, but a classic Georgian landscape with lakes and buildings, and a Victorian terrace and shrubbery. Landscape artists and gardeners in three periods consulted the genius of the place and came up with quite dazzlingly different answers.

PRIOR PARK

DEVON

Lush parkland, spectacular interiors and landscaped gardens characterise Devon's stately homes, built with love, ambition, extravagance and vision over eight centuries.

❶ Saltram House, Plymouth

This great Tudor manor set in parkland and clothed in Georgian finery played a starring role in the 1995 film of *Sense and Sensibility*. There could scarcely be a more suitable stand-in for the fictional Norland, the grand estate inherited by John Dashwood and his grasping wife, Fanny. Whether or not Jane Austen knew the house, she was certainly known of here. From Saltram in December 1815, Frances, Countess Morley, wrote to the author, thanking her for a presentation copy of *Emma*. Austen responded with gratitude, drawing reassurance from this approbation – while the countess confessed in private that she preferred *Pride and Prejudice* and *Mansfield Park*.

The first great house at Saltram was built for the Bagg family in the early 17th century. It was acquired by George Parker in 1712 and rebuilt by his son John and daughter-in-law Lady Catherine, incorporating rococo-style decorations. John II, later Lord Boringdon, brought in Robert Adam, whose Saloon, with its superb plasterwork ceiling by Joseph Rose, is regarded as one of his finest interiors, enhanced by Chippendale sofas and elaborate chandeliers hung in the 19th century. It is no stretch to imagine the great balls that were held here in 'the Age of Elegance'.

Sir Joshua Reynolds, a close friend of Lord Boringdon, advised on the acquisition of Saltram's art collection, which includes ten of his own works. John III, later Earl Morley, employed John Foulston to add an entrance porch and to create the library. His second wife, Frances, added to the art collection with watercolours and copies of Old Masters by her own hand. The ambitious earl overreached himself with industrial projects, and had to rent the house out between 1861 and 1884, as well as selling valuable paintings. Nevertheless, Saltram remained with the family until 1951, when house and contents were accepted by the Treasury in lieu of death duties.

It stands in gardens and a deer park, with a lime avenue, orangery, chapel and the Victorian Gothic Castle folly.
▶ *PL7 1UH. 3 miles E of Plymouth close to A38. NT. Seasonal opening for house; gardens and park open all year.*

❷ Ugbrooke House and Park

Crime writer Agatha Christie met her first husband, Archie, in 1912 at a concert held in this four-square, castellated house with Robert Adam interiors. Before the Dissolution of the Monasteries the estate of Ugbrooke belonged to the Church, but for the past 400 years this has been the home of the Lords Clifford of Chudleigh. At around the time that Adam was remodelling the house in the mid 18th century, Capability Brown worked his wonders on the park. The exquisite chapel and the library are fine examples of Adams's castle style. Furniture and furnishings, paintings, porcelain, military artefacts, tapestries and embroideries abound. Peacefully situated in the valley of the Ugbrook, which falls through a series of lakes, the park offers beautiful walks among mature trees, including giant redwood, with views over Dartmoor.
▶ *TQ13 0AD. 4 miles N of Newton Abbot off A380. Limited seasonal opening of house and gardens; private tours and events.*

❸ Castle Drogo

Tea magnate Julius Drewe had a modest ambition – to build the last great castle in England. The founder of the Home and Colonial Stores grocery chain, Drewe had sometimes stayed with his cousin Richard Peek, rector of Drewsteignton – named for Drogo de Teigne, a Norman baron who came over with William the Conqueror. He had already owned one mock castle, which he acquired in 1890 at age 33, but he dreamed of creating his own. When a genealogist traced his roots back to Drogo, confirming his nobility, the idea crystallised: he would site his castle in a commanding situation, where Baron Drogo himself might have built it. On the advice of William Hudson, proprietor of *Country Life,* he called in Edwin Lutyens to design his new stately home. Built entirely of granite, the castle is an arresting sight, rising up dramatically on a spur above the River Teign, a teasing mix of styles, part Norman, part Tudor (as are many genuine castles), complete with a portcullis, operated by the flick of a switch.

Despite its formidable exterior and hulking stone walls, the interiors have an almost intimate

STAIRCASE, POWDERHAM CASTLE

atmosphere; 17th-century tapestries seem quite at home. Lutyens designed much of the furniture, including one of the first fitted kitchens. (Replicas of the circular beech kitchen table are available from a company set up by Sir Edwin's grandson; sales generate royalties for the National Trust.) There is even a prototype power shower. In the Arts and Crafts-style gardens, also designed by Lutyens, plantings by Gertrude Jekyll still flourish, and there is a croquet lawn for visitors' enjoyment.
▶ *EX6 6PB. 14 miles W of Exeter, signed from A382 and A30. NT. Castle and garden open for most of year.*

❹ Powderham Castle

Five centuries before Julius Drewe dreamed of building a castle (left), Sir Philip Courtenay had much the same idea. In 1391 he established Powderham in a deer park beside the River Exe. The Manor of Powderham came into the Courtenay family with the marriage of Margaret de Bohun to Hugh de Courtenay, son of the 1st Earl of Devon. Six hundred years on, this is home to the 18th Earl and Countess, although the earldom has at times been forfeit and re-created. The castle built for Philip – one of 17 children of that marriage – had an archetypal medieval long hall with six towers, of which only one is still standing. In the Civil War, the castle came under siege as a Royalist stronghold and suffered serious damage. During restoration in the 18th century, the Great Hall was converted to accommodate the Staircase Hall and Marble Hall, with two floors above. Rococo plasterwork on the hall and staircase walls was commissioned by Sir William Courtenay, later 1st Viscount Courtenay of Powderham. James Wyatt designed the Music Room for William, 3rd Viscount and laid down the biggest carpet Axminster had ever made – before the Prince Regent, the future George IV, as was his spoilt way, demanded a bigger one. When William Courtenay became 10th Earl of Devon in 1835, he engaged Charles Fowler to turn the clock back and endow Powderham with 'a character consistent with an ancient castle' – a makeover that included the addition of the State Dining Room and medieval-style gatehouse.

This is the castle that the visitor sees today, set in a lush deer park. Inside, tour guides tell tales of Courtenay family fortunes – of ancestors who found and lost favour with monarchs and paid the price. Wonderful views, 600 deer and teeming wildlife enhance the pleasure.
▶ *EX6 8JQ. 7 miles S of Exeter on A379. Seasonal opening of castle and grounds; usually closed on Saturdays.*

THE HARNESS ROOM, ARLINGTON COURT

❻ Hartland Abbey

The family home of Sir Hugh and Lady Stucley, the 12th-century Hartland Abbey was the last monastery to be dissolved by Henry VIII, in 1539. The first private owner was William Abbot, Sergeant of the Wine Cellar at Hampton Court. The present owner's great grandfather, Sir Hugh Stucley, changed his name from George Buck when he became a baronet, reclaiming a much older family name. The Queen Anne-style makeover to the southern end was ordered by Paul Orchard in 1704, and in the 1770s Paul Orchard II oversaw major rebuilding. Down came the chapel and Great Hall. The house was reduced to the height of the cloisters and remodelled, receiving a friendly Strawberry Hill Gothic façade and two prominent bay windows. Sir George Gilbert Scott designed the Alhambra passage and its vaulted, stencilled ceilings, for Sir George Stucley.

In the abbey's sheltered valley situation, amid an Area of Outstanding Natural Beauty, peacocks and guinea fowl wander the grounds, as donkeys and Black Welsh Mountain sheep crop the grasses. Gertrude Jekyll came here often as a guest and advised Marion, Lady Stucley, on the creation of the baronet's bog garden, Victorian fernery and camellia garden. Staff were depleted in the Great War, and Nature went on the march until the 1950s, when Sir Dennis and Lady Stucley began planting camellias, hydrangeas and eucyrphias.
▶ *EX39 6DT. 16 miles W of Bideford on minor road to Hartland Quay. Limited seasonal opening of abbey, gardens and grounds.*

❼ Killerton House

Sir Richard Acland was a man of principle who put his money where his morals were. This Georgian country house had been the Acland family home until Sir Richard, a Labour politician and a founder of both the Common Wealth Party and CND, handed it over to the National Trust in 1944. It was one of the greatest gifts the Trust had ever received, a house built in the 1770s, set in 2,590ha (6,400 acres) of parkland. The estate included 20 farms, 200 cottages and an Iron Age hillfort.

The Aclands acquired Killerton at the time of the Civil War. The main block of the house was built by the Essex architect John Johnson as a 'temporary residence' or 'stop gap' for Sir Thomas and Elizabeth Dyke Acland, with the intention – never realised – that it should be replaced with a grand mansion by James Wyatt. The horses were more stylishly accommodated, in a stable block

❺ Arlington Court

What better way to tour the grounds of this Regency house than by taking a carriage ride? Arlington Court's stables are home to the National Trust's Carriage Museum and some beautiful working horses. The neoclassical house was built for Colonel John Palmer Chichester. His grandson Sir Bruce Chichester ordered major additions in 1865. It contains the family collection of antique furniture and memorabilia. The National Trust describes it as 'a complete family estate'. The tea room uses fruit and vegetables from the walled kitchen garden and flowers are cut for the house.
▶ *EX31 4LP. 7 miles NE of Barnstaple on A39. NT. Seasonal opening of house and carriage museum; grounds open all year.*

with a cupola above pedimented arches. The interior received a makeover in the 1890s, and in 1924 after a fire. It is presented – in a slightly Mary Celeste fashion – as the home of the dispossessed family as they would have lived in it between the First and Second World Wars.

The spectacular hillside garden was laid out by the great landscape designer John Veitch at the time the house was built, and the grounds are home to species brought to England by plant hunters dispatched by Veitch to far corners of the world.

▶ *EX5 3LE. 6 miles NE of Exeter close to M5. NT. Seasonal opening for house; park and garden open all year.*

❽ Knightshayes Court

'Dear Burges, ugly Burges, who designed such lovely things – what a duck.' So the architect of this Victorian Gothic country house was described by Lady Bute, wife of his patron. Childish, capricious, extravagant, William Burges began work on Knightshayes in 1869 for Sir John Heathcote-Amory, grandson of John Heathcote, whose revolutionary lace-making machine sparked the Luddites' revolt. The house was completed by 1874, although not entirely to Burges's designs. After he and Heathcote-Amory fell out, partly over budget (extravaganzas don't come cheap), Burges was replaced by John Dibblee Crace. A massive tower was planned for the west end but only its base was built. Parts of Burges's work were obscured or removed. There is, though, much of his eccentric genius to enjoy here. The 'medieval' Great Hall comes complete with minstrels' gallery. Smoking room, billiard room, drawing rooms and boudoirs are so richly decorated, the eye is constantly diverted. Burges himself was so myopic that he once mistook a peacock for a person but he knew a hawk from a handsaw when it came to design. Exquisite carvings include the seven deadly sins.

The grounds are no less of a pleasure, with whimsical topiary, a woodland garden, stables and a walled garden planted with fruit and vegetables.

▶ *EX16 7RQ. 2 miles N of Tiverton off A396 Bampton road. NT. Seasonal opening of house and gardens (closed on Fridays).*

❾ Cadhay

This is among the country's top ten manor houses, in the view of *Country Life*. It was begun in 1550 on the site of an earlier house, by John Haydon, and built in a U shape. John Haydon's nephew Robert added the Long Gallery, enclosing the central courtyard, which

became known as the Court of the Sovereigns, due to the carved images of four Tudor monarchs above the doors (Henry VII doesn't get a look in). The Long Gallery dates from the reign of Elizabeth I.

Rupert Thistlethwayte has spent a decade restoring and updating the house, introducing contemporary furniture of his own design to mix with antique pieces. The visitor approaching by an avenue of lime trees will be greeted by the prospect of a pure Tudor building with tall chimneys, leaded windows and stone mullions. Cadhay is run today as a guest house offering bed and breakfast, but there are opportunities to see both house and grounds and to visit the tea room.

▶ *EX11 1QT. 1 mile NW of Ottery St Mary town centre. Friday openings in season.*

❿ Great Fulford

The Fulfords have a history of raising their heads above the parapet. Sir Baldwin de Fulford, crusader, warrior and ardent Lancastrian, was hanged, drawn and quartered by Yorkists in the Wars of the Roses. Staunch Royalists in the Civil War, the family saw their home besieged, garrisoned and left in partial ruins. Often with more dash than cash, they have improved their grand house over centuries, and it is no surprise that Francis, 23rd Fulford of Great Fulford, writer and broadcaster, delivers such colourful polemics. Here he is getting British heritage and government off his chest: 'Great Fulford is listed Grade I by English Heritage and as such is considered by them to be an important part of the National Heritage. This is odd considering that the "Nation" has had no part in creating either the house or the landscape surrounding it. In fact the "Nation", in the guise of Parliament, has done its best to destroy it, either by use of cannon in the Civil War or, more recently, by punitive taxation.'

Well, quite. Great Fulford has been the family seat for 800 years. The house was substantially built in the 1530s and 1570s by Sir Thomas, son of Sir Baldwin, who prospered from his support of Henry VII. Repairs to the damage wrought by roundheads were ordered by Colonel Francis Fulford in the late 1600s. In the 18th century a lake and new drives in the park were added, and in 1805 the house was remodelled. The latest restoration has been in progress since 1910. Tours conducted by Fulford or his wife are 'by definition unique', promising a very personal way to explore a stately home.

▶ *EX6 7AJ. 10 miles W of Exeter just S of A30 near Cheriton Bishop. Private tours only, by appointment.*

SOUTH-WEST ENGLAND

DORSET

The county's treasures include Sir Walter Raleigh's beloved Sherborne, a home filled with Egyptian trophies and 'the nation's finest manor house', according to the magazine *Country Life*.

MAPPERTON HOUSE

❶ Mapperton House and Gardens

The home of the Earl and Countess of Sandwich, in its valley setting, is 'the nation's finest manor house' in the view of *Country Life.* Architectural historian Nikolaus Pevsner noted that, 'there could hardly be a more enchanting manorial group'. Elizabethan in origin, the house was remodelled in the 1660s for Richard Brodrepp, who added two stable blocks and a dovecote. Only the gabled north wing, with its chimneys and finials, reveals the building's Tudor beginnings.

A later Richard Brodrepp added the balustrade, Georgian staircase and north front in the 1700s. Built of Ham stone and completely at one with the landscape, Mapperton is surrounded by gardens, including an Italianate plot laid out by a former owner, Ethel Labouchere, as a memorial to her husband, with grottoes, fountains and stone ornamental birds and animals.

▶ *DT8 3NR. 5 miles N of Bridport off A3066. Limited seasonal opening of house, and tours by appointment; seasonal opening of gardens.*

❷ Sherborne Castle

After a spell in the Tower with his new wife in 1591, for the crime of marrying without Elizabeth I's permission, Sir Walter Raleigh must have found it sweet to bring his bride to Sherborne. Sir Walter's biographer, John Aubrey, tells how the great explorer, poet, smoker and spy saw Sherborne on a trip to Plymouth, fell for its charms and 'begged it as a bon' from the queen. The plan was to renovate a 13th-century castle on the site, but instead he built what Aubrey describes as 'a delicate Lodge in the Park of Brick; not big, but very convenient ... A place to retire from the Court in Summer time, and to contemplate, etc.' When Raleigh again languished in the Tower, charged with treason, James I leased Sherborne to Robert Carr.

This has been home to the Digby family since diplomat Sir John Digby bought it in 1617. He added four wings, staying faithful to Raleigh's style, with square-headed windows, balustraded roofs and heraldic beasts.

The Old Castle was held by the Digbys for the king, and demolished by Cromwell's men in the Civil War. Its ruins stand in grounds landscaped by Capability Brown, who created the 20ha (50 acre) lake in 1753.

Through all his travels, Raleigh had an abiding love for Sherborne, writing to his family, in his Bible, on the eve of his execution: 'Beg my dead

body, which living is denied you; and bury it either in Sherborne or Exeter Church.' His final resting place is St Margaret's, Westminster.
▶ *DT9 5NR. Castle ½ mile SE of town centre. Seasonal opening of house and garden.*

❸ Kingston Lacy

William John Bankes was an explorer, adventurer and Egyptologist, driven into exile after being caught in flagrante with a guardsman in Green Park. He was a friend of Lord Byron and of Sir Charles Barry, architect of the Palace of Westminster. William John's ancestor Sir Ralph Bankes built Kingston Lacy between 1663 and 1665, on a site chosen by Sir John Bankes, his father, after the destruction of the family's Corfe Castle in the Civil War. It was designed by Sir Roger Pratt with interiors by John Webb in the style of Inigo Jones. Using a handsome inheritance, William John commissioned Barry to remodel the building as a grand palazzo. When the scandal forced him to flee abroad, he directed operations at long range through his sister.

Although he could not live in his spectacular creation, William John endowed it with antiquities brought from the Middle East and the Orient, including the largest private collection of Egyptian artefacts in the UK – among them the obelisk from Philae, separated from its twin, that stands in the grounds. He also acquired Rubens' portrait of Maria Di Antonio Serra, which hangs here with works by Van Dyck, Titian, Murillo and Breughel. The gilded ceiling in the Spanish Room is from the Contarini Palace in Venice. In the Library are the giant keys of Corfe Castle, which was torn down by Cromwell's men after Lady Bankes had held it under siege while her husband was away fighting for the king. From the white Carrara marble staircase, statues of Sir John, 'Brave Lady Mary' and Charles I look out onto the gardens. Within an estate of 3,443ha (8,500 acres) stands the Iron Age hillfort of Badbury Rings.
▶ *BH21 4EA. 2 miles NW of Wimborne Minster, S of B3082. NT. Seasonal opening of house; gardens open all year.*

❹ Deans Court

The former Deanery of Wimborne Minster has been home to the Hanham family since 1548, and is now enthusiastically lived in and managed by William and Ali Hanham. Their combined passion for art and antiques drives a programme to conserve the house and its contents. The house has its origins in the reign of Edward the Confessor, before the Norman

Conquest, although the present redbrick building dates from 1725. In the historic gardens visitors will find a stream-fed Saxon fishpond, apiary, orchard, rose garden and herb garden. The kitchen garden is enclosed by a serpentine 'crinkle-crankle' wall. Among many interesting and venerable trees are a Tulip tree planted by an ancestor in 1607, and a magnolia planted in 1870. The Hanhams stage events, such as an annual food festival, and offer courses and tours (by prior appointment).
▶ *BH21 1EE. Deans Court Lane, Wimborne Minster town centre.*

❺ Highcliffe Castle

Lord Stuart de Rothesay was a distinguished diplomat, but he cut no ice with Augustus Pugin. In 1831, Lord Stuart planned a fantasy castle in a romantic clifftop setting where his grandfather, the 3rd Earl of Bute, had built a house that had been lost to landslips. He engaged William John Donthorne as his architect and shipped in materials salvaged from the 16th-century Grande Maison at Les Andelys, medieval stonework and carved oak panels from the ruins of a Benedictine abbey at Jumièges, and stained glass from churches in France, Germany, Switzerland and Belgium.

However, experiencing doubts about Donthorne's work in progress, his lordship called in Pugin, that great exponent of the Gothic style, to consult on the project. Arriving in the afternoon, Pugin rapidly sketched out a revised plan, which he presented over dinner, urging alterations that would entail some demolition of newly erected stonework. He was aged just 24 and at the height of his powers. Lord Stuart hummed. He ha'ed. He said he'd sleep on it. Then, rising early for a breakfast meeting, he found that the bird had flown. Pugin had left in high dudgeon aboard the 6am coach.

The Gothic Revival 'castle' completed to Donthorne's design has been described as 'arguably the most important surviving house of the Romantic and Picturesque style of architecture'. Sadly, like its predecessor, it fell into ruin, after two fires in the 1950s and 1960s. The French furniture and furnishings are lost, but in 1977 Christchurch Borough Council stepped in to buy Highcliffe and renovate it. It now houses a heritage centre, stages exhibitions and events, and some rooms are available for private hire.
▶ *BH23 4LE. Rothesay Drive, Highcliffe. 3 miles E of Christchurch. Castle and visitor centre closed in January; grounds open all year.*

MINTERNE HOUSE

❻ Minterne House

The home of the Churchill and Digby families since 1620 succumbed to dry rot and was rebuilt in 1905 by Leonard Stokes. Now seat of the 12th Lord Digby, it stands amid parkland in the Cerne Valley, in 'a corner of paradise'. A founder of the Arts and Crafts movement, Stokes felt no constraint in designing a house that mixed architectural styles. From the south front it is an Elizabethan manor house with leaded windows and gables, while the windows that look from the north front are Gothic. The interiors are classical Georgian. The house is not open to the public but is available for weddings, private parties and other events.

The valley was landscaped in the 18th century in the style of Capability Brown. In the gardens there is a chain of small lakes, waterfalls and streams. The times to see them are in spring, when the bulbs are in bloom, when the rhododendrons are flowering, and in the season of mists and mellow fruitfulness, when the foliage takes on spectacular colour.

▶ *DT2 7AU. 10 miles N of Dorchester on A352. Seasonal opening of gardens.*

❼ Edmondsham House

This Tudor manor house with Georgian additions stands in 2.5ha (6 acres) of gardens and has been in the same family since the 1500s. The owner, Mrs Julia Smith, personally conducts tours. Among the curiosities are a medieval cockfighting pit, Victorian dairy and stable block and a walled kitchen garden that has been in use for more than a century.

▶ *BH21 5RE. 6 miles W of Fordingbridge on B3078. Limited seasonal opening of house and garden; private tours by appointment.*

COTHAY MANOR

SOMERSET

Fragrant gardens with vivid plantings surround mansions of exquisite character, from homes of Gothic magnificence to an Elizabethan manor once described as 'the most beautiful house in England'.

❶ Cothay Manor

A fine example of a medieval moated manor, Cothay was begun in the 14th century and is today the home of Alastair and Mary-Anne Robb. Since 1993 the Robbs have undertaken sympathetic restoration, with period furniture and fabrics. Visitors taking a tour see a series of historic rooms, including the Oratory, Georgian Hall and Great Chamber. There are stained-glass windows, 15th-century wall paintings and 17th-century panelling.

The surrounding grounds include a yew walk, bog garden, cottage garden, courtyards and river walk. Red and white roses have been planted since the 15th century to celebrate the end of the Wars of the Roses.

▶ *TA21 0JR. 5 miles W of Wellington on minor roads. Seasonal opening of gardens; tours by appointment all year.*

❷ Dunster Castle

Rising above wooded hillsides, the former family home of the Luttrells looms dramatically against the sky. It was in the family for more than 600 years, but its history goes back much further, to its beginnings as a Norman motte-and-bailey castle built by William de Mohun after the Conquest of 1066. The castle came under siege from both sides in the Civil War as Thomas Luttrell flip-flopped between the Parliamentary and Royalist causes. The future Charles II stayed here in May 1645. The words 'God save the King' inscribed on a warming pan recall this visit.

Little remains of the medieval stronghold this once was. When he inherited the Dunster estates in 1867, George Luttrell ordered a remodelling, employing Anthony Salvin to lend it a more Gothic aspect. Salvin added a large square tower on the west side, and a small tower on the east for an asymmetrical effect. Windows of different period styles were installed with the idea that the castle would appear to have grown up over centuries. Victorian mod cons included central heating and updated kitchens. Rooms were knocked through to create the Outer Hall, a first-floor gallery, billiard room, drawing room and library. Casualties included 17th-century panelling stripped from the parlour. Works of art were brought in along with a stuffed polar bear and a brace of Italian cannons.

Geoffrey Luttrell took up residence in 1920 and decorated some rooms in the style of the day. He commissioned a polo ground and enjoyed shooting and hunting. In 1976, Colonel Luttrell gave to the National Trust a Norman-cum-medieval castle transformed into a grand country home. At its heart is a considerably altered Jacobean manor house.

▶ *TA24 6SL. 2 miles E of Minehead on A39. NT. Seasonal opening of castle; garden and park open all year.*

❸ Hestercombe Gardens

One of the most fruitful cross-fertilisations in gardening history was that between the minds of Gertrude Jekyll and her protégé Edwin Lutyens. They collaborated on at least 70 projects, and exchanged ideas on many more, establishing a style that would define the English garden. A Lutyens-Jekyll garden brimmed with hardy shrubs and overflowing herbaceous borders within classical architecture of steps and balustraded terraces. Jekyll was renowned for her colour harmonies and for planting in drifts. Their Edwardian garden at Hestercombe is regarded as their finest creation. By the time Jekyll and Lutyens got to work here, she was nearly blind. He held her in affection and called her Aunt Bumps. Theirs is one of three historic gardens on this site on the southern slopes of the Quantock Hills. The Landscape Garden, rediscovered in 1992, was the creation of Coplestone Warre Bampfylde, a soldier and artist, in 1750. It was said that he had 'the finest taste for laying out ground of any man in England' (which was somewhat to overlook Lancelot 'Capability' Brown). To this was added a Victorian terrace and shrubbery.

The gardens are overlooked by a house built in the 16th century for the Warre family, enlarged and altered in the 1700s and refronted in 1875 for Edward Portman, 1st Viscount Portman. It is in a mix of styles, but might be called 'Italianate', and both house and gardens derive character from the use of dark pink diorite rock, with which the building is faced. The gardens are open all year; there is no public access to the house but it is available to hire for weddings, parties and conferences.

▶ *TA2 8LG. 4 miles NE of Taunton on minor roads off A361.*

❹ Barrington Court

A Tudor manor house begun in the reign of Henry VIII, with a 17th-century stables court, was acquired by the National Trust, in 1907. It had fallen into disrepair after a fire in the early 1800s, but following repairs by Alfred Hoare Powell, the Trust leased it to Colonel A.A. Lyle, of Tate & Lyle, in the 1920s. He turned the house around, and renovated the stable and coach block, built by William Strode and known as Strode House. Barrington Court stands empty now, but a sprung dance floor recalls the time when the Lyles entertained in style. There is the further considerable attraction of an Arts and Crafts-style garden commissioned by Lyle, for which Gertrude Jekyll planned the plantings (see Hestercombe Gardens, left). Presented as a series of walled rooms, it includes a white garden, a rose and iris garden and a lily garden. The restaurant in Strode House is supplied with fruit and vegetables from the kitchen garden.

▶ *TA19 0NQ. 4 miles NE of Ilminster on minor roads. NT. Seasonal opening of house and garden.*

❺ Montacute House

If the empty Barrington Court strikes a note of melancholy, here is a house to lift the spirits, a magnificent Elizabethan mansion hung with portraits and furnished in high style. More than 60 fine Tudor and Elizabethan portraits from the National Portrait Gallery collection are exhibited. The state rooms display period furniture and textiles, including enchanting samplers collected by Douglas Goodhart and bequeathed to the nation.

Grade I listed and a Scheduled Ancient Monument, Montacute is a superb example of a house built at a time when Renaissance classical architecture was the new fashion and Gothic was in decline. Once described as 'the most beautiful Elizabethan house in England', it was begun in around 1598 for Sir Edward Phelips, Master of the Rolls, who opened the indictment against Guy Fawkes. It was designed on the E plan that was a tribute to the Virgin Queen, probably by William Arnold, and topped with Dutch gables and soaring chimneys. The honeyed Ham

SOUTH WEST ENGLAND

Hillstone exterior glows. So many are the glinting bands of windows that, as at Hardwick Hall (see page 104), it appears 'more glass than wall'. A strong Italian influence may be felt. In the second-floor Long Gallery, in niches that divide the windows, there are statues of the Nine Worthies in Roman attire, an idea borrowed from the Palazzo degli Uffizi in Florence.

The garden planting was the creation of Ellen Phelips, who lived at Montacute from the 1840s until 1911, working with her gardener, a Mr Pridham. The 'melted' shape of a giant clipped yew hedge was inspired by the effects of a freak snowfall. In the East Court, vivid plantings by Phyllis Reiss of neighbouring Tintinhull replaced the softer palate of Vita Sackville-West in 1951.

▶ *TA15 6XP. 4 miles W of Yeovil on A3088. NT. Seasonal opening of house; gardens and park open all year.*

❻ Clevedon Court

Here is a family home visited by Alfred Tennyson and William Makepeace Thackeray, who used it as his model for Castlewood in his novel *The History of Henry Edmond*. A manor house begun by Sir John de Clevedon in the early 1300s, it has retained its medieval character through serial alterations. In 1709 the house became the property of Abraham Elton, who was succeeded by four further Sir Abrahams. From 1761, Sir Abraham Isaac Elton, 4th Baronet, ordered extensive changes in the popular Victorian Gothic Revival style. Sir Charles Abraham Elton, 6th Baronet, was a writer, contributing to *The Gentleman's Magazine*. His nephew, Arthur Hallam, died prematurely and was the subject of Tennyson's 'In Memoriam' (the lines ''Tis better to have loved and lost / Than never to have loved at all' – is said to have brought solace to the widowed Queen Victoria). Tennyson came to Clevedon in 1850, the year that 'In Memoriam' was published and he became Poet Laureate. In 1881, the enterprising Sir Edmund Elton, 8th Baronet, set up the Sunflower Pottery in the grounds and the rich blue, green and crackle-glazed Elton ware was soon in demand in America. His grandson Sir Arthur was a pioneer documentary filmmaker, supervisor of films for the Ministry of Information in the Second World War.

The house was presented to the nation in lieu of death duties, it remains the Eltons' family home and contains many family portraits as well as Elton ware.

▶ *BS21 6QU. 1 mile E of Clevedon town centre, close to J20 of M5. NT. Seasonal opening.*

❼ Tyntesfield

Where there's muck, there's money. Here is a spectacular Victorian Gothic pile built by William Gibbs with a fortune made from sales of guano. Gibbs acquired a Regency house, Tyntes Place, in 1843, and splashed out £70,000 on a dazzling rebuilding that would reflect his High Anglican sensibility. He employed John Norton, architect of churches and country houses and a disciple of August Pugin, and in the 1880s brought in another Puginite, Henry Woodyer, to make alterations. When the National Trust acquired the house in 2002, it launched an appeal

to raise funds to prevent it from being sold to private interests. In just 100 days it had received £8.2 million from more than 77,000 donors, with an additional £17.4 million from the National Heritage Memorial Fund. Surrounded by parkland, built of mellow Bath stone and sporting turrets and pinnacles and ecclesiastical-style windows, the house, is under restoration but there is public access to some of the 65 rooms and the exquisite chapel designed by William Blomfeld in the 1870s. Among its glories are mosaics by the Murano glassmakers and mosaicists Salviati. Trust staff have had the extraordinary job of sifting through the possessions of four generations of a family who don't seem to have thrown anything away. By the time the inventory reached 30,000 items, they had catalogued everything from battered Teddy bears and boxes of Christmas crackers to a roll of 19th-century flock wallpaper, a jewel-encrusted chalice and an unexploded Second World War bomb.

In the walled kitchen garden are glasshouses, an orangery and gardeners' quarters. A distinctive aviary, designed in 1880 to house exotic birds, was later converted to a playhouse.

▶ *BS48 1NX. Wraxall. 7 miles SW of Bristol. M5 (Junction 19) via A369 and B3129. NT. Seasonal opening of house, gardens and estate.*

TYNTESFIELD

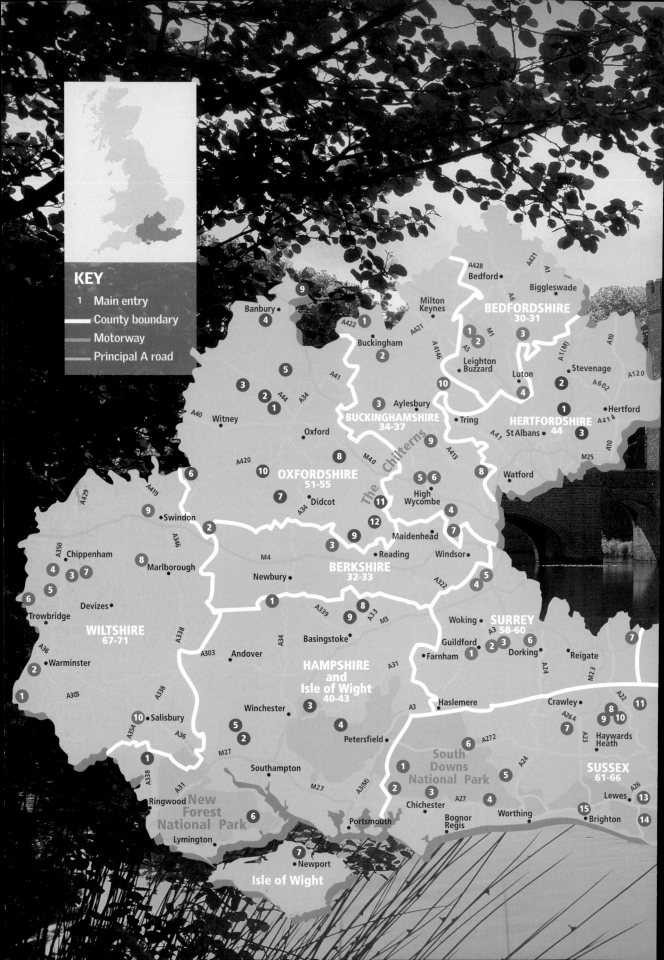

KEY

1 Main entry
County boundary
Motorway
Principal A road

BEDFORDSHIRE
30-31

HERTFORDSHIRE
44

BUCKINGHAMSHIRE
34-37

OXFORDSHIRE
51-55

The Chilterns

BERKSHIRE
32-33

SURREY
58-60

WILTSHIRE
67-71

HAMPSHIRE
and
Isle of Wight
40-43

South
Downs
National Park

SUSSEX
61-66

New
Forest
National Park

Isle of Wight

Bedford
Biggleswade
Milton
Keynes
Leighton
Buzzard
Luton
Stevenage
Hertford
St Albans
Watford
Aylesbury
Tring
Banbury
Buckingham
High
Wycombe
Maidenhead
Windsor
Oxford
Witney
Didcot
Reading
Swindon
Chippenham
Marlborough
Newbury
Basingstoke
Devizes
Trowbridge
Andover
Woking
Guildford
Dorking
Reigate
Farnham
Warminster
Winchester
Haslemere
Crawley
Haywards
Heath
Salisbury
Petersfield
Southampton
Chichester
Lewes
Brighton
Bognor
Regis
Worthing
Ringwood
Lymington
Portsmouth
Newport

A428
A421
A1
A6
A1(M)
A10
M1
A5
A4146
A421
A41
A602
A6
A413
A41
A414
A10
M25
A422
A34
A44
A40
A420
M40
A34
A419
A429
A346
A350
M4
A322
A303
A338
A339
A33
M3
A34
A31
A3
A24
M23
A22
A264
A23
A272
A24
A26
A27
A3(M)
M27
M27
A31
A338
A36
A354
A36
A30
A303
A420
A41

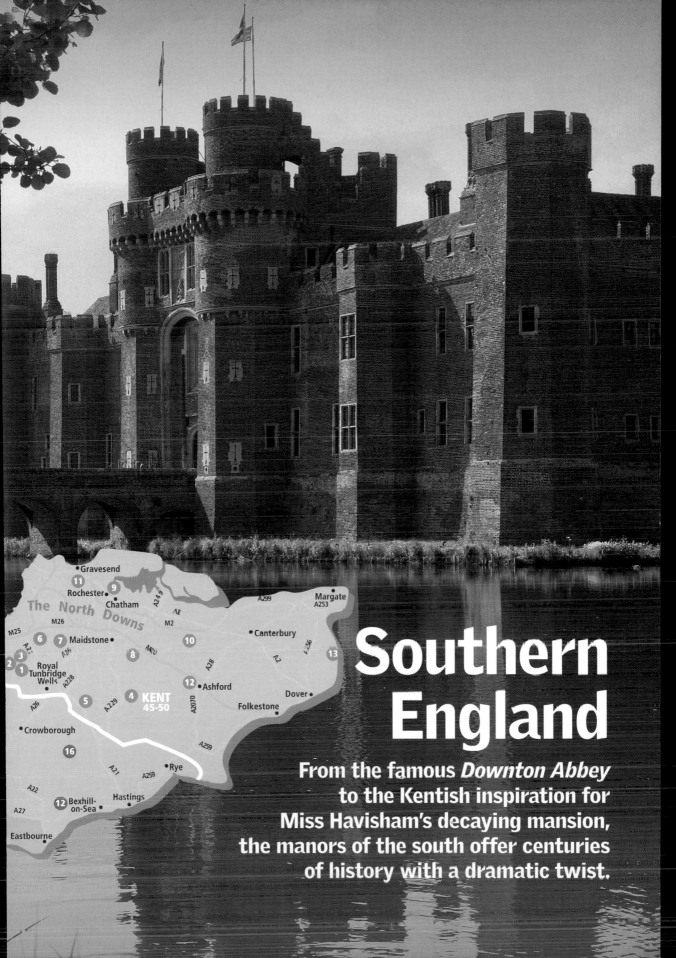

Southern England

From the famous _Downton Abbey_ to the Kentish inspiration for Miss Havisham's decaying mansion, the manors of the south offer centuries of history with a dramatic twist.

The North Downs

KENT
45-50

BEDFORDSHIRE

Eccentric aristocrats created, rebuilt, remodelled and restored Bedfordshire's grand estates over the centuries, leaving a legacy that millions of visitors can enjoy today.

❶ Woburn Abbey

In a bedroom slept in by Queen Victoria at this great 'Treasure House' are etchings drawn by Victoria and Albert, a gift to Anna Maria, 7th Duchess of Bedford, one of the Queen's ladies-in-waiting. The Russell family, Dukes of Bedford, have long associations with royalty. In 1547, Edward VI made a gift to John Russell, the future 1st Earl of Bedford, of a 12th-century Cistercian monastery snatched by Henry VIII in the Dissolution. The stunning stately home of today was rebuilt by Henry Flitcroft for the 4th Duke in 1747. Henry Holland added the south front 40 years later. The 13th Duke, a great showman, inherited a building falling into ruins and set about massive renovations. In 1955 he opened his doors to the paying public – who arrived that first day in two cars and on a bicycle. That early trickle turned into a torrent as more attractions were added, including the Safari Park, which opened in 1970. When criticised for the commercial gambit, the Duke's response was robust: 'I do not relish the scorn of the peerage, but it is better to be looked down on than overlooked.' One of England's

finest art collections includes works by Reynolds, Gainsborough, Van Dyck and Canaletto.
▶ *MK17 9WA. Woburn, 8 miles SE of Milton Keynes close to junction of A4012 and A5130. Abbey seasonal opening; gardens and grounds open all year.*

❷ Woburn Deer Park

As a condition of his licence to keep deer, granted in 1690, Francis, Duke of Bedford, was obliged to send two bucks every year to Trinity College, Cambridge. By the turn of the century, his herd was so depleted that he was forced to cadge two animals from the Duke of Rutland. A century later, the park had been so well replenished that Archduke John of Austria wrote in 1815 that 'we had never seen a park so full of deer'. Herbrand, the 11th Duke of Bedford, as president of the Royal Zoological Society, introduced many exotic deer – nine species now roam Woburn's 1,200 or so walled hectares (3,000 acres), in serene parkland designed by Humphry Repton in 1802. 'Hatband' was less successful in improving the house. His first attempt to install electricity resulted in a fire; the second was hampered by his distaste for the sight

WOBURN ABBEY

of workmen, who had to hide when he came by.
▶ *MK17 9WA. Woburn, 8 miles SE of Milton Keynes close to junction of A4012 and A5130. Open all year.*

❸ Wrest Park

A mansion modelled on the Hotel de Matignon in Paris, with Louis XV interiors, stands in parkland inspired by the gardens of Versailles. The château-style mansion was built for Francophile Thomas, Earl de Grey, in the 1830s on the site of his former ancestral home. The de Grey family owned Wrest Park for almost 700 years, until the death of Auberon Herbert, 9th Baron Lucas, in 1917, killed in action with the Royal Flying Corps. It was sold to a northern brewery owner and mining magnate, John Murray, but by 1934 it had fallen into neglect, and the estate was up for sale. Not until 1939 did an insurance company set up its headquarters here, when much of the parkland was turned over to food production. After the war, Wrest Park was sold to the Ministry of Public Buildings and Works, later the Silsoe Insitute, which occupied the house until 2006. Such worthy use has not enhanced the property, but the central staircase,

Hall, Library and State Rooms are visions of opulence with glorious views. The garden has a baroque pavilion designed by Thomas Archer in 1709, a French-style Orangery, bridges and statues.
▶ *MK45 4HR. 10 miles S of Bedford, 1 mile E of Silsoe, off A6. EH. Open most days; Saturdays and Sundays only in winter.*

❹ Luton Hoo

In an affecting Diamond Jubilee speech, The Queen praised her husband, the Duke of Edinburgh, her 'constant strength and guide'. Their enduring marriage began when she was still Princess Elizabeth, in November 1947. They spent part of their honeymoon at this grand Robert Adam House, and returned for anniversaries before she ascended the throne in 1952. A fire in 1843 left it a burnt-out shell, but it was restored by Sir Julius Wernher, a diamond dealer, and his wife 'Birdie', who commissioned Charles Mewes and Arthur Davis, architects of The Ritz, to design the interior. Today it is a five-star hotel. Adam's ballroom was used in the filming of the 1994 *Four Weddings and a Funeral.*
▶ *LU1 3TQ. 2 miles S of Luton town centre.*

BERKSHIRE

A castle made famous by TV's *Downton Abbey* basks in 1,000 acres of parkland, while another grand mansion survived against all odds to become a model stately home.

❶ Highclere Castle

'How scenical! How scenical!' Benjamin Disraeli was charmed by his first sight of Highclere, which had been remodelled for the 3rd Earl of Carnarvon by the great architect Sir Charles Barry. The Victorian castle, known to millions of viewers of the TV drama series as *Downton Abbey*, stands in 404ha (1,000 acres) of Capability Brown parkland, commanding views across downland and the Kennet Valley.

Highclere has been the seat of the Carnarvon family since 1679. The original house was converted to a classical Georgian mansion in the late 1700s and early 1800s, but the most spectacular transformation was wrought by Barry. The 4th Earl was a member of Disraeli's Cabinet; they would talk politics in the library when 'Dizzy' visited, surrounded by more than 5,000 books. The interiors are sumptuous – the Gothic-style Saloon has leather wall hangings from Cordoba, Spain, the State Dining Room has Van Dyck's equestrian portrait of Charles I, and the Music Room is hung with 16th-century silk embroideries from Italy, under a baroque ceiling painted in the 1730s by Francis Hayman.

Famously, in 1922, the 5th Earl of Carnarvon, with Howard Carter, discovered the tomb of the boy king Tutankhamun, and the 8th Earl and Countess have mounted an Egyptian Exhibition in his honour.

▶ *RG20 9RN. 6 miles S of Newbury on A34. Seasonal opening of house and grounds.*

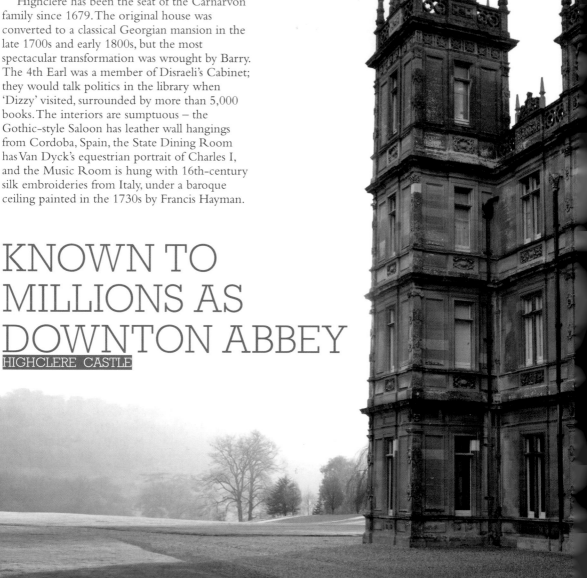

KNOWN TO MILLIONS AS DOWNTON ABBEY
HIGHCLERE CASTLE

❷ Ashdown House

This beautiful, Dutch-style 17th-century house was built for the widowed Elizabeth, Queen of Bohemia, by her admirer, William, 1st Earl Craven. The eldest child of James I and Anne of Denmark, feted as 'the most beautiful princess in Europe', Elizabeth married Frederick V,

Elector of the Palatinate of the Rhine in 1613. In 1619 he ascended the throne, but the couple were exiled in 1620, earning her the nickname 'the Winter Queen'. Elizabeth outlived Frederick by 30 years, and in the early 1660s travelled to London to visit her nephew, Charles II. The Earl of Craven, being smitten with her, and hearing that she 'longed to live in quiet', commissioned the Dutch-born Captain William Winde to build this house for her on the site of a medieval deer park amid the Berkshire downs. She died in 1662 before it was completed, and the quintessentially feminine chalk-block building topped with a cupola and flanked by pavilions is 'consecrated' to her.

▶ *RG17 8RE. On B4000 10 miles E of Swindon. NT. Seasonal opening of house (guided tours only) and grounds; woodland open all year, (Sundays to Thursdays).*

❸ Basildon Park

'Such a house and such a situation. What a casket to enclose pictorial gems!' So rejoiced art collector James Morrison when he bought Basildon Park in 1838. In 1776 Sir Francis Sykes, 1st Baronet, had commissioned John Carr of York to design him a mansion it was built, metaphorically, on sand. A fortune made in service to the British East India Company was dwindling and there were budget constraints. Upon Sykes's death in 1804 the 'Adamesque' interiors were unfinished. Within a few weeks, Sykes's son also died, and at the age of five, his grandson, Francis, 3rd Baronet, inherited the house. By the time he was 14, Francis was entertaining his profligate pal George, the Prince Regent, at Basildon – at no small expense. He married the sensuous Henrietta Villebois, who had affairs with Benjamin Disraeli, Lord Lyndhurst and the painter Daniel Maclise. She was the model for Disraeli's novel *Henrietta Temple: A Love Story*. Maclise's friend Charles Dickens named the villainous Bill Sykes in *Oliver Twist* after Francis, and the humiliated cuckold sold his 'casket' to Morrison.

In 1910 it was acquired by press baron Lord Iliffe. In 1929 developers offered to ship the whole house to the US for anyone who could find $1 million – they had no takers. Troops were billeted at Basildon in the Second World War. It was damaged by fire, and by 1952, when the 2nd Baron and Lady Iliffe embarked on restoration, it was a wreck. Yet in 1978 they presented a perfect house and grounds to the National Trust.

▶ *RG8 9NR. 7 miles NW of Reading on A329. NT. Seasonal opening.*

SOUTHERN ENGLAND

STOWE TEMPLE OF BRITISH WORTHIES

BUCKINGHAMSHIRE

The gardens at Stowe saw in a new and enduring era of landscape design, while a few miles south, the fairytale Waddesdon Manor presents an exotic Victorian take on horticultural beauty.

❶ Stowe Landscape Gardens

'Spontaneous beauties all around advance, /Start ev'n from Difficulty, strike from Chance; /Nature shall join you, Time shall make it grow/A Work to wonder at – perhaps a STOWE.' Alexander Pope's epistle to Richard Boyle, 3rd Earl of Burlington, is a celebration of Stowe and a tribute to Boyle for inspiring a taste for a new style of gardening in the 18th century. Richard Temple, 1st Viscount Cobham, employed the great architects and landscapers Charles Bridgeman and William Kent, and conceived the gardens as a formal stage set. Structures in the grounds were designed by the architects John Vanbrugh and James Gibbs.

In 1841, Capability Brown became head gardener and swept away the formality, creating landscapes that brought sightseers flocking. Temple was a radical Whig who retired from

politics in protest at the policies of Robert Walpole. His garden is charged with hidden meaning, a polemic against his opponents. Above the door of the Gothic Temple he wrote: 'Thank God I'm not a Roman!' Thank God for the geniuses who created this Elysium with more than 40 temples and monuments in a landscape of lakes and valleys! Stowe has been a public school since 1922. The National Trust acquired the gardens in the 1980s.

▶ *MK18 5EQ. 3 miles NW of Buckingham off A422. NT. Open all year.*

❷ Claydon House

When Ralph, 2nd Earl Verney, ordered the rebuilding of the family's 17th-century ancestral home, it was his ambition to upstage Viscount Cobham in his mansion at Stowe. Vain rivalry would bankrupt both men.

Verney engaged stonemason and woodcarver
Luke Lightfoot to let rip on the rococo interiors.
He created a pure extravaganza of foliage and
drapery, festoons, vines and garlands, cherubs,
cornucopias … . The pièce de resistance is the
Chinese Room with fretwork teahouse and a
frieze depicting a tea ceremony. Sadly, after ten
years, Verney and Lightfoot fell out over matters
of money and taste. Sir Thomas Robinson
bemoaned 'such a work as the world never saw',
and urged Verney to engage Joseph Rose, Robert
Adam's stuccoist, instead. Money ran out. Verney
ran off. The remaining house is still home to the
family today. It presents to the visitor an austere
front with little hint of what lies within. It is,
furthermore, not half the house it once was – just
the surviving west wing, a wing and other parts
having been demolished by Verney's niece in 1792.
▶ *MK18 2EY. 6 miles S of Buckingham, off A41
Aylesbury-Bicester road or A413 Aylesbury-
Buckingham road. NT. Seasonal opening of house
and garden.*

❸ Waddesdon Manor

**When Queen Victoria visited Baron
Ferdinand de Rothschild's country house,
she was so intrigued by an electric**
chandelier that it is said she spent ten minutes
switching it on and off. The modern visitor
is more impressed by what appears to be a
Renaissance château magically transported
from the Loire. The 45-room manor, built
between 1874 and 1889, was designed by the
architect Gabriel-Hippolyte Destailleur, who had
valuable experience in château restoration. Mod
cons included hot and cold running water and
central heating.

The purpose of this supremely elegant and
ambitious building was to house de Rothschild's
art treasures, including Sèvres porcelain, clocks,
sculpture, 18th-century British portraits and
17th-century Dutch landscapes. The interiors are
lavishly furnished and fitted with beautiful
French antiques, reflecting the 'goût Rothschild'.
Elie Lainé created the Victorian gardens, with a
parterre, shrubs, rose garden and specimen trees.
There are statues and a rococo aviary of exotic
birds. The Proserpina fountain from the Ducal
Palace of Colorno, Parma, and seasonal carpet
of bedding plants make a splash. When James
de Rothschild died in 1957, he bequeathed
Waddesdon, lock, stock and 81ha (200 acres)
to the National Trust.
▶ *HP18 0JH. 6 miles NW of Aylesbury on A41. NT.
Limited opening all year for house and gardens; entry
to house by timed ticket.*

❹ Cliveden

**The first-ever rendition of 'Rule Britannia'
was given here in 1740 for Frederick, Prince
of Wales, who rented the house for £600**
a year and staged theatrical and musical
performances. Cliveden had close associations
with royalty since Lord Orkney entertained
George I here. In the time of society hostess
Nancy Astor, guests included Charlie Chaplin,
Winston Churchill, Rudyard Kipling and
Mahatma Ghandi. Yet Cliveden is known above
all as the place where John Profumo, Secretary of
State for War, met good-time girl Christine
Keeler in 1961, and began an affair that nearly
brought down the Macmillan government.

In 1666 the Duke of Buckingham engaged
William Winde to build him a riverside mansion.
It was twice rebuilt in the 1800s after fires. In its
present Italianate form it was the creation of
Sir Charles Barry, completed in 1852. In 1893
Cliveden was sold to the American billionaire
William Waldorf Astor, who passed it to his son
Waldorf on his marriage to Nancy. Harold
Nicolson found a 'ghastly reality about it all'. He
enjoyed seeing it, 'But to own it, to live here,
would be like living on the stage of the Scala
theatre in Milan.' It is now a hotel.
▶ *SL6 0JA. 4 miles N of Maidenhead on A4094
Woodburn road (M4 Junction 7). NT. Limited
seasonal opening of house, partial access by timed ticket;
gardens open daily mid-February to December;
woodland open all year.*

❺ West Wycombe Park

**Sir Francis Dashwood, 2nd Baronet, MP,
libertine, liked to live it large. He founded
the aristocratic Hellfire Club** and held
bacchanalian orgies in West Wycombe Caves.
The house he inherited in 1724, at the age of 16,
was an unassuming Carolean box. A series of
Grand Tours filled his head with fancies and he
set about creating an Italianate pleasure palace.
Work begun in 1740 was not completed until
1800, nearly 20 years after his death, and the
building reflects the march of fashion in
architecture, from Palladianism to neoclassicism.
The house is bookended to east and west by
porticos inspired by the Villa Capra 'La Rotonda'
in Vicenza and the Temple of Bacchus in Baalbek.

The interiors revel in Greek and Roman
mythology, with painted ceilings copied from
palazzi. In the Music Room, The Banquet of the
Gods is copied from Palazzo Farnesina in Rome.
The Triumph of Bacchus and Ariadne is
celebrated in the Blue Drawing Room. Paintings,

silk hangings, tapestries and antiques abound. The grounds are strewn with classical follies. At the centre of a swan-shaped lake is the Temple of Music. The landscaping by Thomas Cook was extended by Humphry Repton. In death as in life Sir Francis did not efface himself. The model for his Mausoleum, located on the hill overlooking his playground, is Constantine's Arch in Rome.
▶ *HP14 3AJ. 2 miles W of High Wycombe, off A40. NT. Seasonal opening of house and grounds.*

➏ Hughenden Manor

'Excruciating' was how architectural historian Nikolaus Pevsner judged this redbrick edifice, home to Queen Victoria's beloved prime minister, Benjamin Disraeli, and his wife, Mary Anne. Disraeli himself was delighted with 'the romance many years realising' of Edward Buckton Lamb's remodelling and 'dramatising' of a modest late 18th-century stuccoed house. Under Lamb, out went classical Georgian features; in came hybridised baronial Gothic. It was a fine place for Disraeli to entertain a sovereign with whom he would grow very close, and Queen Victoria visited often.

Many of Disraeli's books, paintings and furniture remain in the house. In the Library is a collection of Disraeli's novels, which included *Henrietta Temple* (see Basildon Park, page 33). Despite his earlier passion for Henrietta Sykes, he was devoted to his wife. When he once remarked that he had married her for money, she riposted, 'Ah, but if you had to do it again, you would do it for love.' The gardens have been restored to Mary Anne's own design.
▶ *HP14 4LA. 2 miles N of High Wycombe on A4128. NT. Seasonal opening of house and gardens; park open all year.*

➐ Dorney Court

It is claimed that the first pineapple to be raised in England was grown here, and presented to Charles II in 1661. Since 1629, 13 generations of the Palmer family have lived in this enchanting, many-gabled, 15th-century manor house, surrounded by 40.5ha (100 acres) of gardens. The panelled rooms are full of period furniture in oak and 17th-century lacquer, family portraits, tapestries and needlework. Dorney

CHEQUERS

means 'island of bees' and the estate is still famous for its delicate honey.
▶ *SL4 6QP. 3 miles NW of Windsor on B3026. Seasonal opening.*

⑧ Chenies Manor

This 15th-century manor house, previously known as Chenies Palace, played host to both Henry VIII and Elizabeth I and their courts. At its heart, the manor is a part-fortified brick hall house, built by Sir John Cheyne in the mid 1400s. The building was extended by John Russell, Earl of Bedford, in the 16th century. The antiquary John Leland found it 'so translated that little or nothing of it yn a maner remaynith untranslated … a great deale of the House in ben newly set up made of Bricke and Timber.'
In 1829 Edward Blore created a series of interiors, which contain Georgian and later furniture. The house feels both homey and historic, with big fireplaces, family portraits, beamed ceilings, four-poster beds – and tiny priest hole.
Architectural historian Nikolaus Pevsner found Chenies 'beautifully mellow under the trees by

the church, and architecturally a fascinating puzzle'. In summer, the gardens are resplendent.
▶ *EWD3 6ER. 4 miles E of Amersham on A404. Limited seasonal opening.*

⑨ Coombe Hill (Chequers)

The public cannot visit Chequers unless by invitation of the prime minister, whose official country residence this is. However, the curious who climb Coombe Hill can have sight of this ancient and historic house. Chequers was restored and enlarged in 1565. In the 1800s it was updated for the Greenhill-Russells in the Gothic style by William Atkinson – only to be returned to its Tudor magnificence for Arthur and Ruth Lee after 1909. In the Long Gallery a stained-glass panel commissioned by Lord and Lady Lee reads: 'This house of peace and ancient memories was given to England as a thank offering for her deliverance in the great war of 1914–1918 as a place of rest and recreation for her Prime Ministers for ever.' It was their hope that 'the high and pure air of the Chiltern hills and woods' would encourage saner government. Coombe Hill was given to the National Trust in 1965.
▶ *3 miles NW of Great Missenden, off A413 Amersham-Aylesbury road. NT car park 1 mile W of Dunsmore.*

⑩ Ascott House

The name de Rothschild is a byword for wealth and opulence, but this is no baronial pile, more 'a palace-like cottage', as it appeared to Gladstone's daughter Mary in the 1880s. The Jacobean farmhouse was known as Ascott Cottage when it was bought by Baron Mayer de Rothschild in 1873 as a country retreat. It was taken over as a hunting box the following year by Leopold de Rothschild, who employed George Devey to transform it into a family home. It was extended in the 1930s, but when Anthony de Rothschild inherited Ascott in 1937, he ordered a remodelling that would simplify it and create a background against which the family treasures would shine. In 1949 Anthony presented the house, collection, and 105ha (261 acres) to the National Trust. Since 1961 Ascott has been home to Sir Evelyn de Rothschild, who drew on Victorian influences to create the present setting for a collection that includes paintings by Reynolds and Gainsborough, 18th-century French and English furniture, and some 400 pieces of Chinese ceramics.
▶ *LU7 0PR. Near Wing, 3 miles SW of Leighton Buzzard on A418. NT. Limited seasonal opening.*

The fruits of their labours

Always more than a vegetable plot, the kitchen garden was a focus of experiment, innovation and surprising variety.

When Celia Fiennes made her pioneering journeys *Through England on a Side Saddle* in the late 17th century, she saw at Coleshill in Wiltshire 'many steps and tarresses and gravel walkes with all sorts of dwarfe trees, fruit trees with standing apricock and flower trees, abundance of garden roome and filled with all sorts of things for pleasure and use'. She tells of pots of 'fine orange citron and lemon trees' with no astonishment. The modern consumer, accustomed to buying fruit and vegetables the year round from all over the world, might be surprised to know what choice and abundance was available to the nobility in the 1600s, with no air miles.

Stately homes, with their farms, deer parks and game habitats, poultry yards, livestock, fish ponds, duck ponds, rabbit warrens, dovecotes, hives, vineyards, brew houses, dairies, orchards and kitchen gardens, glasshouses and orangeries, were largely self-sufficient food factories. Manure was plentiful; even songbirds might go into a pie.

The kitchen garden would be imaginatively planted, with flowers for cutting, medicinal and culinary herbs, pleached vines and espaliered fruit trees. Enclosing walls – sometimes heated by furnaces and horizontal flue pipes – created a micro-climate in which tropical fruits would flourish. These were not confined to the potager, but were also a feature of the pleasure gardens, where they could be admired for their rarity and beauty.

In his *Paradisi in Sole Paradisus Terrestris* of 1629, apothecary John Parkinson catalogues several dozen fruit varieties, including 48 apples, 19 peaches, 29 cherries, plums, currants, quinces, medlars, gooseberries, grapes and filberts.

Traditionally the kitchen garden would have four main beds or 'quarters' around a central feature such as a dipping pond for watering and perhaps a fountain. The beds would be planted in rotation with brassicas, legumes, root crops and salad. Fruit trees might be grown in a quincunx pattern, with a tree at each of four corners and a fifth in the middle.

A kitchen garden was usually located near the house until the late 18th century when it began to be put at some remove. The garden designer Humphry Repton created decorative walks to a mini Eden with gazebos and shady paths under trained fruit trees.

Glasshouse delights

By the Victorian era new techniques enabled the construction of glasshouses. James Paxton was head gardener to the Duke of Devonshire at Chatsworth in Derbyshire, where he built greenhouses and installed the Great Stove – a huge conservatory now demolished – before designing the Crystal Palace at Hyde Park for the Great Exhibition of 1851.

When fruits and vegetables were harvested they might be bottled, pickled, dried, crystallised, made into jams, jellies – even into ice creams and sorbets. Before refrigeration, stately homes would have an ice house, deep underground, storing ice from the Baltic Sea, transported by carriage, wrapped in straw.

The stately home kitchen garden was at its peak in the early 1900s when traditional cultivation and new technology combined to make possible the growing of the rarest fruits, vegetables and flowers. In the memoir of her childhood at Kingston Lacy in Dorset at that time, Viola Bankes recalled 'yellow guavas and melon trained to grow upright on walls ... all kinds of berries in mouth-watering profusion, even huge, sweet strawberries in February'.

AVEBURY MANOR KITCHEN GARDENS, WILTSHIRE

HAMPSHIRE & ISLE OF WIGHT

The county's elegant houses offer lovely views over the countryside, collections of art and world-class museums; there are famous cars, a children's playhouse and even the Duke of Wellington's funeral carriage.

❶ Breamore House

This perfect E-plan Elizabethan manor house on the edge of the New Forest has been in the same family for ten generations. Built of red brick with stone quoins, for William Dodington, it was completed in 1583 and has been little altered since. The Dodingtons' granddaughter, Anne, married Robert Greville, Lord Brooke, in 1660, the year of the Restoration of the Monarchy. In 1748, the 8th Lord Brooke sold the house and part of the estate to Sir Edward Hulse, Baronet, whose descendants live here today, custodians of the building and possessions collected over centuries. The Great Hall looks out over the Avon Valley to the forest beyond. It is hung with 17th-century Brussels tapestries and four paintings from the studio of Van Dyck, of the children of Charles I, Charles II, James II and Mary, mother of William III. On a more intimate scale is the Regency West Drawing Room, looking out over the park. The two Tudor bedrooms have period oak furniture and tapestry hangings. The amusing Clock Tower dates from 1860. Here, too, is a countryside museum.
▶ *SP6 2DF. 3 miles N of Fordingbridge on A338. Limited seasonal opening of house and museum.*

❷ Broadlands

Lord Mountbatten introduced the young Princess Elizabeth to his nephew Philip in 1939, and upon their marriage in 1947, he offered his stately home as a romantic honeymoon retreat. The original manor belonged to Romsey Abbey before 1066, and was sold by Henry VIII in 1547 to Sir Francis Fleming. Later, it was owned by the St Barbe family, and much improved by Sir John St Barbe, before passing to his cousin Humphrey Sydenham in 1723. When the South Sea Bubble burst, Sydenham lost everything and in 1736 sold Broadlands to Henry Temple, 1st Viscount Palmerston. Temple swept away the formality of the grounds to create 'a gentle descent' to the River Test – the 'broad lands'. In 1767 began a transformation as Lancelot Brown and Henry Holland created the Arcadian park and Palladian mansion seen today. It was Henry Temple, 2nd Viscount Palmerston, who proposed that Brown exploit the 'capabilities' of the Tudor and Jacobean manor – a word that the architect

and landscaper used so often that it became his nickname. Broadlands is home to Lord and Lady Brabourne.
▶ *SO51 9ZE. Just S of Romsey town centre. Seasonal opening.*

❸ Avington Park

The estate of 'Afintun' belonged to Winchester Cathedral until Henry VIII gave it to Edmund Clerke. When George Brydges, Groom of the Bedchamber to Charles II, acquired the house, he enlarged and improved it to make it fit for a king and his mistress Nell Gwyn. This was not the only time Avington accommodated illicit royal lovers. When the Duke of Buckingham and Chandos inherited the property, he played host to George IV and the widowed Maria Fitzherbert, a Catholic, whom the king married in secret, in contravention of the Royal Marriages Act. Avington today is a splendid Georgian manor with classical portico surmounted by statues, sweeping lawns, a lake, and gilded, mirrored interiors.
▶ *SO21 1DB. 5 miles NE of Winchester, off B3047. Limited opening in August and September.*

❹ Hinton Ampner

What appears at first sight to be an elegant Georgian country house dates in its present form from the 1960s. It was remodelled by Ralph Dutton, 8th and last Lord Sherborne, in 1960, after a catastrophic fire. The house contains a wealth of Georgian and Regency furniture, Italian works of art and beautiful artefacts. Everything has a meaning for its former owner. Gardens laid out by Dutton are a masterpiece of 20th-century design. People say the place feels 'still lived in', although its owner died in 1985, leaving the property to the National Trust.

Hinton Ampner's history is long – mention is made in the Domesday Book of a house on the site. A Tudor manor here, reputedly haunted, was pulled down at the end of the 18th century, after a new house had been built next to it. This was rebuilt as a Victorian fantasy, and then again in the Georgian style. It offers lovely views of the South Downs.
▶ *SO24 0LA. 9 miles E of Winchester on A272. NT. House and gardens open most of year (usually closed on Fridays).*

MOTTISFONT ABBEY ROSE GARDEN

❺ Mottisfont Abbey

Part of the incalculably rich haul that came to Henry VIII with the Dissolution of the Monasteries, this former Augustinian priory, was the king's gift to William, Lord Sandys, the Lord Chancellor. Rather than demolish it, Sandys used the nave as the centrepiece of his new house. In the mid 1700s Sir Richard Mill transformed the house into a Georgian mansion, yet left many of the monastic remains intact. In 1934, Maud and Gilbert Russell took up residence, commissioned improvements, and made Mottisfont a centre of their artistic and political circle. The county house we see today is mostly Maud's creation as she commissioned artist friends to embellish her home. The illusion of Gothic architecture in the Salon was created by Rex Whistler to evoke the medieval architecture of the priory. The mosaics inside and outside the house, including that of an angel with Maud's face, are the work of Boris Anrep, with whom she had an affair. Society portraitist Derek Hill donated a collection of early 20th-century art to the National Trust to be displayed here, where the pictures form part of a programme of exhibitions. The formal grounds include a walled rose garden.
▶ *SO51 0LP. 5 miles N of Romsey on A3057. NT. Seasonal opening of the abbey; gardens have limited opening all year.*

❻ Beaulieu Palace House

Time has not stood still at Beaulieu, home to the Montagu family and one of the most vibrant of the stately homes of England.
The 13th-century Palace House was the Great Gatehouse of Beaulieu Abbey, built by Cistercian monks on land given to them by King John – and taken from them by Henry VIII. The abbey was originally known as Bellus Locus Regis, 'the beautiful place of the king', and that great Tudor fat cat duly confiscated it in the Reformation. In 1538 he granted it to Sir Thomas Wriothesley, 1st Earl of Southampton, ancestor of Edward Douglas-Scott-Montagu, 3rd Baron Montagu, who inherited Palace House in 1951. With the 25-year-old Montagu's inheritance came a collection of historic cars, and in 1952 he opened the National Motor Museum in the grounds. In 1956 he launched the first country-house jazz festival, and set about making his ancestral pile pay, with scant regard for the carping of his patrician peers.

Palace House was substantially remodelled in the Gothic revival style by Victorian architect Sir Arthur Blomfield, although he kept some medieval features. It is rated as one of the 'Top Ten Treasure Houses of England' online, the finest houses and palaces, containing important art works and antiques. The gardens include a

41

fragrant Victorian flower garden and ornamental kitchen garden with 1870s vine house. The National Motor Museum has grown to a collection of 250 vehicles, among them Del Boy's three-wheeled Reliant Regal (from the TV series *Only Fools and Horses*), buses, roadsters, dragsters … more *Top Gear*, less *Pride and Prejudice*.

▶ *SO42 7ZN. 6 miles E of Brockenhurst on B3055.*

❼ Osborne House

'A Sicilian palazzo with garden terraces, statues and vases shining in the sun, than which nothing can be more captivating.'
Benjamin Disraeli, Queen Victoria's pet prime minister, was enraptured by her seaside retreat. In 1845, Victoria and Albert had bought an estate overlooking the Solent. An existing Georgian house was demolished and, with the help of Thomas Cubitt, architect, Albert designed this grand Italianate villa, mixing Roman, Florentine and Palladian styles. A grand marble corridor linked the family pavilion to a wing intended for visitors and members of the household.

The recently restored interiors were also mostly to Albert's design, but he had no hand in the creation of the Durbar Room. The jewel in Osborne's crown was added after his death. It was begun in 1890, after Disraeli made Victoria Empress of India. Decorated by Indian craftsmen, with Moghul-style plasterwork, it was designed by Bhai Ram Singh with advice from John Lockwood Kipling, father of Rudyard.

In the grounds, the Swiss Cottage is not so much a playhouse as a lesson in domesticity, contrived by Albert to teach his children and their cousins good housekeeping.

Victoria died at Osborne in January 1901, with her children and grandchildren gathered around her huge canopied bed. Edward VII gave the house to the nation in 1902.

▶ *PO32 6JX. 1 mile SE of East Cowes, off A3021. EH. Seasonal opening.*

❽ Stratfield Saye

For his military service and the defeat of Napoleon at Waterloo in 1815, the Duke of Wellington was granted a fortune to build himself a palace to rival Blenheim (see page 51). The Iron Duke chose the estate of Stratfield Saye, home of the Pitt family, and a house built around 1630 by Sir William Pitt, Comptroller of the Household to James I, faced in stucco by George Pitt, 1st Baron Rivers, in the 1700s. Wellington planned to pull the house down and to build a fabulous 'Waterloo Palace', but the scheme

promised to be too expensive so he contented himself with commissioning alterations. A conservatory and outer wings were added, as were water closets in many rooms, and central heating (when Victoria and Albert came to stay, she found the place too hot).

Among the duke's effects on show are his spectacles and slippers, and paintings including one of his charger, Copenhagen. The horse carried him for 18 hours in his most decisive battle. An exhibition in the stables includes the duke's massive, ornamental funeral carriage, cast in bronze from cannons captured at Waterloo. Copenhagen lived out his days at Stratfield Saye, dying in 1836, aged 28. He was buried with military honours, and is commemorated by a gravestone in the Ice House Paddock beneath a turkey oak grown from an acorn planted in 1843 by the housekeeper Mrs Apostles. Among the trees in the Pleasure Grounds are Wellingtonias, which were introduced to Britain in 1853, a year after the duke's death, and named in his honour.

▶ *RG7 2BT. 10 miles S of Reading on minor roads, off A33. Limited seasonal opening of house (by guided tour only) and grounds.*

❾ The Vyne

Henry VIII brought his first queen, Catherine of Aragon, to stay here – and returned with his second wife, Anne Boleyn. His Lord Chamberlain, William, the 1st Lord Sandys, built the original house from a group of medieval structures, as well as adapting Mottisfont Abbey (page 41). Although Sandys was distressed when the king divorced Catherine, he was obliged to receive Anne with good grace – as he would later be obliged to escort her to the Tower. Elizabeth I visited the 3rd Lord Sandys, and from here wrote a letter commanding the Earl of Huntingdon to take Mary, Queen of Scots into custody.

From 1650, for 350 years, The Vyne was home to the Chute family, who, among many alterations, added a classical portico by John Webb, a pupil of Inigo Jones's. The style is a mix of Tudor, Palladian, Georgian Gothic and Victorian Revival. Impressive interiors include the carved Oak Gallery. In the Stone Gallery are objects brought back by John Chute when he made the Grand Tour in the 18th century. The house, set in gardens and meadows, is filled with textiles, tiles, carvings and paintings. In the Tudor Gothic chapel, stained-glass images of Henry and Catherine have a peculiar brilliance. In the gardens and grounds are an ornamental lake, woodlands and wetlands.

▶ *RG24 9HL. 3 miles N of Basingstoke on minor roads, off A340. NT. Seasonal opening (closed Fridays).*

JOHN CHUTE'S
STAIRCASE HALL

THE VYNE

HERTFORDSHIRE

A Victorian Gothic fantasy of a house opens its gardens to the music-loving public, while other stately Hertfordshire gems are better known for their royal connections.

❶ Brocket Hall

The third house to have stood on this site, Brocket Hall has many associations with British prime ministers. It was built for Sir Matthew Lamb in 1760 by James Paine. The Prince Regent, the future George IV, visited often – and no wonder! Elizabeth, a social climber and wife of Sir Matthew's son Peniston Lamb, was his mistress. He gave her the painting by Reynolds that hangs in the ballroom – and gave her husband the title of Lord Melbourne. The wife of William, 2nd Lord Melbourne, Lady Caroline Lamb, famously had an affair with Lord Byron. William became Queen Victoria's first prime minister and she stayed often at the Hall. In 1848 it passed to Melbourne's sister, who married Lord Palmerston, another future prime minister. He died here aged 81. Baroness Thatcher spent time at Brocket, writing her memoirs. This is one of England's finer stately houses but it is not a family home. It is available for private events and has a Golf Academy.
▶ *AL8 7XG. 2 miles W of Welwyn Garden City.*

❷ Knebworth

'It was a dark and stormy night; the rain fell in torrents – except on occasional intervals, when it was checked by a violent gust of wind.' Here is Knebworth's most celebrated resident, the novelist and MP Edward Bulwer-Lytton, 1st Baron Lytton, putting pen to paper in 1830 to tell the tale of gentleman criminal *Paul Clifford*. Knebworth has been the seat of the Lytton family since 1490. A redbrick quadrangle house had been through various incarnations and reduced to just the west wing when Bulwer-Lytton inherited it in 1843. His mother had disapproved of his marriage to Irish beauty Rosina Doyle Wheeler and had withdrawn his allowance, so he had turned his hand to fiction, averring that 'the pen is mightier than the sword'. He engaged H.E. Kendall Junior and John G. Crace to rebuild the house, which is of a piece with his prose, an overwrought Victorian Gothic fantasy topped with towers and pinnacles, adorned with heraldic beasts and gargoyles.

Further additions were made to the house by Robert, 1st Earl Lytton in the late 19th century. The interiors are in a riotous mix of styles, mostly the work of Crace, and of Sir Edwin Lutyens, Robert's son-in-law.

Lutyens laid out the Italianate gardens, with lawns and avenues of pollarded limes. A maze, organic walled kitchen garden, rose garden, golden garden, wilderness walk and Gertrude Jekyll Garden (designed in 1907, planted in 1982) provide perennial interest – not to speak of the miniature railway, dinosaur park, classic-car rallies… and the annual Salvo Fair of architectural salvage. But Knebworth's greatest claim to fame is as an open-air music venue, 'the stately home of rock' since 1974.
▶ *SG3 6PY. Access Knebworth from Junction 7 of A1(M). Limited seasonal opening.*

❸ Hatfield House

Hatfield House's predecessor, Hatfield Palace, was built for the Bishop of Ely in 1485. Henry VIII, took it over as a home for his children, Mary, Elizabeth and Edward. Princess Elizabeth was confined here by her older sister and was sitting reading under an oak tree in 1558 when news was brought to her that Mary had died and she was queen. Although this house is not the building she knew, the Palace Great Hall in which she held her first Council survives.

When James I inherited Hatfield, he did not care for it, and proposed to Robert Cecil, chief minister of the Crown, that he exchange it for his home, Theobalds (now a hotel). Cecil can't have cared for it, either. In 1607 he demolished three wings and used the materials to build a new house to designs by Robert Lyminge, modified by others, among them perhaps a young Inigo Jones.

Hatfield is today the home of the 7th Marquis and Marchioness of Salisbury. Visitors find a stupendous Jacobean manor retaining mementoes of Elizabeth, including gloves and a pair of silk stockings believed to be the first in England. An illuminated parchment roll in the Library traces her ancestry back to Adam and Eve. In the Marble Hall is the 'Rainbow Portrait' of her.

The gardens were laid out in the early 17th century by the great plant hunter John Tradescant the elder, who imported flora never before seen on these shores. They include orchards, fountains and water parterres.
▶ *AL9 5NQ. Hatfield signposted from Junction 4 of A1(M). Limited seasonal opening.*

KENT

Castles in miniature, gardens spilling over with summer flowers, bizarre collections and a manor with one of the world's finest rooms: Kent's stately homes are the pride of the county.

❶ Penshurst Place

'The most complete surviving example of 14th-century architecture in England', Penshurst was the birthplace of the brilliant Sir Philip Sidney, poet, soldier and courtier to Elizabeth I. An earlier house was transformed into a country mansion by Sir Stephen de Penchester in around 1340, and in the 1390s it was fortified against a feared invasion by the French. In the 15th and 16th centuries it was owned by the Dukes of Buckingham, and upon the execution of the 3rd Duke, in 1521, the estate, as property of a traitor, was seized by the Crown. Henry VIII stayed here when he was wooing Anne Boleyn at Hever Castle. His son, Edward VI, granted it to the son of his tutor, his childhood friend Sir Henry Sidney. Sidney's wife, Mary, was the sister of Sir Robert Dudley, Earl of Leicester, a favourite of Elizabeth I's. The queen visited often and the Queen Elizabeth Room is named in her honour. In the State Dining Room is a painting of her being whirled off her feet by Dudley as they dance the volta.

Sir Philip Sidney turned Penshurst into a Tudor palace, adding a wing of private rooms with an Italian loggia. The old Great Hall with its vast roof has been described as one of the world's finest rooms. The Elizabethan gardens have been spared later remodelling and restored, complete with a mile-long yew hedge.

▶ *TN11 8DG. 6 miles NW of Royal Tunbridge Wells at junction of B2176 and B2188. Seasonal opening.*

❷ Hever Castle

The childhood home of Anne Boleyn was in a state of decay when American millionaire William Waldorf Astor first saw it in 1903. An idealised dream of a castle, moated, crenellated and complete with drawbridge and portcullis, it owes its perfect existence to Astor's wealth and vision, an important piece of Tudor history revived. In 1451, the 13th-century fortress of William de Hever was bought by Sir Geoffrey Bullen, whose grandson, Thomas Boleyn, would become an ambassador and treasurer for Henry VIII. Thomas and his wife, Elizabeth Howard, had two daughters, Mary and Anne. Both became ladies-in-waiting, Anne to Catherine of Aragon. She became Henry's mistress, and upon his

divorce, his second wife. The marriage lasted just three years. On May 19, 1536, at Tower Hill, Anne Boleyn commended her soul to God and laid her head on the block. Two years later, upon Thomas Boleyn's death, Hever was taken by the Crown. Henry gave it to his fourth wife, Anne of Cleves, as part of her divorce settlement. It was a mouldering wreck when Astor stepped in, employing legions of craftsmen and labourers to rebuild, panel and furnish it, under the architect Frank Pearson. He poured a fortune into the project, adding a 'Tudor village', Italian Garden with 'Pompeian Wall', digging an 18ha (35 acre) lake. What was achieved in just two years is astonishing – and all so nearly lost.

▶ *TN8 7NG. 10 miles NW of Royal Tunbridge Wells on minor roads. Seasonal opening.*

❸ Chiddingstone Castle

Denys Bower was a troubled eccentric, a passionate and gifted collector, a lonely stranger to mop, bucket and duster. In 1955 he bought for £6,000 a building that began life as the timber-framed Tudor house of the Streatfeild family. Chiddingstone was remodelled in the 1800s by William Atkinson for Henry Streatfeild, in the style of a medieval castle. Bower hoped to make a profit by displaying his collections. What better setting for Jacobean paintings, Japanese armour, swords and Buddhist and Egyptian artefacts (including a mummified cat and a 5,000-year-old funerary boat). His life story is a sad one – but, then, as a Buddhist and reincarnation of Bonnie Prince Charlie, he should have known that the First Noble Truth is suffering. Born in 1905, by the age of 45 he had been through two marriages. In the late 1950s he shot his fiancée, Anna, after she jilted him, then turned the gun on himself. Thirty years his junior, Anna had persuaded him that she was the Comptesse de Estainville. In reality, she was the daughter of a Peckham bus driver. Both survived, but Bower spent four years in Wormwood Scrubs. On his death in 1977 his friend Ruth Eldridge formed the Denys Eyre Bower Bequest to care for his collections in trust. The castle and park, the collections, the very English eccentricity of it all, make for compelling interest.

▶ *TN8 7AD. Off B2027, 8 miles W of Tonbridge. Seasonal opening.*

SOUTHERN ENGLAND

❹ Sissinghurst Castle

'Never, never, never. Not that hard little plate at my door ... as long as I live no Nat. Trust or any other foreign body shall have my darling.' In Sissinghurst: an Unfinished History, Adam Nicolson tells how his grandmother Vita Sackville-West recorded in her diary her opposition to National Trust ownership of Sissinghurst. Five years after her death in 1962, her son Nigel, burdened with death duties, placed the property in the Trust's hands, while the Nicolsons continue to live there. The garden created by Vita and her husband, Harold Nicolson, around the ruins of an Elizabethan palace, is the most loved and visited in England. It was planned as a series of themed 'rooms' (a 'succession of privacies'), a garden for all seasons. Vita confessed that it broke her back, her fingernails, sometimes her heart. It was 1930 when the couple came here from Knole, her childhood home, which had passed to her uncle as male heir. They bought a farm and the remains of a building once used to house Napoleonic prisoners of war. Their associations with the aristocratic, literary and artistic Bloomsbury Group, their way of life and their love affairs are

part of the intrigue. This is a deeply romantic place. The white garden is world famous. From the top of the evocative four-storey brick tower, there are lovely views over the Weald. The room in which Vita wrote, in winter bundled up in coats, is just as she left it. She remains a presence.
▶ *TN17 2AB. 14 miles W of Ashford on A262. NT. Seasonal opening of house and garden; estate open all year.*

❺ Scotney Castle

A Victorian country manor built in the Elizabethan style shares picturesque grounds with a partially ruined castle.
French knight Lambert de Scoteni owned an estate here in the 12th century, but the castle was not begun until 1378, by Robert Ashburnham. In 1835, his grandson, Edward Hussey, commissioned Anthony Salvin to build a new castle on a terrace above the old, with sandstone quarried from the slope below. A garden was created by William Sawrey Gilpin, whose uncle, William Gilpin, was the great exponent of the Picturesque style, which was more natural, romantic and rough around the edges than the landscaping of Capability Brown. The Picturesque movement extolled ruins and the old castle was partially dismantled, purely for the effect. It sounds like vandalism, but in summer, when it is swagged with wisteria and climbing roses, the visitor sees the point. The old castle is located on an island in a lake. The 'new' has been open to the public since 2008.
▶ *TN3 8JN. 12 miles SE of Tonbridge on A21. NT. Seasonal opening of house, old castle and garden; estate open all year.*

IT BROKE HER BACK, HER FINGERNAILS AND HER HEART...
SISSINGHURST GARDEN

6 Knole

'It has the tone of England; it melts into the green of the garden turf, into the tawnier green of the park beyond, into the blue of the pale English sky,' wrote Vita Sackville-West of the family home. For Vita, Knole had 'a deep inward gaiety of some very old woman who has always been beautiful, who has had many lovers'. Henry VIII was one who took a shine to the old lady. Originally a grand Episcopal palace, it was built for Thomas Bouchier, Archbishop of Canterbury, who acquired the Knole estate in 1456. The king grabbed it in the Reformation in 1538.

In 1566, Elizabeth I gave Knole to Thomas Sackville, 1st Earl of Dorset, who transformed it into a Renaissance mansion. In the late 17th century, the 6th Earl amassed a collection of Stuart furniture and textiles, and in the 18th, John Sackville, 3rd Duke of Dorset, hung the house with Old Masters from Italy, as well as portraits by English artists, including Reynolds and Gainsborough. The grey Kentish ragstone building presented to some a gloomy aspect. The 17th-century diarist John Evelyn was brought low by this 'greate old fashion'd house', while in the 18th century, Horace Walpole concluded that it had 'neither beauty nor prospects'. Vita saw it through different eyes and used it as the setting for her novel *The Edwardians*. It is a 'calendar house', having 365 rooms, of which 18 are open to the public. Murals on the stunning Great Staircase depict *The Five Senses*, *The Triumph of Peace over War*, and *The Four Ages of Man*. The deer park is a Site of Special Scientific Interest.
▶ *TN15 0RP. 2 miles SE of Sevenoaks. NT. Seasonal opening.*

7 Ightham Mote

Here is another historic Kent house rescued by an American – one with far less deep pockets than the saviour of Hever (see page 45). Portland, Maine, has many charms, but for the businessman Charles Henry Robinson, it had nothing to compare to this very ancient, timbered, moated country house in olde England. He first had sight of his dream house in its peaceful valley setting as a young man on a cycling tour before the First World War. In 1953 he saw it advertised for sale and bought it from a consortium of businessmen. Regretting his rashness, he wrote to withdraw his offer – but forgot to post the letter. The house dates from *c*.1320 and had been little changed since the addition of a new chapel in the 16th century completed a quadrangle. To architectural historian Nikolaus Pevsner this was 'the most complete small medieval manor house in the country'. More than 70 rooms are arranged around the central courtyard, including the Great Hall, discreetly modernised by Richard Norman Shaw in the early 20th century, the old and new chapel, 15th-century drawing room with a Jacobean fireplace, and the library. This was Robinson's favourite room, and has been kept as a memorial to him by the National Trust, to whom he presented the restored house in 1985. He might have just gone out for a turn around his 5.7ha (14 acres), to sit in the 19th-century North Lake and Woodland Garden, and admire the view of the house. In the 1990s Ightham Mote was once more on the critical list, with deathwatch beetle on the march, acid rain eating away at the masonry, and damp ruining the plaster. How it was brought back from the brink is the subject of a permanent exhibition. Both the house and its dog kennel are Grade I listed.
▶ *TN15 0NT. 3 miles SE of Sevenoaks, off A227. NT. Seasonal opening.*

8 Leeds Castle

A castle straight out of fairytales sits on an island, lapped by and mirrored in an artificial lake on which black swans glide. The first castle here was built by Robert de Crèvecoeur on land given to his father by William the Conqueror. Since that time it has been rebuilt and embellished several times. Most of what we see today was created in the 19th century for the Wykeham-Martin family, who acquired the castle as a ruin.

Crèvecoeur means 'heartbreak', and this is a place of heartbreaking beauty. It came into royal ownership in 1278 when Edward I bought it for his queen, Eleanor of Castile. It was probably Edward who created the lake, adding a barbican spanning three islands and the 'Gloriette' with apartments for the royal couple. Henry VIII transformed the castle into a palace for Catherine of Aragon. His portrait hangs in the Banqueting Hall. The castle's last private owner was the Hon. Olive, Lady Baillie, an heiress, who bought it in 1926 and engaged architects Armand-Albert Rateau and decorator Stéphanie Boudin to transform the interiors. She bequeathed the castle to a charitable foundation and it must work for its living, offering gift shops, a restaurant, B&B, golfing and conference facilities (Tony Blair held Northern Ireland peace talks here in 2004). A strange curiosity is a museum of dog collars.
▶ *ME17 1PL. 6 miles E of Maidstone, close to Junction 8 of M20. Open all year.*

RESTORATION HOUSE

9 Restoration House

Dickens used this as the model for Satis House, Miss Havisham's decaying home in *Great Expectations*, but visitors will not find dismal brick, walled-up windows or rusted bars. Situated in the town centre, this house was created in the late 1500s or early 1600s, incorporating two medieval buildings. Its name recalls the night Charles II stayed here on his triumphant return to England in 1660, but it could as well describe the labour of love that it is for its present owners. The building was condemned when Robert Tucker and Jonathan Wilmot viewed it in the early 1990s. It had bankrupted the comedian Rod Hull. They have brought it back to life, filled it with period furniture, and uncovered details that they believe were hastily contrived by the lawyer Francis Clerke – marbling, japanning, French doors – in honour of the royal visit. The façade was added ten years after the Restoration. The exterior is of red brick with tall chimneys, Dutch gables and windows of widely varying styles. Inside are tapestries said to have been a gift from the appreciative Charles II. The King's Bedroom, which still has 17th-century window glass, was embellished in the Victorian era, with a mural illustrating Tennyson's Idylls of the King. All this and a large walled garden with boxwood parterre, herbaceous borders, picturesque greenhouse and a pond overhung with quinces.

▶ *ME1 1RF. Crow Lane, Rochester town centre. Seasonal opening of house and garden on Thursdays and Fridays.*

⑩ Belmont House

Upstairs and down, historic clocks tick and whirr and chime. 'O let not Time deceive you, / You cannot conquer Time', as W.H. Auden was fond of reminding us. Time ran out for Colonel John Montresor in June 1799 in Maidstone prison. He had been falsely accused of dipping into army coffers, died in custody and was posthumously exonerated. In 1780, Montresor had bought Belmont, a Georgian house in an elevated position with views over the North Downs. He enlarged the park and engaged Samuel Wyatt to build a neoclassical main block, using an orangery to connect it to the earlier house. Sold from under him by the War Office, Belmont was acquired by General George Harris (later Lord Harris), as reward for his part in the defeat of the Sultan of Mysore in 1798. The house remained in the Harris family until 1995. Mementoes recall the role played by successive generations in the expansion of the Empire. The grounds are made up of a pinetum, a walled garden, woodland, lawns and kitchen garden. Most interesting is the largest private collection of clocks in Britain, brought together by George St Vincent, 5th Baron Harris of Seringapatam, Mysore and Belmont in the county of Kent. At his death, aged 95, in 1984, he had 340 timepieces from all over the world, with emphasis on England from the mid 1600s to mid 1700s. Harris was Master of the Worshipful Company of Clockmakers, so he could keep them all ticking over.
▶ *ME13 0HH. 5 miles SW of Faversham on minor roads. Seasonal opening of house at weekends (tours only – specialist clock tours on last Saturday of month); gardens open daily.*

⑪ Cobham Hall

This large redbrick Elizabethan house with tall chimneys and octagonal towers was built for the Cobham family. The flanking wings were added after a visit from Elizabeth I, when the mortified family feared that it hadn't measured up. One-time home to the Earls of Darnley, it has been a girls' school since 1960. Darnley portraits adorn the walls and the interiors are impressive. The hall is also used as a wedding venue and is open to the public on certain days in season. The grounds were laid out by Humphry Repton in the 1790s, to great renown, with an Ionic temple, grotto and aviary.
▶ *DA12 3BL. 5 miles SE of Gravesend on minor roads. Guided tours of house and grounds.*

⑫ Godinton House and Gardens

In Tate Britain's collection there is a painting by Robert Braithwaite Martineau, *The Last Day in the Old Home.* It portrays the family of a feckless squire who gambled away his inheritance. The model for the squire was Martineau's friend John Leslie Toke; the work was painted here in 1862. The Tokes acquired the original house in the late 1400s. In the early 17th century Captain Nicholas Toke put his stamp on it, building a Jacobean house with distinctive gables around the medieval great hall and Tudor rooms, adding an east wing, installing a staircase of elaborately carved chestnut, and creating the Great Chamber that is one of the house's idiosyncratic marvels. A frieze shows soldiers performing pike drill, as Toke's troops did in the Civil War. He was a great character, and in his 90 years outlived five wives.

In the Georgian era his son John added a further wing, and planted the parkland with numerous trees. Martineau's pal J.L. inherited the house in 1666. When Ashley Dodd bought the property in around 1900, he called in Reginald Blomfield to update it. Blomfield also redesigned the delightful gardens and planted one of the longest yew hedges in England. House and gardens are managed by a trust.
▶ *TN23 3BP. 2 miles NW of Ashford town centre. Limited seasonal opening of house; gardens open daily March to end October.*

⑬ Walmer Castle

One of a trio of Henry VIII's artillery forts, with Deal and Sandown, Walmer was built against a feared invasion from France or Spain. By the time it was completed, the threat of foreign incursions had diminished. From 1708 it became the official residence of the Lords Warden of the Cinque Ports, a ceremonial office often held by prime ministers or members of the royal family. William Pitt and the 2nd Earl Granville created the lovely gardens. The 1st Duke of Wellington was Warden from 1829 until his death here in 1852. His bedroom is much as he left it, complete with camp bed, the armchair in which he died, and a pair of Wellington boots. The Queen Mother was Lord Warden until her death in 2002 and loved to stay in the summer. Some of her rooms are open to the public, and one of the gardens within the 19th-century walled garden, designed by Penelope Hobhouse, was a gift for her 95th birthday.
▶ *CT14 7LJ. 1 mile S of Deal. EH. Seasonal opening.*

OXFORDSHIRE

The mansions that grace the Oxfordshire landscape are romantic, magnificent – even labyrinthine – but above all, full of treasures, from Old Masters and Pre-Raphaelite paintings to heritage roses.

① Blenheim Palace

Here is Queen Anne's reward to John Churchill for victory at the Battle of Blenheim in 1704 – grander than any royal residence. Churchill, Duke of Marlborough, was a mean, self-seeking man, but a military genius. His wife, Sarah Jennings, was an attendant and intimate of Queen Anne. Through her, Churchill became one of the most powerful men in England, imposing his views on the ailing queen. For his supremacy at Blenheim in the War of Spanish Succession, Anne granted him the royal estate at Woodstock, on which to build a palace. John Vanbrugh was commissioned, and a model was presented to the queen. Sarah, who had dreamt of a comfortable country house, lamented 'the madnesse of the whole Design'. In spite of her objections, Vanbrugh, with Nicholas

Hawksmoor, set out to build a baroque mansion in the highest style.

Work stopped in 1712 when the Marlboroughs fell from grace and went into temporary exile. The house was eventually completed at the duke's own expense, costing in all an incredible £300,000. Vanbrugh declared it a work of 'beauty, magnificence and duration'. Above all, it is triumphal. On the ceiling of the Great Hall, Sir James Thornhill painted a map of Blenheim battlefield. Heroic murals celebrate military might. At the end of an avenue, in parkland laid out by Capability Brown in the 1760s, stands a 41m (134ft) Column of Victory.

In November 1874, the most famous Churchill of all, another great war tactician, Winston Spencer, was born here.

▶ *OX20 1PP. 8 miles N of Oxford on A44. Seasonal opening of house; park open all year.*

BLENHEIM PALACE

❷ Ditchley Park

A vision of Georgian perfection, this mansion was built in 1722 for the 2nd Earl of Lichfield, whose mother, Charlotte Fitzroy, was the illegitimate daughter of Charles II. It is the work of Francis Smith of Warwick, modified by James Gibbs, who trained in Rome under Carlo Fontana, master of the baroque. The richly decorative interiors were by William Kent and Henry Flitcroft. From 1760 the park took on a more 'natural' aspect. Stiff Leadbetter added the Great Temple. In 1933, Ronald Tree, an Anglo-American and a Conservative MP, bought the estate. He and his wife, Nancy, set about a programme of meticulous restoration. A young Geoffrey Jellicoe was brought in to remodel the grounds. He created an Italianate sunken garden and reinstated parts of Gibbs' design. Winston Churchill came to stay before the Second World War, and also in wartime when Chequers – the Prime Minister's country residence in Buckinghamshire – was deemed too vulnerable.

Portraits of both Charles II and Barbara Villiers, Charlotte Fitzroy's mother, hang in the White Drawing Room. Ditchley is today available for hire as a conference venue and for private group visits by arrangement. It is home to a foundation dedicated to promoting Anglo-American accord.

▶ *OX7 4ER. 7 miles SE of Chipping Norton on A44.*

❸ Chastleton House

Here is the birthplace of croquet as a competitive sport. The croquet lawn was laid down in the 1860s by Walter Whitemore-Jones, author of the definitive rules of the game. A Jacobean country house, Chastleton was built of sandstone, around a central courtyard, for wool merchant Walter Jones in 1607–12. Architectural historian Nikolaus Pevsner paid it a backhanded compliment, describing the decoration as 'blatantly nouveau riche, even barbaric, uninhibited by any consideration of insipid good taste'. The Long Gallery, which would have been hung with portraits and tapestries, is rather bare. Jones's descendants let his wealth run through their fingers in the Civil War, so they could not afford to update the building.

In 1955 it passed to a relative of the Joneses, art historian Professor Alan Clutton-Brock. It was very run down, 'held together' by cobwebs, but otherwise scarcely changed when the National Trust acquired it from his widow in 1991. The interior layout is labyrinthine, with numerous rooms, including the Great Chamber. In the library is displayed a Bible that Bishop William Juxon placed in the hands of Charles I as he awaited execution.

▶ *GL56 0SU. 4 miles SE of Moreton-in-Marsh on A44. NT. Seasonal opening.*

❹ Broughton Castle

'About the most beautiful castle in all England.' 'Still the most romantic house imaginable.' This medieval ironstone castle in lush countryside, has been owned by the Fiennes family, Barons Saye and Sele, since the 14th century. In his 2009 book *The Music Room*, a paean to his childhood home, William Fiennes describes a house with medieval beginnings, transformed in Tudor times into a stately home. His ancestor William Fiennes, 1st Viscount Saye and Sele, opposed Charles I, raising troops to

ROUSHAM PARK GARDENS

fight at Edgehill. At one time, Royalists besieged and occupied his castle. In the small Council Chamber, 'a room that hath no ears', clandestine meetings were held to plot against the king. In the Oak Room a tall cartouche bears a Latin inscription expressing the view that 'there is no pleasure in the memory of the past'. Was it placed here by William upon the Restoration of the Monarchy? Relationships with royalty were not always sour. On show are the rooms in which James I and Anne of Denmark slept in 1604.

In the 19th century the castle was falling into decay and Sir George Gilbert Scott was called in by the 16th Lord to restore it. Many films have used it as a backdrop, including *Lady Jane* and

The Madness of King George. The 1300 Great Hall was the scene of a dance in *Shakespeare in Love*. The gardens were created by Lord and Lady Saye and Sele with advice from Lanning Roper, the American designer, who urged, 'Let the borders spill.' The heritage roses are a particular delight.

▶ *OX15 5EB. 3 miles SW of Banbury on B4035. Seasonal opening.*

❺ Rousham House and Garden

'The garden is Daphne in little, the sweetest little groves, streams, glades, porticoes, cascades, and river, imaginable; all the scenes are perfectly classic.' Horace Walpole came to Rousham in 1760 and was transported. House and garden are the work of William Kent, a pioneer of English landscape design. The house has been in the ownership of the same family since Sir Robert Dormer bought the manor of Rousham in the 1630s. In 1719, Dormer's grandson, Colonel Robert Dormer-Cottrell, set about transforming his property. Charles Bridgeman laid out the grounds over 18 years. When Rousham passed to Robert's brother James, he brought in Kent, who built two wings and the stable block, and added crenellations. The south front is almost as he left it, although some of the interiors have been altered.

The gardens remain today pure Kent, a series of Arcadian set pieces, with ponds and cascades in Venus's Vale, the Cold Bath, the seven-arched Praeneste, the Temple of the Mill, and the 'Eyecatcher', a contrived ruin rising against the sky, all sitting within a bend in the River Cherwell. In the house there are collections of fine Jacobean and 18th-century furniture, paintings and statuary. The Library won a sceptical Walpole around: 'It reinstated Kent with me; he has no where shewn so much taste.'

▶ *OX25 4QU. 11 miles N of Oxford off A4260. Gardens open every day; house by arrangement.*

❻ Buscot Park

'Any reservations you may have … must be laid fairly and squarely at my door … for the Trust plays no part in the day-to-day running of Buscot Park, nor the vermilion reds or the Germolene pinks we may choose.' Charles, 3rd Lord Faringdon, describes the characterful family home that he tends on behalf of the National Trust, complete with the Faringdon Collection. His great-grandfather Alexander Henderson bought this late 18th-century house in 1859. He enlarged it and called in Harold Peto to lay out the Italianate water garden. A successful financier, Henderson became 1st Lord Faringdon in 1916. He filled his house with precious furniture and paintings, bringing together works by Rembrandt, Rossetti and Murillo among others. For Burne-Jones's paintings of *The Legend of Briar Rose* in the Saloon, the artist himself designed the framework of carved and gilded wood.

Alexander's grandson and heir, Gavin Henderson, 2nd Lord Faringdon, was a socialist and pacifist. In his time, Buscot became an intellectual hothouse, buzzing with debate. He added to the collection, which continues to grow as the house evolves. It is a special place – no museum but palpably alive.

The present Lord Faringdon, came to live here at age 16, following the death of his parents. He commissioned Ellen-Ann Hopkins to paint the witty murals in the tearoom, depicting the Faringdon family with their lurchers, the black swans from the lake and flowers from the Four Seasons Garden. A novelty is a 62 seat 1930s theatre still used for public performances.
▶ *SN7 8BU. 3 miles NW of Faringdon on A417. NT. Seasonal opening.*

❼ Ardington House

A 'swagger house', in the words of architectural historian Nikolaus Pevsner, Ardington dates from 1720 and is a superb example of Georgian architecture. It was built by the Strong brothers for the Baring banking family and has been their home ever since. Full of family portraits, the house also contains paintings and furniture from a variety of periods. The staircase is magnificent. Today it is principally a wedding and conference venue.
▶ *OX12 8PY. 2 miles E of Wantage on A417. Open for six weeks in summer for tours. Private tours at other times by arrangement.*

❽ Milton House

This tall, elegant, classically inspired redbrick Restoration mansion stands in parkland, overlooking a lake. It was begun in around 1663, and was sold to Bryant Barrett, lacemaker to George III, in 1764. Barrett commissioned Stephen Wright, Master Mason of the Office of Works, to add wings and more service accommodation. The extensions included a new chapel for the recusant Catholic family. His friend the bishop Richard Challoner often celebrated mass here. The classical exterior and its first-floor situation were intended to disguise its use, so it should blend in with the main house.

Both library and chapel are Strawberry Hill Gothic. A precious stained-glass panel depicts Christ enthroned. The Chinese wallpaper in the bedroom adjacent to the chapel dates from the 17th century. A 17th-century oak staircase rises majestically from ground floor to attic.

The house passed by descent to the present owner, Anthony Mockler-Barrett.
▶ *OX14 4EN. 3 miles SW of Junction 7 of M40 on A329. Limited seasonal opening for guided tours only; open all year for group tours by arrangement.*

❾ Mapledurham House

'There's Toad Hall ...' said the Rat. 'Toad is rather rich, you know, and this is really one of the nicest houses in these parts, though we never admit as much to Toad.' The reader of *The Wind in the Willows*, turning to Ernest Shepard's illustrations of Toad Hall, will see that it is Mapledurham to the life. The author, Kenneth Grahame, lived not far upstream, in Pangbourne, and would have known the house. Its original Elizabethan staircase may have been the one down which poor Mr Toad was bundled under house arrest. It is a survivor of an interior modernised in 1868; the H-plan exterior is unspoilt.

The house was begun for Sir Michael Blount in 1588 when he became Lieutenant Warden of the Tower of London. It was completed by his son, the Royalist Sir Richard. Sir Richard's son Charles was a Royalist and apparently a spendthrift in the manner of Mr Toad. In 1635 he had to sell his possessions to pay off his creditors.

In the Civil War his depleted house was besieged, sacked and sequestered by Parliament. Sir Charles was killed the following year, fighting for the king at the Siege of Oxford and the heir, Michael Blount, was murdered, aged 19, by a footman, at Charing Cross. Michael's brother Walter recovered the property, which passed to his cousin, Lyster. Poet Alexander Pope would visit to court Lyster's daughters, Teresa and Martha (who styled themselves Zephalinda and Parthenissa). At first more attracted to Teresa, he was later drawn to Martha's 'resistless charms'. He wrote romantic and outrageous letters to them both.

The house that passed down to John Joseph Eyston came with a lot of history – including a remnant of the original medieval manor. Since 1960 he has restored it as a family home, which he shares with his wife, Lady Anne, and their three children.
▶ *RG4 7TR. 4 miles NW of Reading off A4074. Seasonal opening, weekends and bank holidays.*

⑩ Kingston Bagpuize House

The history of this elegant house goes back 1,000 years, but what we see today is a remodelling carried out in 18th-century Georgian style. It was the home of the Fettiplaces, a prominent Oxfordshire family, until 1917. It is today the home of Virginia Grant and her two children. The gardens were restored by Virginia and her late husband, Francis. She continues the labour of love. The house is a venue for weddings and corporate functions.

▶ *OX13 5AX. 6 miles W of Abingdon on A415. Open all year for groups and private tours.*

⑪ Stonor Park

In a gentle fold in the Chilterns, behind a redbrick Georgian façade with Gothic centrepiece, stands one of Britain's oldest manor houses. The history of Stonor is intertwined with that of the devoutly Catholic Lords Camoys, who have lived here for 850 years. In the Reformation they were recusants, refusing to attend Anglican worship. It was a perilous stance. St Edmund Campion, a Jesuit priest, was sheltered here in the reign of Elizabeth I.

Visitors can see the room in which he printed a pamphlet on 'Ten Reasons' to prefer the Catholic faith, before he was hanged, drawn and quartered in 1581.

In 1975 the 6th Lord Camoys sold up, but the family bought the estate back and have been restoring the house ever since. Bright interiors contain antique furniture and ceramics. Pictures of saints hang alongside family portraits and Italian Old Master drawings. The tower of a chapel begun in the 13th century is the earliest example of fine brick architecture in the southeast. Mass is still celebrated here. The *Stations of the Cross,* carved by a Polish prisoner of war, was a gift from Graham Greene, whose religious sensibility runs through his novels. Fallow deer graze in the park.

▶ *5 miles N of Henley-on-Thames on B480. Henley to Watlington road. Limited seasonal opening.*

⑫ Greys Court

'Framed like a picture by the rarest and stateliest of trees ... stands a comparatively modern house and erected among the remains of a vast old castellated mansion, belonging first to the noble family of Gray ... then to the house of Knollys.' So Mary Russell Mitford described Greys Court in 1851. It is very ancient in its origins, dating from the 1300s. Sir John de Grey negotiated a licence to crenellate in 1347. The house passed to the Crown in 1485 and was granted to Robert Knollys, who had lived there since 1503, for an annual rent of a red rose at midsummer. Henry VIII secured it for Robert's son Francis, later Treasurer to Elizabeth I and attendant to the captive Mary, Queen of Scots. His son William is said to have been the inspiration for Malvolio, the butt of Shakespeare's wit in *Twelfth Night.*

Little remained of the oldest part of Greys when Sir Felix Brunner came to the rescue in 1937. What survives is part of a wing of an Elizabethan mansion, built of brick and flint with three gables, and an unmatched, bow-windowed 18th-century extension, probably by Henry Keene. The drawing room has some fine rococo plasterwork attributed to Thomas Robert of Oxford in around 1750 and there are panels of 16th and 17th-century Swiss stained glass on the landing. Outside there is a donkey wheel in use until the First World War for drawing water.

Greys Court remained home to the Brunners until recently and still has a lived-in feeling. Walled gardens are set among medieval ruins.

▶ *RG9 4PG. 3 miles W of Henley-on-Thames on minor roads. NT. Seasonal opening.*

SOUTHERN ENGLAND

BANQUETING ROOM, BRIGHTON PAVILION

Pavilioned in splendour

At legendary house parties thrown by society hostesses renowned for their hospitality, excess was the order of the day.

Sir Christopher Hatton danced attendance on Elizabeth I. He was her devoted Lord Chancellor and built Holdenby in Northamptonshire in her honour and vowed that he would not live there until she had graced it with her presence. She never came.

Hatton was not the only courtier to commission a 'Prodigy House' fit to entertain Gloriana. Sir John Thynne built Longleat in Wiltshire; Sir William More rebuilt Loseley House in Surrey; Sir William Cecil splashed out on Burghley House in Lincolnshire and received Elizabeth a dozen times. If the cost of creating a palatial residence did not bankrupt these noblemen, the expense of hosting the queen and her court, on one of her great road shows known as 'progresses', was bound to do so. And yet they craved royal patronage and the status it conferred.

Royalty would also push the boat out. Guests joining George IV in his Banqueting Room at Brighton Pavilion could expect to be presented with 70 courses. As Prince Regent he employed a French chef, Marie-Antoine Carême, who produced towering confectionery centrepieces. In January 1817, George sat down with the Grand Duke Nicholas of Russia to a feast of 127 dishes. Carême's *pièces montées* included an Italian pavilion, Swiss hermitage, an oriental pavilion of nougat, and a pastry of the Pavilion.

Of course, it was very much about show, as many of the great country-house parties were. Guests enjoyed hunting and shooting, horse-riding, feasting, dancing, promenading, musical recitals, sparkling conversation, games of 'Sardines' and treasure hunts, carriage-driving, social climbing and bed-hopping. A country house was ideal for illicit trysts, in well-appointed bedrooms and hidden bowers.

In the 'Golden Age' of the country-house party, from the 1860s to the First World War, London society left the city at the close of 'the season' for weeks of leisure, spent visiting one another at their ancestral piles. Armies of cooks, valets, butlers, ladies' maids, housemaids, gardeners, gamekeepers and grooms serviced their every need.

House parties presented great opportunities for power-mongering and guest lists were carefully compiled. Lady Tweedsmuir, Mrs John Buchan, wrote that the clever hostess would bring together 'one or two Cabinet Ministers ... there might be a Viceroy or high official from a far-off corner of the Empire ... a diplomat home on leave, a painter, and almost certainly a musician ... a sprinkling of women famous for their beauty, or wit, or both.'

Putting on the Ritz

At Polesden Lacy in Surrey, in the early 20th century, Margaret Greville established herself as the 'prima donna' of party-giving. Her life revolved around entertaining high society, including Edward VII, for whom she provided a ritzy suite of rooms.

Even after the Great War there were stellar events. In the 1920s, the American-born Olive Wilson Filmer, Lady Baillie, at Leeds Castle in Kent, entertained such diverse guests as Edward VIII and Charlie Chaplin, Douglas Fairbanks Jnr and the Grand Duke Dimitri of Russia.

At Cliveden in Buckinghamshire, Nancy Astor held court with a group of political intellectuals. She was famous for her rapier wit, saying of herself, 'My vigour, vitality and cheek repel me. I am the kind of woman I would run from.' Winston Churchill felt the same way. In one of their memorable exchanges she told him, 'If you were my husband, I'd poison your tea,' to which he replied, 'Madam, if you were my wife, I'd drink it.' In the 1930s Maud Russell made Mottisfont in Hampshire a Mecca for literary and artistic friends, including her lover, Ian Fleming, creator of James Bond.

Lord Berners, composer, artist, practical joker, upstaged them all at Faringdon House, a Palladian villa in Oxfordshire now rented privately. In the 1930s this gay and infinitely amusing lord created a salon for a circle of artistic and intellectual friends that included Beerbohm, Sassoon, Waugh, Cecil Beaton, Dali, Margot Fonteyn and H.G. Wells. A composer and artist, Berners entertained in outlandish style. For one party he dyed the plumage of his fantail pigeons in pastel shades to create what Nancy Mitford described as 'a cloud of confetti in the sky'.

> The Prince Regent sat down with the Grand Duke Nicholas of Russia to a feast of 127 dishes that included an oriental pavilion made of nougat
> BRIGHTON PAVILION

SURREY

Sweet music, fine food and finer art characterise Surrey's elegant houses. All had their place in history, though one – that can be glimpsed from Windsor Great Park – shaped the events of the modern world.

THE LOSELEY ESTATE

❶ The Loseley Estate

When James I stayed at Loseley, he was so well pleased that he commissioned portraits of himself and his queen, Anne of Denmark. They are by his court painter, John de Critz, and hang in the Great Hall, where the panelling is believed to have come from Henry VIII's lost pleasure palace, the incomparable Nonsuch. This unspoilt Elizabethan mansion was built in the 1560s by a courtier, Sir William More, as a place to entertain the queen, when she deemed an earlier house inadequate. It has been in the More-Molyneux family for 500 years. The Drawing Room ceiling was commissioned especially for James I's visit. The fireplace, carved from local chalk, is to a design by Holbein; cushions are said to have been worked by Elizabeth I herself. Here are such curiosities as George IV's coronation chair. Fine china and paintings abound. The visitor has a sense of both pride of possession and the impulse to share. The exterior incorporated stone reclaimed from the Cistercian Waverley Abbey at Farnham, suppressed by Henry VIII in the Reformation. Within the walled gardens, a series of 'rooms' display plantings of roses, herbs and vegetables. The Loseley herd of Jersey cattle, which grazes the park, supply the well-known dairy products.
▶ *GU3 1HS (include Stakescorner Road for Sat Nav). 2 miles SW of Guildford, off B3000. Seasonal opening.*

❷ Clandon Park

The 2nd Lord Onslow commissioned the Venetian Giacomo Leoni to build this Palladian mansion in the 1730s, in the peaceful Surrey countryside. It is noted in particular for its magnificent two-storey, balconied Marble Hall beneath a frescoed ceiling. Lord Onslow had made a 'prudent' marriage to Jamaican heiress Elizabeth Knight, and no expense was spared. The National Trust has done a fine job in rescuing a house and gardens that had fallen into decay. It is a wedding venue and available for corporate functions, with a restaurant in the undercroft.
▶ *GU4 7RQ. 3 miles E of Guildford off A246. NT. Seasonal opening.*

❸ Hatchlands Park

Pianofortes once played by Bach, Mahler, Elgar, Chopin and Liszt, a piano made for Marie Antoinette, virginals from the court of Charles II – this pristine Georgian redbrick mansion is home to the Cobbe Collection of more than 40 of the finest historic keyboard instruments, 12 of them owned or performed upon by great composers. Hatchlands was built in 1758 for Admiral Boscawen, a veteran of naval conflict who famously advised his men: 'Never fire until you see the whites of their eyes.' His architect was Stiff Leadbetter, whose style has sometimes been described as 'lacking flair', and the exterior is rather restrained, but what lies within is music to the eyes.

Here is the earliest known work of a young Robert Adam, including the ceiling in the Saloon, with a frieze celebrating Boscawen's seagoing adventures. This is the main exhibition room, hung with Old Masters. The Adam fireplace is flanked by caryatids carved by Flemish sculptor John Michael Rysback.

Hatchlands was left to the National Trust in 1945. Alec Cobbe is the tenant, and he has filled it with his art treasures, his furniture, and the instruments that are his delight, all in perfect tune. The house stands within 163 hectares (400 acres) of informal grounds, partly laid out by Humphry Repton, with a small parterre designed by Gertrude Jekyll.
▶ *GU4 7RT. 5 miles E of Guildford, off A246. NT. Seasonal opening.*

❹ Fort Belvedere

What began life as an elaborate folly was to be the scene of one of the most momentous events in the recent history of British royalty. When Prince William Augustus commissioned Fort Belvedere in 1750, it was to be essentially picturesque, its only practical purpose that of a summerhouse. In 1828, Sir Jeffrey Wyattville enlarged the structure, adding an octagonal room in which George IV would dine. In 1911 it was converted into a residence – presented, in 1929, by George V to his son Edward, Prince of Wales. Even as king, Edward VIII stayed frequently, and it was here, on December 10, 1936, that he renounced the throne to marry an American divorcee, Wallis Simpson. In 2011, letters came to light, written by Wallis to Ernest, the husband she was divorcing, which reveal that she still loved him. She had enjoyed being the king's mistress but had not dreamt that she would marry 'Peter Pan'. She wrote, 'None of this mess and waking emptiness is my doing.' An abdication of responsibility, one might say. The house, situated in Windsor Great Park, is in private hands.
▶ *SL5 7SD. 8 miles S of Windsor close to junction of A30 and A329.*

SOUTHERN ENGLAND

❺ Great Fosters

This Elizabethan country house has been a hotel since the 1930s, when the Sutcliffe family converted it, retaining its character. Jacobean fireplaces, panelling, Flemish tapestries, mullioned windows, a 17th-century oak staircase to the tower all speak of its age. In the early 1900s Great Fosters was owned by Baroness Halkett, lady-in-waiting to Queen Alexandra, passing to the Earl of Dudley and then to the Hon. Gerald Montagu. The garden was part of a 1918 redesign by W.H. Romaine-Walker, including topiary, a knot garden, archery pavilion and swimming pool. The Drake sundial may have been a gift from Sir Francis Drake in the days when Elizabeth I stayed here. In 1931 the Ascot Ball was held here. Charlie Chaplin and Orson Welles were among early guests.
▶ *TW20 9UR. 1 mile SW of Staines, off M25 Junction 13, 1 mile S of Egham.*

❻ Polesden Lacey

'She was so shrewd, so kind and so amusingly unkind, so sharp, such fun, so naughty, altogether a real person, a character, utterly Mrs Ronald Greville and no tinge of anything alien.' So wrote Elizabeth Bowes-Lyons, wife of George VI, to Osbert Sitwell, on the death of Margaret Greville. The illegitimate daughter of an Edinburgh brewer, Margaret created a fabulously grand house here in which to entertain royalty. In 1906, Captain the Hon. Ronald Greville acquired for his new bride, Margaret McEwan, a regency villa designed by Thomas Cubitt. Mrs Greville engaged Charles Mewès and Arthur Davis, architects of The Ritz, to create opulent Edwardian interiors, with an additional suite of rooms to accommodate Edward VII.

After the death of her husband in 1908, Margaret continued to cultivate friends in high places. She grew very close to Queen Mary, consort of George V, and to Elizabeth Bowes-Lyons before her marriage to the future king (the couple honeymooned here in 1923). Her jewellery included the Empress Josephine's emeralds and a diamond ring that once belonged to Catherine the Great. To her friend Elizabeth she left Marie Antoinette's necklace. But the greatest bequest of all was of this spectacular house, paintings, and park to the nation.
▶ *RH5 6BD. 4 miles SW of Leatherhead, off A246. NT. Limited opening of house all year; gardens open all year.*

POLESDEN LACEY

❼ Titsey Place and Gardens

A grasshopper crest above the front door gives a clue to the house's origins. This is the emblem of the Gresham family, City merchants in Tudor times. John Gresham acquired the manor of Titsey, in the foothills of the North Downs, in 1534. His son Thomas was founder of the Royal Exchange, where a grasshopper adorns a weather vane. The estate passed through the female line to the Leveson Gowers.

The original Tudor house received a Georgian makeover, but the face it now presents is neo-Tudor, grey rendered, the work of James Wyatt's assistant William Atkinson in 1826. A battlemented tower was added by Squire Granville Leveson Gower in the latter 1800s. Obsessed with ancestry, he filled the place with family portraits, decorated it with heraldry, and compiled and printed *The Genealogy of the Family of Gresham*. He and his brother, William laid out the gardens. The last generation of Leveson Gowers, set up a charitable trust to preserve the estate for public enjoyment. This faintly eccentric property is in the care of a godson, David Innes. Restoration work continues.
▶ *RH8 0SD. 3 miles NE of Oxted on B269. Seasonal opening.*

SUSSEX

The manors of Sussex conceal four centuries of triumph and tragedy, but now all is tranquil within their walls. Certainly Rudyard Kipling found no 'ancient regrets or stifled miseries' at his cherished Bateman's.

❶ Uppark House and Garden

When Sarah Wells worked as a housekeeper here, her brilliant son Herbert George was given use of the library. He had been forced to leave school, and was apprenticed to a draper, but he continued his own education, burying himself in Plato's Republic and Thomas More's Utopia. Fired with a passion for literature, he went on to write such innovative novels as *The Time Machine* and *The War of the Worlds*.

A grand 17th-century house in the Dutch style, with a portico by Humphry Repton, who landscaped the gardens in the Picturesque style, Uppark was rescued after a fire in 1989. Interiors are Georgian, and house a collection brought together on the Grand Tour. An 18th-century dolls' house is presented with its contents. The surrounding woodland and South Downs views are as 'the father of science fiction' would have seen them when he turned up between menial jobs, 'the bad shilling back again', loving the place, disliking the social inequality it represented. The servants' quarters appear as they were in Victorian times when Sarah laboured here.
▶ *GU31 5QR. 5 miles SE of Petersfield on B2146. NT. Seasonal opening.*

❷ Stansted House and Park

'A house seeming to be a retreat, being surrounded by this woods, thro' which there are the most pleasant agreeable visto's cut, that are to be seen any where in England.' Daniel Defoe was writing in 1724, but his description serves today. Situated in the South Downs National Park, Stansted was begun as a hunting lodge 800 years ago and has been much altered over centuries. A 17th-century house that burnt out in 1900 was rebuilt in replica by Sir Reginald Blomfield, in the style of Sir Christopher Wren, with colonnaded portico and roof cupola. Inside, though, this is an Edwardian home, and the visitor is invited to imagine a hive of industry 'below stairs', as well as to see how the Ponsonbys, Earls of Bessborough, lived, from the time they bought Stansted in 1924. A former owner in the early 19th century, Lewis Way, built the Regency Gothic chapel that is at the centre of a group of historic walled gardens. Its stained-glass window makes an appearance in Keats's *The Eve of St Agnes* – 'A casement high and triple-arch'd … All garlanded with carven imag'ries.' The chapel's resplendent decorations were created by Harry Goodhart-Rendel in the 1920s.
▶ *PO9 6DX. 4 miles NE of Havant off B2147. Seasonal opening.*

❸ Goodwood House

Charles de Keroualle was the illegitimate son of Charles II by his French mistress, Louise de Keroualle. He loved hunting and gambling, and visited Goodwood from the age of 17 to ride to hounds. When he bought and enlarged this Jacobean house on the Sussex Downs in 1697, it was for use as a hunting lodge. The house was extended in the 18th century, with the addition of a Palladian-style, Portland stone south wing. The north wing that followed was partly demolished 50 years ago because of dry rot. James Wyatt added Regency state apartments and a round tower.

Goodwood might not have measured up in the eyes of Louise, whose rooms at Whitehall were praised for being 'ten times' richer and more sumptuous than the queen's, but it is one of England's finest stately homes and one of the most unusual, rising over just two storeys. This is the seat of the Dukes of Richmond, Lennox, Gordon and Aubigny, whose art collection is one of the best in any English country house. Fine pieces of English and French furniture, Gobelin tapestries and Sèvres porcelain adorn interiors restored by the duke's heir, the Earl of March and Kinrara.
▶ *PO18 0PX. 6 miles NE of Chichester. Limited seasonal opening.*

❹ Arundel Castle

From the walls of the picture gallery in this magnificent castle, generations of Howards, Dukes of Norfolk, look down. For 850 years this has been their stately home, and their exploits fill many pages of the history books. The 2nd Duke, Lord Howard of Effingham, joined Sir Francis Drake in fighting off the Spanish Armada in 1588. Others fell foul of royalty and lost their heads.

The castle was badly damaged in the Civil War. Some 200 years later, in 1846, Victoria and

Albert spent three days here. Bedroom and library furniture were specially commissioned for their stay. Today's castle is a Victorian re-creation by Henry, 15th Duke of Norfolk. It was completed in 1900 and although it is largely a Gothic revival fantasy, it has kept touch with its medieval roots, and suits of armour seem perfectly at home. Greatest of the enormous rooms is the cavernous Baron's Hall, with oak hammerbeam roof. Among a wealth of treasures are portraits by Van Dyck, Reynolds and Gainsborough, tapestries, clocks and some personal possessions of Mary, Queen of Scots.
▶ *BN18 9AB. 8 miles E of Chichester, off A27 Brighton road. Seasonal opening.*

❺ Parham

In the Green Room of this lovely Elizabethan manor hangs a painting of a kangaroo by George Stubbs, who worked from a skin and skull brought back from Captain Cook's great voyage of 1771. In the Long Gallery, which runs the width of the house, the Parham Troop of Yeomanry was drilled for the Napoleonic Wars. It contains antique furniture, needlework, paintings, antiques and objets d'art, under a ceiling by Oliver Messel, dating from 1968. Only three families have owned Parham since it was founded in 1577. Today it is the property of a charitable trust and is the family home of Lady Emma Barnard. The place was dying on its feet when her grandfather, the Hon. Clive Pearson, bought it in 1922 and began to breathe new life into it. The family's collection of historic needlework is one of its special charms. The approach is through the deer park with views of the downs.
▶ *RH20 4HS. 3 miles S of Pulborough on A283. Seasonal opening.*

❻ Petworth House and Park

J.M.W. Turner's talents were little recognised when George Wyndham, 3rd Earl of Egremont, perceived his brilliance. Turner visited Petworth often, and in 1809 was commissioned to make paintings of the house and park, which he did over the next decade. One-time seat of the powerful Percy family, Dukes of Northumberland, Petworth is home to the National Trust's finest collection of pictures. In 1682 the estate passed by marriage to the 6th Duke of Somerset, who rebuilt it in a French-inspired style, with a very long, rather plain façade. When Daniel Defoe saw it in 1724, he noted that 'the duke's house … is certainly a compleat building in itself, and the apartments are very noble, well contriv'd and richly furnish'd'.

However, 'The house stands as it were with its elbow to the town, its front has no visto answerable'. There is no want of 'visto' now. After the house passed to the Wyndhams, Turner's patron called in Capability Brown to landscape the estate and create the deer park, today grazed by the largest herd of fallow deer in England. In 1879 Anthony Salvin remodelled some rooms and added an east porch. Turner hangs here with family portraits and Old Masters. There are fine carvings by Grinling Gibbons, murals by Louis Laguerre. Visitors can see servants' quarters and kitchens, including a 1,000-piece batterie de cuisine. Lord and Lady Egremont live in the south wing.
▶ *GU28 0AE. 7 miles E of Midhurst on A272. NT. Seasonal opening.*

❼ Nymans

Leonard and Maud Wessel created a Gothic fantasy house so perfect it appeared to have stood since the Middle Ages. In truth, it was built for them by Walter Tapper, and was begun in 1923 on the site of a house built by Leonard's father, Ludwig. Nymans burnt out in 1947, the flames devouring the library of antique botanical books that reflected the Wessels' passion for their garden. When their dream went up in smoke, they departed, but their daughter Anne, the Countess of Rosse, later occupied surviving ground-floor rooms. These can be seen as she left them, furnished with antiques and tapestries and filled with fresh flowers from the gardens that surround the ruin. The gardens are laid out as a series of 'rooms', including a walled garden, rose garden, top garden and sunken garden, in a lovely situation in the High Weald.
▶ *RH17 6EB. 5 miles S of Crawley on B2114. NT. Seasonal opening of house; gardens open all year.*

❽ Saint Hill Manor

A stately manor like no other, this was the home of L. Ron Hubbard, founder of the church of Scientology, and before him the Maharajah of Jaipur. Hubbard lived and worked here from 1959 to 1966 and mementoes of him are among Saint Hill's curiosities. A Scotsman, Gibbs Crawfurd, built the original sandstone house in 1792, to which a later owner, Edwardian archaeologist Edgar Marsh Crookshank, added a loggia overlooking a garden planted with 100 rose varieties. The most amusing caprice is the Monkey Room. In the late 1940s Mrs Anthony Drexel Biddle, wife of the American ambassador, converted this room into a private cinema and

VISITORS CAN SEE SERVANTS' QUARTERS AND KITCHENS
PETWORTH HOUSE

had John Spencer Churchill produce paintings of monkeys to adorn the walls. He spent three months sketching at the London Zoo, another three months painting, on strips of canvas, the 145 anthropomorphic monkeys of 20 species that cavort here. A capuchin under a tree bears a cheeky resemblance to the artist's uncle, Sir Winston. Black Spanish marble columns in the entrance hall were the contribution of the Maharajah. Hubbard began restoration to return the house to its original condition; the work continues today. Saint Hill sits in beautiful parkland overlooking a lake. The castellated sandstone college of Scientology overlooks the drive.

▶ *RH19 4JY. 2 miles SW of East Grinstead off B2110. Open all year for guided tours.*

❾ Gravetye Manor

The initials R and K over the main door commemorate Richard Infield and his new bride, Katharine Compton, for whom he built this beautiful manor in 1598. More famously, this was the home, from 1884 to 1935, to William Robinson, great exponent and pioneer of the English natural garden style – more honest simplicity, less statuary and sham. Sitting in a peaceful valley in an estate of 405ha (1,000 acres), Gravetye became a hotel after Peter Herbert bought it in 1958. The Elizabethan manor house and the gardens Robinson created are for the pleasure of hotel and restaurant guests.

▶ *RH19 4LJ. 4 miles SW of East Grinstead off B2110.*

❿ Standen

Perhaps this is more a statement home than a stately one. The Arts and Crafts movement's social principles would seem inimical to the 'us' and 'them' ethos of the grand country house. And yet Standen has stature. It embodies the same high craftsmanship and 'truth to materials' as we see in more grandiose residences. It is the result of collaboration between William Morris, leading light of the movement, and architect Philip Webb. Designed in 1891 for James Beale, a solicitor, it has the expected superb furniture and fittings. William Morris wallpaper, fabrics and tiles, Pre-Raphaelite paintings, ceramics by William de Morgan, metalwork by W.A.S. Benson, Ashbee and Benson silver tableware – there is much to admire. The family were Unitarians, and the Beale children were kept busy working a bead curtain for the morning room, while being read to from

The Swiss Family Robinson. Bougainvillea, oleander and plumbago flower in the conservatory. The hillside garden brims with wild flowers, rhododendrons, azaleas and roses.

▶ *RH19 4NE. 2 miles S of East Grinstead. NT. Open all year (but closed some Mondays and most Tuesdays).*

⓫ Hammerwood Park

A house built by Benjamin Henry Latrobe, later architect of the White House and Capitol, Washington DC, was once owned by rock band Led Zeppelin. In 1792, John Sperling engaged the young Latrobe to transform a simple ironmaster's house. Hammerwood was Latrobe's

money to buy it and, with some funding from English Heritage, has since restored it. It must have felt like climbing a very long stairway to heaven, but this is now his family home, hosting concerts and dinners, offering B&B, and welcoming visitors.

▶ *RH19 3QE. 4 miles E of East Grinstead on A264. Limited seasonal opening.*

⑫ Herstmonceux Castle

The visitor approaching this glowing, moated, many-towered edifice is presented with a vision of outward perfection. The castle was built in around 1441 for Sir Roger Fiennes, Treasurer to Henry VI. Its fabric is red Flemish brick – innovative in its time – with stone dressings. Defences of arrow slits were for show. This was a grand country mansion that would have crumpled under bombardment. What nearly did for it was not siege from without, but sabotage from within. In 1776–7 Robert Hare swept away the interiors to use the materials for another property. Some original features survive; others were brought in when Lt Col Claude Lowther came at last to the rescue in 1911–12, with further restoration by Sir Paul Latham in the 1930s. The Royal Greenwich Observatory took up residence in 1946, departing in 1988. The castle is now the Bader International Study Center of Queen's University, Canada. The best way to appreciate the glorious building is from the surrounding parkland and Elizabethan gardens, at their most beautiful when the rhododendrons and azaleas are in bloom. Herstmonceux hosts many events, including England's Medieval Festival in August.

▶ *BN27 1RN (not for satnav, leads to closed entrance). E of Hailsham, minor roads off A271. Seasonal opening of grounds. Group booking for castle tours.*

⑬ Glynde Place

Order, order. Everything is of the highest order in the Elizabethan home of the 7th Viscount and Viscountess Hampden, where an ancestor is commemorated in the Speaker's Room. Henry Brand, 1st Viscount, was a Victorian Speaker of the House of Commons and an art collector. The gabled house with towering chimneys, set high in the Downs, was built in 1569 by William Morley, from local flint and chalk, and Caen stone. A descendant, Colonel Harbert Morley, is also remembered here. He was active for Parliament in the Civil War and was one of the judges at the trial of Charles I,

first complete work and one of only two in Britain, a rare early example of the English Greek revival style, raised as a temple to Apollo. House and park are described as 'an essay in perspective'. The estate passed through several private hands before Led Zeppelin bought it in the 1970s as a place to make and record music, and hang out with family. In their long absences dry rot did its worst. Vandals did what vandals do. Thieves stripped lead from the roof. By 1976 the house was boarded up. Could it be true that the affluent rockers had just forgotten they even owned the place? 'In need of modernisation' read the caveat when it was advertised for sale in *Country Life* in 1982. This understated the case. David Pinnegar, 21, a physicist and recent graduate, scraped up the although he refused to sign the death warrant. Upon the Restoration of the Monarchy, Morley begged a pardon, and secured it from Lord Mordaunt for £1,000.

The house was updated in the Georgian era by Richard Trevor, Bishop of St Albans, to whom it passed by marriage. His additions included the two fierce wyverns that guard the gateway. Among many art treasures is one of Allan Ramsay's portraits of George III in the Great Hall. Up a 17th-century staircase is the Gallery, with wood carving in the style of Grinling Gibbons and works by Lely and Canaletto. The visitor can wander through the flower-filled courtyard garden, over lawns, through carpets of wild flowers and the sculpture garden. Events might include an evening of opera in the Marble Hall, with world-class singers from nearby Glyndebourne.

▶ *BN8 6SX. 3 miles E of Lewes off A27. Closed for restoration until 2013 season, except for scheduled events.*

⑭ Firle Place

This has been the seat of the Viscounts Gage for more than 500 years. An ancestor, Sir Thomas Gage, introduced to Britain the plum that bears his name – the greengage. Firle was begun in 1473 by Sir John Gage and built upon over centuries. Sir William Gage, 7th Baronet, inherited the house in 1713 and had the exterior clad in Caen stone (possibly plundered from the dissolved priory in Lewes) to lend it the appearance of a classical French château. The interiors, with Georgian finish, looking onto a courtyard shaded by fig trees, are hung with many important paintings, including works by Gainsborough, Reynolds, Van Dyck, Raphael, Zoffany and Teniers. A screen of fluted Ionic columns in the drawing room is the work of William Kent; the Long Gallery probably of Colen Campbell. Some 120ha (300 acres) of gardens and parkland surround the house. In a private walled garden there is one of the original greengage trees planted by the family. To the monks of Chartreuse, who supplied a tree to Sir Thomas, it would have been known more poetically as Reine Claude. The centrepiece of the late 19th-century garden is a Victorian fountain designed by Austin Sealy. In 2009, antiques worth £1 million were stolen from Firle, a crime described by Lord Gage as 'crass'. It would, he said, 'prevent members of the public viewing this historic porcelain'.

▶ *BN8 6LP. 5 miles SE of Lewes on A27. Open to the public from the 2013 season.*

⑮ Brighton Royal Pavilion

George, Prince of Wales, was not a man to stint himself, and when it came to creating a pleasure palace, he went the whole hog. In the mid 1780s, the 'Prince of Whales' rented a small farmhouse in Brighton, where the climate and the practise of 'dipping' in sea water were said to be therapeutic. Henry Holland was commissioned to transform the house into a villa known as the Marine Pavilion. It was a modest indulgence of the Prince's love of art and architecture – and nothing compared with what was to come. In 1815 he called in John Nash to create a magnificently idiosyncratic oriental fantasy in which to hold court. Tented roofs, minarets, domes and pinnacles were added, the interior lavishly decorated and opulently furnished. Of the great dome over the Banqueting Hall, Sydney Smith remarked that it 'looked for all the world as if the Dome of St Paul's had come down to Brighton and pupped'. The Pavilion reflects the Prince Regent's love of beauty and excess. It is a complete work of art, furnished with French, English and Chinese furniture, adorned with gilded dragons, carved palm trees and faux bamboo staircases.

▶ *BN1 1EE. City centre. Access Brighton by A23. Open all year.*

⑯ Bateman's

'It was the heartbreaking Locomobile that brought us to the house called "Bateman's". We had seen an advertisement of her, and we reached her down an enlarged rabbit-hole of a lane.' Rudyard Kipling relates in *Something of Myself* how he and his wife Carrie ('the Committee of Ways and Means') first saw the house that would be their home for more than 30 years. Entering, they felt the 'Feng Shui' to be good, 'no shadow of ancient regrets, stifled miseries, nor any menace'. Bateman's was built for a local ironmaster in the 17th century. Kipling's own description of it cannot be bettered: 'Behold us, lawful owners of a grey stone lichened house – ad 1634 over the door – beamed, panelled, with old oak staircase, and all untouched and unfaked. It is a good and peaceable place.' The Jacobean interiors, with their leaded windows, would permit no modern furniture. What visitors see is pure Kipling, from his upstairs study to the library, family portraits, Indian rugs and oriental miniatures, the gardens that he laid out, and his Rolls-Royce Phantom in the garage.

▶ *TN19 7DS. Near Burwash, 7 miles E of Heathfield on A265. NT. Seasonal opening.*

STOURHEAD

WILTSHIRE

Lions, libraries and experimental photography are among Wiltshire's stately home surprises, but it is the landscaped gardens, planted and crafted in a tribute to nature, that are one of their greatest attractions.

❶Stourhead

'To build, to plant, whatever you intend, /To rear the column, or to arch the bend, /To swell the terrace, or to sink the grot; /In all, let Nature never be forgot.' Alexander Pope's verse laid down the foundation for a guiding principle of landscape architecture – that designers should work within the natural context. 'Consult the genius of the place,' he urged. When Henry Hoare II reared the column and sunk the grot at Stourhead between 1741 and 1780, he had the genius – or spirit – of the place very

much in mind. Claude Lorrain's painting *Landscape with Aeneas at Delos* may have been his model. Working with Henry Flitcroft, he raised the Pantheon and the Temples of Apollo, Flora, Ceres and Hercules, around a man-made lake, planting specimen trees and shrubs from around the world, never losing sight of nature.

Holland's father, also Henry, acquired the estate in 1717, and in 1721 called in Colen Campbell to demolish the original manor house and rebuild in the grand Italian style. The work was completed by 1724, apart from a portico, which was not added until 1838. In 1816 William

THE GRACEFUL, DREAMY CLOISTERS OF THE NUNNERY
LACOCK ABBEY

Wilkins added a Grecian-style lodge to the landscape for Sir R. Colt Hoare, who designed the Regency library himself. Henry II ('the Magnificent') was a great art collector, and over 200 years the house has been increasingly filled with treasures. Some interiors were destroyed by a fire in 1902 but were restored. Many of the contents were saved, and the walls are hung with family portraits, landscapes and Old Masters. Henry Hugh Arthur Hoare gave Stourhead to the National Trust in 1946, his one son and heir having died of war wounds in 1917.

▶ *BA12 6QD. Stourton, off B3092, 3 miles NW of Mere on A303. NT. Seasonal opening of house; gardens open all year.*

❷ Longleat

'I've seen the lions at Longleat' proclaimed the bumper stickers when the Wiltshire estate opened its Safari Park in 1966. And while 'I've seen the library at Longleat' does not have the same resonance, the Red Library – one of seven in this beautiful, high-Elizabethan mansion – is truly magnificent. Its gilded interior, its ornate ceiling, its opulence and bookishness are a bibliophile's dream. There are almost 5,000 books in this library alone (the entire Longleat collection numbers 40,000).

The first privately owned stately home to welcome the paying public, back in 1947, Longleat was begun by Sir John Thynne, who bought the medieval Augustinian priory previously standing on the site with the intention of knocking it down and building a grand country home. His new house burnt down. Thynne was twice imprisoned in the Tower by Edward VI. Nothing daunted, after his release in 1551, he built what would become one of the greatest 'prodigy houses' – palatial dwellings to host Elizabeth I. It stood two storeys tall. The third storey was almost certainly added by Thynne's son John. Apart from a few baroque embellishments, the exterior is little changed, although many of the interiors were redesigned in the late 19th century.

Longleat owes much of its success to the enterprise of Alexander Thynn, the flamboyant 7th Marquis of Bath, who was born in 1932. Lord Bath handed the family firm over to his son, Ceawlin, Viscount Weymouth, in 2010, but his murals can still be seen – perhaps even admired – and it is hard to imagine that he will really retire to his 'chair and slippers'. Children love the adventure park, and there is a fiendish maze.

▶ *BA12 7NW. 4 miles W of Warminster, off A362. Seasonal opening.*

❸ Lacock Abbey & Fox Talbot Museum

The graceful, dreamy cloisters of a 13th-century Augustinian nunnery survive beneath a residence bought from Henry VIII by Sir William Sharington, embezzler of the Bristol Mint. Sir William demolished the abbey church but retained the beautiful medieval fabric of the abbey at ground level. He added a stables courtyard, brewery and an octagonal tower with a room for his art treasures and an upper banqueting hall. This must have drained his finances, already depleted by a spree in which he bought 14 manors. As master of a mint, he could indulge in a spot of quantitative easing, debasing the coinage and supplying funds for a doomed plot by Thomas Seymour against the boy king Edward VI. Seymour was beheaded. Sharington bought himself a pardon. In the 1750s his descendant John Ivory Talbot commissioned Sanderson Miller to make alterations in the Gothic revival style, adding a parapet and cupolas to the abbey façade.

Despite Sharington's notoriety, Lacock is most identified with William Henry Fox Talbot. He used the oriel window in the South Gallery to create the earliest surviving photographic negative, in 1835. It is displayed in situ, together with family portraits, including one of the knave Sharington. Relics of Fox Talbot's experimental work can be seen throughout. In 1944 the abbey, with Lacock village, passed to the National Trust. The abbey played a starring role in the 2008 film *The Other Boleyn Girl*.

▶ *SN15 2LG. 3 miles S of Chippenham on A350. NT. Open all year.*

❹ Corsham Court

On his travels around Europe, diplomat Sir Paul Methuen collected works of Italian Masters, and Flemish, Dutch and French paintings. They hung in his London home while Nathaniel Ireson remodelled his E-plan Elizabethan house for him, making over the north front in Palladian style in 1747. Thirteen years later Sir Paul called in Capability Brown to improve both house and parkland. Brown doubled the bay windows of the projecting wings, and created a gallery for Sir Paul's art treasures in the east wing, lit by large windows on the east front. Paul Cobb Methuen inherited Corsham in 1795 and engaged John Nash to make improvements. There followed a catalogue of error and trial, as the project went more than four times over budget, design flaws resulted in damp and dry rot, and Methuen sued. In 1844

Frederick Methuen married Anna Sanford, who came with a dowry of more Italian Masters. Thomas Bellamy was commissioned to remodel the north front once more, and returned it to its Elizabethan origins.

Examples of Nash's work survive in the riding school and stables, the gabled domestic quarters and dairy. The tower on the north front, the Dining Room, Music Room and Grand Staircase are Bellamy's. Among the works on show is Sir Anthony Van Dyck's *The Betrayal of Christ*. In the 'Octagon Room' – today a misnomer – is a sleeping cupid by Michelangelo. Chippendale chairs and Adams mirrors that were commissioned for the gallery are still there, and in the State Dining Room hang portraits of the family with their beloved pets, by Sir Joshua Reynolds. Displays of ceramics fill the corridors. In the grounds is an arboretum of specimen trees planted by Brown, including a huge, spreading Oriental plane on the lawn.

▶ *SN13 0BZ. Corsham town centre, 4 miles SW of Chippenham. Limited seasonal opening.*

❺ Great Chalfield

With its moat, barns and gatehouse, terraced gardens and topiary houses, old roses and ponds, this is one of the most pleasing medieval manors in Britain. It dates from c.1470 and was built for Thomas Tropnell, a highly litigious lawyer and 'perilous, covetouse man'. He pressed his claim for Great Chalfield and rebuilt the manor house and church with stone from his own quarry. By the 1800s parts of the house were derelict and the Great Hall had been adapted as farm workers' quarters.

George Fuller acquired the house in 1878, and in the early years of the 20th century restoration began under the auspices of his son, Major Robert Fuller. The Great Hall received a minstrel's gallery and Edwardian makeover. During restoration, a mural was discovered on the wall of the dining room, probably of Tropnell, depicting him with five fingers and a thumb to suggest that he was grasping. He clearly had a sense of self-parody and humour expressed in the figures of armed soldiers, griffons and a monkey on the rooftops. At the smaller end of the 'stately' spectrum, Great Chalfield offers much to delight. In 1943 it passed to the National Trust, but Robert Fuller's grandson Robert Floyd and his family continue to live here.

▶ *SN12 8NH. 4 miles W of Melksham off B3107. NT. Limited seasonal opening of house and gardens; house by guided tour only.*

❻ Peto Garden at Iford Manor

Iford Manor was the home of Harold Ainsworth Peto, architect and landscape gardener, from 1899 to 1933. A medieval house looks out from behind a classical 18th-century façade over the hillside garden Peto created, with terraces, steps, sculpture, artefacts collected on his travels, and long views across the valley. In summer the gardens and cloister play host to jazz concerts and opera. The house is not open to the public but can be appreciated from the grounds.

▶ *BA15 2BA. Bradford-on-Avon. Limited seasonal opening of gardens; open for groups at other times by arrangement.*

❼ Bowood House and Gardens

Beautiful Bowood, once home to leopard and orang utan, is not half the house it used to be. In 1725, Sir Orlando Bridgeman, 2nd Baronet, bought a hunting lodge and grounds from the Crown and built a new house. When he could not pay his debts the property passed to Richard Long, MP. In 1754 it was bought by the Earl of Shelburne, who commissioned Henry Keene to extend the building. The 2nd Earl, William Petty, prime minister from 1782 to 1783, later 1st Marquis of Lansdowne, filled Bowood and his London house with paintings and classical sculpture. Robert Adam was commissioned to decorate the showpiece rooms at Bowood, adding a huge drawing room, an orangery and a menagerie for wild beasts. Capability Brown's landscaping of the park is one of his finest creations. In 2007 the legend that he 'drowned' a village to create the lake gained credence when divers found the remains of two cottages.

In a controversial move the 8th Marquis demolished the 'big house' at Bowood in 1955, complete with Adam's interiors, and engaged F. Sortain Samuels to convert the 'little house' extension into a more comfortable home. In the remaining house, home to the Marquis and Marchioness of Lansdowne, are such oddities as Queen Victoria's wedding chair and Napoleon's death mask. The visitor can see Adam's orangery, C.R. Cockerell's 19th-century chapel and neoclassical library, a wealth of tapestries, sculpture, watercolours including work by Turner, exhibitions of furniture, costumes, jewellery, and the room in which Dr Joseph Priestley – natural philosopher, clergyman, chemist, inventor of soda water – discovered oxygen.

▶ *SN11 9NF (for satnav). 5 miles SE of Chippenham off A4. Daily seasonal opening.*

❽ Avebury Manor

When Vita Sackville-West visited Avebury in the 1920s, she wrote to her husband, Harold Nicolson, that she coveted this house, which has its very own megalithic stone circle. She would later be content with Sissinghurst (see page 46). In the 1540s, when William Sharington of Lacock Abbey (page 69) was busy coining it in at the expense of Bristol Mint, this was one of the manors he acquired. He sold it to William Dunch, an auditor at the London Mint, in 1551. It was updated in the Elizabethan style, and over centuries it passed through a variety of private hands. In the late 1700s Adam Williamson, a Governor of Jamaica, took up residence and created a Palladian room. The manor was a farmhouse for some years until 1902 when it was acquired by Lt Col Leopold and Mrs Nora Jenner, who carried out meticulous restoration. It was the Jenners who entertained Vita here, and laid out the gardens with circular yew hedge, in the style of Gertrude Jekyll.

The ancient standing stones must have been a big attraction for Alexander Keiller, an archaeologist and heir to a marmalade fortune. He arrived in the 1930s and converted the stables into a museum in which many of his finds can still be seen. In the 1940s Keiller sold both the stone circle and the museum to the National Trust. In 2011, a team of historians, designers and volunteers refurbished the manor for a television series, *The Manor Reborn*. Nine rooms have been finished to evoke the families and individuals who lived here in different eras.

▶ *SN8 1RF. 7 miles W of Marlborough. NT. Seasonal opening (by timed ticket).*

❾ Lydiard House and Park

Perhaps the most amazing thing at this house is the likeness of Lady Diana Spencer that hangs in the Dressing Room. This is not 'our' Lady Di but a forebear, yet the expression is so similar, it makes the spine tingle. A former Elizabethan manor, the ancestral home of the St John family, Viscounts Bolingbroke, is presented as a museum. Visitors will find a supremely elegant Palladian house with Inigo Jones-style façade, in formal parkland, on the site of a former Elizabethan manor. It was a ruin when Swindon Corporation took it on in 1943 and restored it, opening it to the public in the 1950s.

In 2005 work began to return the 18th-century landscaped park to its former glory, with the reinstatement of a lost lake, and the renovation of the Coach House, an ice house and ornamental fruit and flower walled garden. The State Rooms are open to the public. The Georgian interiors, with stucco ceilings, contain family portraits and furnishings. The Drawing Room is papered with 18th-century damask flock, and the ceiling is copied from one by Inigo Jones in the Queen's House, Greenwich. An effigy of the 5th Viscount Bolingbroke is seated at his desk in the Library, no doubt dashing off a letter of complaint to the Great Western Railway: 'Dear Sirs, about that infernal factory hooter …' Among the St John monuments in next-door St Mary's Church, the Golden Cavalier shines out.

▶ *SN5 3PA. 4 miles W of Swindon town centre. Open all year (house closed most Mondays).*

❿ Wilton House

'I was seized with a fierce palpitation of the heart, the wellspring of life was dried up within me, and I walked in constant fear of falling to the ground.' The French author Stendhal describes how Florence worked upon his senses in 1817. The susceptible visitor to Wilton might expect to have a touch of 'Stendhal syndrome', confronted with so much art, so much grace and beauty. The seat of the Earl and Countess of Pembroke, Wilton was granted to William Herbert, 1st Earl, by Henry VIII, when Wilton Abbey was dissolved. Herbert began to build in its place a splendid country house around a central courtyard. It is said, on scant evidence, that Hans Holbein the Younger drew up the design – a great entrance porch, which was removed and transformed into a garden pavilion by James Wyatt in 1801, is known as the 'Holbein Porch'.

In the 1630s, Isaac De Caus began work on the gardens, creating a variety of water features. In 1647 the 4th Earl engaged John Webb, a pupil of Inigo Jones's, to transform the house to a plan made earlier by Jones. Their Palladian south front looks onto the lake, and behind it are the state rooms. The great showpiece is Jones's dazzling Double Cube Room, which was designed to display the Van Dycks. Extravagantly decorated, it contains Chippendale furniture. The grounds are world renowned. The Palladian Bridge over the River Nidder was designed by the 9th Earl, with Roger Morris. Built partly on a fortune made from carpets, Wilton is indeed a stately pile. It has starred in several films, including *The Madness of King George*, *Mrs Brown* and *The Young Victoria*.

▶ *SP2 0BJ. 3 miles W of Salisbury, off A36. Seasonal opening of house and grounds.*

SOUTHERN ENGLAND

Enfield

M25

M1

A110

A10

A406

A1

A5

A410

A409

Harrow

A4180

Hampstead
Heath

2 1

A10

Barking

A13

INNER LONDON
74-77

A40

A4020

10

7 3

5 4

A102

17

M4

9

5 8

8

A4

7

6

4 5

6

15

A4

Richmond
upon Thames

A316

1

Richmond
Park

A3

3

14 13

A205

16

A20

A21

A222

11

2

Kingston
upon Thames

Croydon

A232

A21

A308

12

A24 A217

A23

Bromley

A3

A243

A22

A23

A233

KEY

1 Main entry

County boundary

Motorway

Principal A road

London

The city's grand houses were once fine country seats, built on the fringes of the bustling centre. Their art and artistic treasures are rivalled only by their parks and gardens, havens of tranquillity for Londoners today.

INNER LONDON

There is a special elegance to London's grand houses, set in some of the loveliest – and grandest – spots of the capital. Their interiors are spectacular, their gardens an oasis of calm for city visitors.

❶ Lauderdale House and Waterlow Park

Lauderdale House was begun by Sir Richard Martin, Master of the Mint and three times Lord Mayor, as a timber-frame building at the top of Highgate Hill, in 1582. It was the finest country house in Highgate, and acquired its name from the Scottish Royalist Earl of Lauderdale, when it came to him by inheritance. Its most famous resident, in 1670, was Nell Gwyn, mistress of Charles II.

In 1760 the house was rebuilt in the Georgian neoclassical style. It became home to philanthropist and politician Sir Sidney Waterlow, who in 1889 presented the house to the London County Council, with its park as 'a garden for the gardenless', a place 'for the enjoyment of Londoners'. Both house and park are indeed enjoyed today, hosting jazz and classical concerts, poetry and open-air theatre. Lauderdale House served as a park tearoom and keepers' flats for 70 years, until a fire in 1963 destroyed the roof and much of the interior. It lay derelict until, in 1978, it was reopened by the late Yehudi Menuhin, virtuoso violinist, as a centre for arts and education. At the top of the park stands a statue of Sir Sidney, hat in one hand, a key in the other, and equipped with an umbrella in case it should rain.
▶ *Highgate Hill, N6 5HG. Archway tube.*

❷ Kenwood House

Thank goodness for Guinness! Had it not been for the brewing magnate Lord Iveagh, this beautiful Robert Adam house could have been swept away. It stands on an airy hilltop, surrounded by parkland in the style of Humphry Repton, looking over sylvan Hampstead Heath, with London at its feet. It was begun in the early 1600s, with an orangery added in around 1700. In 1764, Adam began to remodel it for William Murray, the future 1st Earl of Mansfield, and his wife, Elizabeth. A neoclassical makeover entailed the addition of pilasters and a portico, and stucco cladding for the exterior, and, within, such rich embellishment. The Great Room, or library, its exuberant ceiling supported by massive columns, is one of Adam's most lavish interiors. By 1925 most of the contents of this great house had been sold off and it was facing demolition when

Lord Iveagh stepped in. Stout fellow! On his death in 1927 he bequeathed Kenwood to the nation with an art collection that includes Rembrandt's self-portrait, along with works by Vermeer, Gainsborough, Reynolds and Turner. Furniture is being reintroduced.
▶ *Hampstead Lane, NW3 7JR. EH. House closed for renovation until autumn 2013; gardens open all year.*

❸ Kensington Palace

Kensington was just a village in 1689 when joint monarchs William and Mary bought a Jacobean manor named Nottingham House for the 'esteem'd very good Air'. Sir Christopher Wren remodelled and extended the building, and a part of Hyde Park was transformed into a formal garden. The palace has been variously occupied, improved and neglected by royalty ever since. Queen Anne ordered the building of a 'summer supper house', which is today the Orangery Restaurant – possibly a unique collaboration between Nicholas Hawksmoor and John Vanbrugh.

State rooms were added for George I, with ceiling paintings by William Kent.

George II was the last reigning monarch to live here. The gardens enjoyed by Londoners took shape under the guidance of his Queen Consort, Caroline of Ansbach. On her death in 1737, the king let much of the building fall into disuse. George III chose Buckingham Palace for his residence, and not until 1798 was Edward, Duke of Kent, granted apartments here. They had been unoccupied for 28 years and he commissioned the architect James Wyatt – then Surveyor General to the Board of Works – to bring them back to life. In 1818 the Duke's daughter, Princess

LUMINOUS LACE LIGHT SCULPTURE, STONE HALL, KENSINGTON PALACE

GLORY AND GRANDEUR HAVE BEEN REVIVED

SPENCER HOUSE

Victoria, was born here. After her accession to the throne the building again fell into decay, and by the late 1800s it was threatened with demolition. Instead, the 'empty, bare, dreary, comfortless' palace was restored in time for Victoria's 80th birthday. The Palace is now home to another William, whose bride, Kate Middleton, fell in love with the 'wonderful peace' of an apartment that was once occupied by Princess Margaret.

▶ *Kensington Gardens, W8 4PX.*
High Street Kensington tube.

❹ Spencer House

After a grand dinner at this splendid house the ladies would withdraw to Lady Spencer's first-floor salon, while the gentlemen had the luxury of the fantastical Palm Room. Spencer House is the only surviving 18th-century aristocratic family palace in London. It was built for John, 1st Earl Spencer, a forebear of Princess Diana's. Ranging in style from Rome to Athens, it was begun to a Palladian design by John Vardy in 1756. The façade has a decorative pediment and seven upper bays split by Tuscan columns. The exterior and ground-floor interiors are Vardy's work, but in 1758 James 'Athenian' Stuart, sculptor and architect newly returned from Greece, stepped in to work on the upper floor. Some of the state rooms – the Morning Room, the Music Room, the Ante Room (the Spencers' 'little eating parlour') and the Library – although very grand, have the authentic feeling of a family home. The Palm Room, adorned with carved and gilded palm trees, symbolic of marital fertility. It did the trick! The Spencers had one son and four daughters. The eldest, Georgiana, as Duchess of Devonshire, was famed for her beauty, notorious for her affairs. Her brother, George, the 2nd Earl, ordered some remodelling of the house by Henry Holland, who added Ionic columns and laid out the garden. In the Blitz, original fixtures were removed for safekeeping. Recently, the glory that was Greece and the grandeur that was Rome have been revived for visitors to see on most Sundays, by arrangement and by guided tour.

▶ *27 St James's Place, SW1A 1NR. Green Park tube.*

❺ Apsley House

With the swanky address 'Number One, London', this grand house at Hyde Park Corner was home to Arthur Wellesley, Duke of Wellington. The duke bought it from his elder brother in 1817, two years after his historic victory at Waterloo. It was built in red brick by Robert Adam in 1771–8 for the Lord Chancellor, Lord Apsley. Wellington employed Benjamin Wyatt to enlarge it to accommodate his growing art collections.

Visitors stepping inside are greeted by Antonio Canova's giant nude of Napoleon as Mars the Peacemaker in the hall stairwell. Made in 1802–10, the figure stood in the Louvre before it was bought by the British government and presented to the duke by the Prince Regent. Wellington attracted such largesse. Among 200 paintings are 83 works, some by Goya, Rubens and Velazquez, captured from Joseph Bonaparte's baggage train after the Battle of Vitoria. They were the property of the Spanish royal family, and were granted to him by Ferdinand VII. Sèvres porcelain was a gift from Louis XVIII; a 1000 piece silver service from the Portuguese. The No 1 address harks back to the time when this was the first house within the Knightsbridge toll gate. Although house and contents were given to the nation in 1947, the family continue to occupy apartments.

▶ *149 Piccadilly, W1J 7NT. Hyde Park Corner tube. EH. April to early November open Wednesday to Sunday; November to March open Saturday and Sunday.*

❻ Fulham Palace

Henry Compton, Bishop of London, was an enthusiastic botanist. In the reign of William and Mary, he planted the gardens here with specimen trees from all over the known world. Using specially designed stoves, he was able to propagate spice bush and swamp bay, sweet gum and scarlet haw.

For centuries this riverside palace was the home of successive bishops of London – the last departing in 1975. A Tudor redbrick manor house overlooks a court with a 19th-century fountain. The gardens are the thing, though, right in the metropolis and protected as a historic landscape. Sadly, much of Compton's work was undone on the orders of one of his successors, Bishop Robinson. Many of his exotic plantings were rooted out by 'ignorant persons'. The restored Tudor walled garden has a glorious wisteria. The palace and gardens are looked after by the local council and a trust. Entrance is free, although there is a charge for guided tours.

▶ *Bishop's Avenue, SW6 6EA. Putney Bridge tube. Open all year, palace Saturday to Wednesday (gallery for exhibitions, or by arrangement), gardens daily; walled garden weekdays, guided tours only at weekends.*

❼ Leighton House

Frederic, Lord Leighton, built this house as a place to live and paint, and as a spectacle, an exercise in self-advertisement, a 'private palace of art'. It was to reflect his status as a widely travelled gentleman, collector, aesthete, artist and, from 1878, president of the Royal Academy. Leighton designed the original house with George Aitchison, and spent the next 30 years extending and embellishing it. Visitors gawped at his Arab Hall, modelled on the 12th-century Palace of La Zisa in Palermo, with golden dome, fountain, and more than 1,000 antique Islamic tiles, mostly from Damascus. A writer for American magazine *Century* reported: 'In every square foot of space there hangs or lies some work of art ancient or modern, peculiarly rare, choice, lovely. One feasts the eye perpetually upon forms of beauty.' In April 2010 Leighton House reopened after an 18 month restoration that soaked up £1.6 million.

▶ *12 Holland Park Road, W14 8LZ. High Street Kensington, Olympia or Holland Park tube. Open all year (closed on Tuesdays)*

LONDON

77

OUTER LONDON

A Gothick masterwork, a hunting lodge that's home to the Royal Ballet School, a pet cemetery, tulip stairs, a house of Art Deco perfection – London's surroundings are home to all manner of delights.

1 Marble Hill House

Twickenham in the 18th century was a magnet for the smart set, including artists, writers, society figures and politicians. Among them was Henrietta Howard, Countess of Suffolk, mistress of the Prince of Wales, later George II. She ordered the building of this house in parkland stretching down to the Thames. It was designed in the fashionable manner of a Palladian villa, after consultation with Roger Morris and Colen Campbell, with the aid of Henry Herbert, Earl of Pembroke, Lord of the Bedchamber to the prince. Charles Bridgeman designed the gardens. Six years after the house was completed, the Countess wed George Berkeley MP, and enjoyed eleven years of married life before his death. She lived another 32 years here. In the gilded Great Room, which has five architectural capricci by Giovanni Paolo Pannini, she entertained Alexander Pope, Jonathan Swift, Horace Walpole and John Gay.

Marble Hill was later briefly home to another royal paramour, Maria Fitzherbert, mistress of the future George IV. From 1825 it was owned by General Jonathan Peel, brother of the prime minister, Sir Robert. It had stood empty for years when the Cunards bought it in 1898 with a view to redeveloping the site. Local feelings ran high and the family was persuaded to sell. In 1965 the Greater London Council began restoration. Everything the visitor sees of the interior today has been reproduced for English Heritage as closely as possible to the original, including hand-painted Chinese wallpaper and a chinoiserie collection. The house has facilities for weddings and other functions.

Richmond Road, TW1 2NL. St Margaret's rail. EH. Seasonal opening at weekends and by guided tour only.

2 Strawberry Hill House

'All Gothicism and gold, and crimson, and looking-glass', was how poet Thomas Gray described the gallery designed for this house by his old Eton schoolmate Horace Walpole. In 1747, Walpole bought Chopp'd Straw Hall, a Thameside cottage, 'a little-play-thing house … the prettiest bauble you ever saw', and set about rebuilding it as a home for his art collection – a project that would continue for almost half a century. Bucking the trend for neoclassicism, Walpole took for his inspiration the architecture

MARBLE HILL HOUSE

of Gothic cathedrals – vaulting, stained glass, tombs and quatrefoil windows. He added battlements and pinnacles and a round tower. In the gloomy hall, the stairwell is lit by a single lantern. Dark corridors lead to rooms of dazzling brilliance. Walpole was the author of the first Gothic novel, *The Castle of Otranto*, which came to him as the remnant of a dream. At Strawberry Hill he set up Britain's first private printing press and ran off a guidebook to his home, for the use of servants in showing around the permitted four visitors a day. His seminal creation set a trend for 'Strawberry Hill Gothic'. 'It is charming,' he wrote to a friend, 'to totter into vogue.' The whole is a jaw-dropping flight of fantasy by the man who coined the term 'serendipity'. Virginia Woolf said of him 'He was mischievous and obscene; he gibbered and mocked and pelted the holy shrines with nutshells.' He was 'the best company in the world – the most amusing, the most intriguing'. Recent restoration has brought Strawberry Hill back to life, with new gilding, silks and damasks.

▶ *268 Waldegrave Road, Twickenham, TW1 4ST. Strawberry Hill rail. Seasonal opening.*

❸ White Lodge

A hunting lodge built for George II by Roger Morris in 1727 is today home to the ballet. George's wife, Caroline, often stayed at the lodge, remote from his infidelities. On her death in 1737, it passed to Robert, 1st Baron Walpole, then to Caroline's daughter, Princess Amelia. The princess became Ranger of Richmond Park in 1751 and closed it to all but a few friends, until a court order forced her to reopen it. Prince Albert Edward, the future Edward VII, kicked his heels here when his father, Prince Albert, chose this secluded location for a kind of educational hothouse. The future Edward VIII, who was born here, also hated the seclusion. For Edward's brother Albert and Elizabeth Bowes-Lyon, the future George VI and Queen Elizabeth, by contrast, was not seclusion enough. They made their home here in 1923, but stayed for just a year because they felt too exposed. Since 1955 the lodge has been occupied by the Royal Ballet Lower School, its graceful Palladian style ideally suited to the dance. For the visitor there is a Museum and Ballet Resource Centre, devoted to the history of both the White Lodge and ballet. Anna Pavlova's death mask rivets the attention.

▶ *Sheen Gate, Richmond Park, TW10 5HR. Mortlake rail (15 minutes' walk). Museum visits by advance booking.*

❹ Chiswick House

Richard Boyle, 3rd Earl of Burlington, 'the Apollo of the arts', made three Grand Tours, imbibing the work of Andrea Palladio, consulting Palladio's architectural treatise. He was at the forefront in the revival of Palladian architecture, and for his efforts was lampooned by the anglophile William Hogarth, whose engraving, *The Man of Taste*, satirised the pretensions of Burlington and his set. How he must have hated Chiswick House!

The first and among the finest example of neo-Palladian design in Britain, the villa, completed in 1729, drawing inspiration from a Greek temple, was the result of a collaboration between Burlington and William Kent. Their homage to Palladio was not intended as a residence, but as a grand pavilion for the old Jacobean Chiswick House, in which to entertain and to show off Burlington's art collections. Thus Lord Hervey's comment: 'Too small for a house, too big to hang on a watch chain.' No expense was spared in creating the interiors. The Red Velvet Room ceiling celebrates *The Triumph of the Arts*. Above the Blue Velvet Room floats the Goddess of Architecture. The coffered dome in the Upper Tribunal is modelled on the ancient basilica of Maentius.

In 1758 the property passed to the Cavendish family. The racy and beautiful Georgiana, Duchess of Devonshire, used it as a retreat. Celebrated visitors over the years included Handel, the Whig statesman Charles James Fox (who died here) and Queen Victoria and Prince Albert. After long years in the doldrums, in the 1950s the house came through Middlesex Council to the Ministry of Works, and restoration began. Visitors can judge for themselves if 'the architect Earl' was indeed 'a man of taste'.

▶ *Burlington Lane, W4 2RP. Turnham Green tube. Limited seasonal opening.*

❺ Chiswick House Gardens

'Mahomet imagined an Elysium,' said Horace Walpole, 'but Kent created many.' The Elysium that William Kent created here with the Earl of Burlington. (above) was the birthplace of the English Landscape Movement. The pair swept away Renaissance formality in favour of a freer and more fluid design. Sculptures and such architectural details as Ionic and Doric columns were placed in 'natural' spaces. Bollo Brook was landscaped to create the illusion of a lake. The 5th Duke of Devonshire commissioned the stone bridge across it, built in 1774 and attributed

to James Wyatt. The Italian Garden and Walled Garden were contributions of the 6th Duke. He bought the adjoining estate and commissioned Samuel Ware to design a large conservatory. Completed in 1913, it set a trend for great glasshouses that found its ultimate expression in the Crystal Palace. It contains what is believed to be the oldest camellia collection in England.

Chiswick House Gardens represent 'one of England's greatest contributions to Western culture', said English Heritage's chief executive, following a £12.1 million restoration that entailed the planting of hundreds of new trees and the replacement of statues that left with the Devonshires. There is an original bowling green and a cricket pitch, in use at weekends in summer.

▶ *Burlington Lane, W4 2RP. Turnham Green tube. EH. Open all year.*

❻ Kew Palace

This redbrick, four-storey Jacobean mansion was built for a Flemish-born London merchant, Samuel Fortrey, as a private home, in 1631. A lovers' knot with the entwined initials S and C over the door recalls the love between Samuel and his wife, Catherine de Latteur. The house is a palace in name only. With its curving gables it would not look out of place in old Amsterdam, and indeed it was originally known as The Dutch House.

George III spent some of his childhood here, and it was to Kew that he retreated in his madness. On display is a turquoise silk waistcoat that was one of the last items he wore before his death in 1821. In his illness he always wore a dressing gown and waistcoat with sleeves of damask.

The smallest of the royal palaces, Kew was first rented to the monarchy in 1728, in the reign of George II. George III bought it from the Levett family. After Queen Charlotte died in her bedroom here, her granddaughter, Princess Victoria, ordered that it remain just as she left it. The ground and first floors have undergone a programme of restoration to take them back to their Georgian heyday. The palace's history is explained in the People's Library. George III was a great family man. On display are cartoons of this much-caricatured king, jigsaw maps used by the governess to educate his 15 children, and an elegant doll's house. The Queen's Garden has been re-created around the palace.

▶ *Royal Botanic Gardens, Kew, TW9 3AB. Kew Bridge rail. An additional entrance fee is required. Seasonal opening.*

❼ Syon House

'9th June, 1658. I went to see the Earl of Northumberland's pictures ... the last of our blessed Kings (Charles I), and the Duke of York, by Lely.' Almost two years to the day before the triumphant return of Charles II, diarist John Evelyn contemplated Lely's painting of Charles I, which still hangs here in the silk-lined Red Drawing Room, with other portraits of the Stuart royal family. The doomed king's children stayed at Syon House while he was held at Hampton Court.

The abbey of Mount Zion was home to Bridgettine monks until Henry VIII seized it. In place of the abbey church, Edward Seymour, Duke of Somerset, built a palatial home in the Italian Renaissance style. Syon passed to the Percy family by marriage in 1594. Earls and Dukes of Northumberland, the Percys seem always to have been in the thick of history. More than one of them literally lost his head. Ralph Percy, 12th Duke, today leads a relatively uneventful life at one of London's last surviving ducal residences and country estates.

In the 1760s, the 1st Duke engaged Robert Adam, who here laid down what has become known as the Adam style, integrating decoration with furniture, fixtures and fittings. Imperial Rome is evoked in the Great Hall, Ante Room and Dining Room. The Red Drawing Room has 293 medallions painted on the ceiling by Giovanni Battista Cipriani. The beautiful, book-lined Long Gallery has a view over the Thames's last tidal water meadow. Capability Brown designed the gardens, including many rare trees and an ornamental lake. The highlight of the park is the Conservatory. Built in 1826 and designed by Charles Fowler, it was an inspiration for Joseph Paxton's Crystal Palace 25 years later.

▶ *London Road, Brentford, TW8 8JF. Syon Lane rail. Limited seasonal opening of house; daily seasonal opening of gardens.*

❽ Osterley Park and House

Robert Adam was not without his critics. Horace Walpole made reference to 'Mr Adam's gingerbread and sippets of embroidery'. The Drawing Room at Osterley Park was 'worthy of Eve before the fall'. Admirers of the great architect see here, through different eyes, some of the best surviving examples of Robert Adam interiors. The original Elizabethan mansion was built around a courtyard for Sir Thomas Gresham, founder of the Royal Exchange. In 1713 Osterley was acquired by Sir Francis Child, a banker, and the Child family

ANTE ROOM, SYON HOUSE

THE CHERRY GARDEN, HAM HOUSE

called in Adam in 1761 to remodel the house as an impressive statement and a place to entertain. Externally, the most distinctive feature is a 'transparent portico', an Ionic pedimented screen approached by a broad flight of steps.

Osterley today is effectively a showcase of Adam's work, with some of the original furniture. The 9th Earl of Jersey gave the house to the National Trust in 1949, but removed the most valuable pictures – works by Rubens, Poussin and Van Dyck, which were all later destroyed in a fire. The Rubens ceiling painting over the Great Staircase is a copy. Other paintings are on loan from the V&A. The 40m (130ft) Long Gallery, described by Henry James as 'a cheerful upholstered avenue into another century', is a panoply of Adam's evolving style. In the Tapestry Room are wall hangings designed by François Boucher for the Gobelin manufactory. The formal park is graced by Adam's beautiful Garden House.

▶ *Jersey Road, Isleworth, TW7 4RB. Osterley tube. NT. Seasonal opening of house and park.*

❾ Boston Manor House

'As to dinner, it was so perfect that it was impossible to know a single thing on the table, and that, you know, must be termed a proper dinner for such a party.' The guests at Boston House for which so exotic a feast was served were William IV and Queen Adelaide, who came to dine with Colonel James Clitherow and his family in 1834. The colonel's sister Mary wrote in detail of the event. James and Jane Clitherow had been friends with the Duke and Duchess of Clarence before the duke's accession; a personal invitation to the coronation hangs in the house.

This redbrick Jacobean manor, close to the M4, was built in 1623 for Lady Mary Reade and sold in the 1670s to the Clitherows, who extended it. In 1924 it was bought by Brentford council. For so long closed to public view, it has been subject to restoration by the London Borough of Hounslow, working with English Heritage, and the Dining Room and State Rooms are now open. The State Rooms have their original magnificent, decorative plaster ceilings. The Drawing Room ceiling depicts 19 allegorical figures representing the Five Senses, Four Elements, Three Virtues, Peace and Plenty, War and Peace, and Father Time flanked by cupids. A Jacobean mantelpiece portrays an angel interceding to prevent Abraham from sacrificing Isaac. The exterior can be admired from the surrounding public park.

▶ *Boston Manor Road, TW8 9JX. Brentford rail, Boston Manor tube. Seasonal opening (weekends and bank holidays).*

⑩ PM Gallery and House

Situated close to Ealing studios, and with authentic interiors, Pitzhanger Manor, Sir John Soane's country villa, has more than once appeared in films. It has doubled as Kensington Palace and the Tate Gallery, and featured in the 2002 version of *The Importance of Being Earnest*. Soane bought the house and surrounding park in 1800, when he was architect to the Bank of England. The Gurnell family had added to the old house a Georgian wing by Soane's early mentor, George Dance the Younger. Soane pulled down all but Dance's wing and set about building his 'dream house', a weekend retreat and a home for his antiques and paintings. He conceived it as 'a sort of portrait', a showcase of his style, with restrained classical detail, inspired colour schemes and use of space and light. Four statues top Ionic columns to the fore. In the grounds, Soane created romantic ruins. The intimate neoclassical interior manifests his signatures – curved and painted ceilings, inset mirrors and false doors. The appearance echoes that of his London home in Lincoln's Inn, today housing the Soane Museum, where the many design drawings for Pitzhanger are held. Having passed through several hands, the building served as Ealing borough's lending library from 1901 until 1984, when the library moved out and restoration began. A 1940s library extension built on the site of Soane's 'Roman' ruins is now the PM Gallery, exhibiting contemporary art.
▶ *Walpole Park, Mattock Lane, W5 5EQ. Ealing Broadway rail and tube. Open most of the year (closed on Sundays and Mondays).*

⑪ Ham House and Garden

William Murray was a close friend of James I's son Charles, and as his whipping boy he took his punishments for him. In 1637 William was rewarded by a grateful Charles I with the manors of Ham and Petersham and a title, Earl of Dysart. He greatly extended this riverside house, built by Sir Thomas Vavasour, Knight Marshal to James I, adding the Great Staircase, Hall Gallery, Long Gallery and North Drawing Room. His daughter Elizabeth and her second husband, John Maitland, Duke of Lauderdale, brought Ham House to a degree of splendour, furnished, according to John Evelyn, 'like a great prince's'. Their portrait, by John Lely, hangs here. Van Dyck's three-quarter-length portrait of Charles I so pleased the king that he asked the artist to make a copy for Murray, and presented it to him in a beautifully ornate frame.

It hangs in the Long Gallery with similarly framed Stuart portraits. Precious silk wall hangings are rare survivors from the 1600s. Elizabeth supported the future Charles II in his exile, and was a member of the secret Sealed Knot society, while overtly courting Cromwell. Bishop Burnet wrote that she 'had a restless ambition, lived at a vast expense, and was ravenously covetous'. Upon the Restoration, a suite of rooms was created for the queen, Catherine of Braganza. Visitors can see the silk-covered, gilded recliner sleeping chair in which she could kick back. Although Ham House is now a museum, it is deeply atmospheric. It remained in family hands until the National Trust took it over in 1948 and it is one of the greatest surviving houses from the 17th century.
▶ *Ham Street, TW10 7RS. NT. Seasonal opening of house (closed on Fridays); gardens open all year.*

⑫ Hampton Court

In the reign of William III, 'Hampton Court put on new clothes, and, being dressed gay and glorious, made the figure we now see it in.' The monarch most associated with the palace is Henry VIII, but Daniel Defoe was writing, in 1724, of its transformation for William and Mary. Henry VIII's Lord Chancellor Cardinal Wolsey, hoping to curry favour, made him a gift of the palace. Henry commissioned new royal suites, laid out hunting grounds, tennis courts, bowling alleys – but still set his face against Wolsey, who had failed to secure him a divorce. The gay and glorious new look was the work of Sir Christopher Wren, for the only joint monarchs in British history who planned a Renaissance-style residence to rival Versailles. Only the vast Great Hall was to be spared, but budget restraints prevailed, and with Mary's death from smallpox in 1694, work stopped, resuming in 1698. Under Wren and William Talman, the east and south façades of the palace were translated from Tudor redbrick to grand baroque. The Chapel Royal, the Great Hall and parts of the exterior, including Wolsey's gatehouse, are among Tudor survivors. The Great Hall is hung with Henry's tapestries, under a lavishly decorated hammerbeam roof. The sublime chapel, the apogee of Tudor interiors at the palace, is still used for worship. Its carved blue and gold ceiling is a wonder. In the grounds, Britain's oldest surviving hedge maze, designed in 1690 by George London and Henry Wise, continues to tantalise visitors.
▶ *East Molesey, KT8 9AU. Hampton Court rail. Boats from Westminster, Richmond and Kingston in summer. Open all year.*

⓭ Southside House

The home of the Pennington Mellor Munthe family, on the south side of Wimbledon common, is not one of those houses where time has stood still. Its clutter, eclecticism and eccentricity speak of generations of occupation. It was built in 1687 for Robert Pennington, who shared Charles II's exile in Holland. On the death of his son from the plague, Pennington retired to salubrious Wimbledon and commissioned Dutch architects to build a house, incorporating an existing farmhouse. It is, then, Restoration at its heart, although with a Georgian Music Room prepared for a visit by Frederick, Prince of Wales, in 1750. In the bedroom where he slept, complete with four-poster, is a necklace worn by Marie Antoinette.

In the Second World War, Southside was the home of Hilda Pennington Mellor and her husband Axel Munthe, a Swedish doctor and author of the bestselling book *The Story of San Michele*. Bombs damaged both front and back of the house, and on his return from heroic exploits behind enemy lines, their son Malcolm threw himself into the task of rebuilding it, creating a double-height, galleried, baroque hall with frescoes. The Dining Room is hung with works by Van Dyck and Hogarth. Off the Tapestry Room is a powder cubicle in which guests could have their periwigs dusted. The imposing Georgian-style entrance is flanked by statues of Plenty and Spring, said to be likenesses of Robert Pennington's wife and daughter. Visitors have included Lord Byron, Lord Nelson and Emma Hamilton. With more than three centuries of mix-and-match history to explore, the visitor is endlessly diverted. The pet cemetery in the romantic, mature garden touches the heart. The house, along with the family's manor, Hellens in Herefordshire (see page 113) is run as a trust.
▶ *3–4 Woodhayes Road, SW19 4RJ. Wimbledon rail and tube. Limited seasonal opening, guided tours only.*

⓮ Cannizaro Park

The society hostess and heiress Sophia Johnstone was 'very short and fat with rather a handsome face, totally uneducated but full of humour and vivacity'. Her marriage to the impoverished Sicilian aristocrat Francis Platamone, Duke of Cannizzaro, in 1814, must have tried that humour. It brought him a fortune and Sophia a title, but brought neither of them happiness. He returned to Italy with his mistress; she consoled herself with music and took up with 'a fiddler from a second-rate theatre in Milan',

a strapping young man who 'plundered her without shame'. Warren House, built for a wealthy London merchant in the early 1700s, became Cannizzaro (now Cannizaro) House when the unhappy duke and duchess took up residence, entertaining the Duke of Wellington and Mrs Fitzherbert, mistress of George IV.

It is today a hotel and stands upon the public park that used to be its gardens, which evolved over 300 years, with plants from around the world. Adopted by Merton Council in 1949, the park is especially lovely when the rhododendrons and azaleas put out the flags. There are woodland walks, spreading lawns, and, of course, an Italian Garden. Visitors can take tea on the terrace.
▶ *West Side Common, SW19 4UE. Wimbledon rail and tube. Park open all year.*

⓯ The Queen's House

James I is said to have given the manor of Greenwich to his wife, Anne of Denmark, as an apology for publicly swearing at her for shooting one of his hunting dogs. In 1616, Inigo Jones received from the queen his first major commission. He had recently returned from three years in Italy, and this was England's first fully neoclassical building, modelled on the Medici villa at Poggia a Caiano near Florence. Anne did not live to see its completion in 1638. After her death, Charles I gave it to his queen, Henrietta Maria, before she went into exile in the Civil War. In 1805, George III gave it to the Royal Naval Asylum, for the education of the orphaned children of seamen. Daniel Asher Alexander added colonnades and flanking wings for dormitories. Little survives of Jones's interior except the ironwork of the 'tulip stairs' – the first geometric, self-supporting, spiral staircase in Britain – and the painted woodwork and marble floors of the Great Hall, a perfect cube rising through the centre of the north side.

The house is today home to a collection of fine art, which includes portraits of the Tudors and a painting, by an unknown artist, of the lost Tudor Palace of Placentia, which the Queen's House overlooked and outshone. When Queen Mary bade Christopher Wren build a retirement home for seamen on the site of the palace, it was not to interfere with her 'visto' of the river from the Queen's House, so he did away with the centre and built two distinct wings. Seen together the three buildings form one of the greatest architectural set pieces, best viewed from across the river.
▶ *SE10 9NF. Greenwich rail or Cutty Sark DLR. Open all year.*

🄶 Eltham Palace

'When we came to the hall, all the retinue was assembled ... In the midst stood Henry, aged nine, already with certain royal demeanour; I mean a dignity of mind combined with a remarkable courtesy.' The scholar Erasmus describes a visit to the childhood home of the future Henry VIII, in 1499. Henry and his court would celebrate Christmas here, enjoying masques and other entertainments. Since that time the building has changed beyond recognition. Eltham had been a royal residence since the time of Edward the Confessor. In the Civil War every deer in the park was slaughtered, every tree felled. Only the medieval Great Hall survives. Charles II bestowed the palace upon Sir John Shaw, who rebuilt it with an orangery and aviary. It was a ruin by the 18th century, a great attraction for aficionados of the Picturesque, and painted by J.M.W. Turner.

In 1933, Sir Stephen Courtauld and his wife Virginia acquired the lease, and Eltham became once more a place of gaiety, song and dance. Paul Paget and John Seely were commissioned to create an Art Deco masterpiece. The Great Hall was restored, with the addition of a minstrels' gallery. Ginnie Courtauld's oval bedroom, the Italianate drawing room, and the dining room with ceilings of aluminium leaf are by the Mayfair decorator and marchese Peter Malacrida. The couple's pet lemur had its own quarters, decorated with tropical forest scenes. Arts and Crafts gardens were laid out. After the Courtaulds left in 1944, in one of those bizarre changes of use, the palace became an army educational facility before English Heritage began restoration in 1995.

▶ *Court Yard, SE9 5QE. Eltham or Mottingham rail. EH. Limited seasonal opening; open on Sundays in winter.*

🄷 Charlton House Peace Garden

'I went to visit my worthy neighbor, Sir Henry Newton, and consider the prospect one ... of the most noble in the world; so as, had the house running water, it were a princely seat.' Newton's father, Sir Adam Newton, was tutor and then secretary to Henry, Prince of Wales, son of James I and Anne of Denmark. His visitor in June 1653 was diarist John Evelyn. Newton senior had, said Evelyn, built the house with his royal pupil in mind. It is one of Britain's finest examples of Jacobean domestic architecture, probably designed by John Thorpe, who had served as Clerk of the Works at the Palace of Placentia in Greenwich until 1601. An extension built by Norman Shaw in 1877 served as a library until it was closed by Greenwich council in 1991. There is now a smaller library in the old chapel.

The house is today used as a community centre and the grounds are mostly parks. A Peace Garden has been planted in the former Rose Garden, and from there the handsome redbrick building with mullioned windows can be enjoyed. Here too are the Mulberry Tea Rooms and one of several contenders for the title 'oldest mulberry tree in Britain', planted, apparently, in 1608, on the orders of the future Charles I, who would have been aged eight. A summerhouse, which now overlooks the road, is attributed to Inigo Jones. It was built around 1630, and was once used as a public convenience.

▶ *Charlton Road, SE7 8RE. Charlton rail. Open all year.*

🄸 Eastbury Manor

'A little beyond the town, on the road to Dagenham, stood a great house, ancient and now almost fallen down, where tradition says the Gunpowder Plot was at first contrived.' Daniel Defoe, writing in 1726, records the persistent rumour that the owners of Eastbury Manor were in league with Guy Fawkes. 'Tall, dark and handsome' would describe this three-storey Elizabethan gentry house, built on an H-plan with a cobbled courtyard and towering chimneys. It was completed around 1573 for a City merchant, Clement Sysley, on part of the demesne of Barking Abbey, seized in the Reformation. The last remnant of the powerful abbey, the Curfew Tower, stands within a mile, by St Margaret's church.

Outwardly, the house has changed little, although it was in a poor state of repair, and part used for livestock, when the National Trust took it over in 1918. Some frescoes have been restored, notably the fishing scenes in the Painted Room. The spiral wooden staircase to the turret is a rarity, as is the attic, where exposed beams show the construction of the roof. The Great Hall has an original brick fireplace. In the walled garden are bee holes, from which honey was extracted. When the manor was first built it stood on rising ground with views across marshland to the Thames. Today, it is surrounded by modern housing. As to Eastbury's link with the events of November 5, 1605 ... true or false? 'Unlikely,' according to the Gunpowder Plot Society.

▶ *Eastbury Square, Barking, IG11 9SN. Upney tube. NT. Open most of year (Mondays, Tuesdays and occasional Saturdays)*

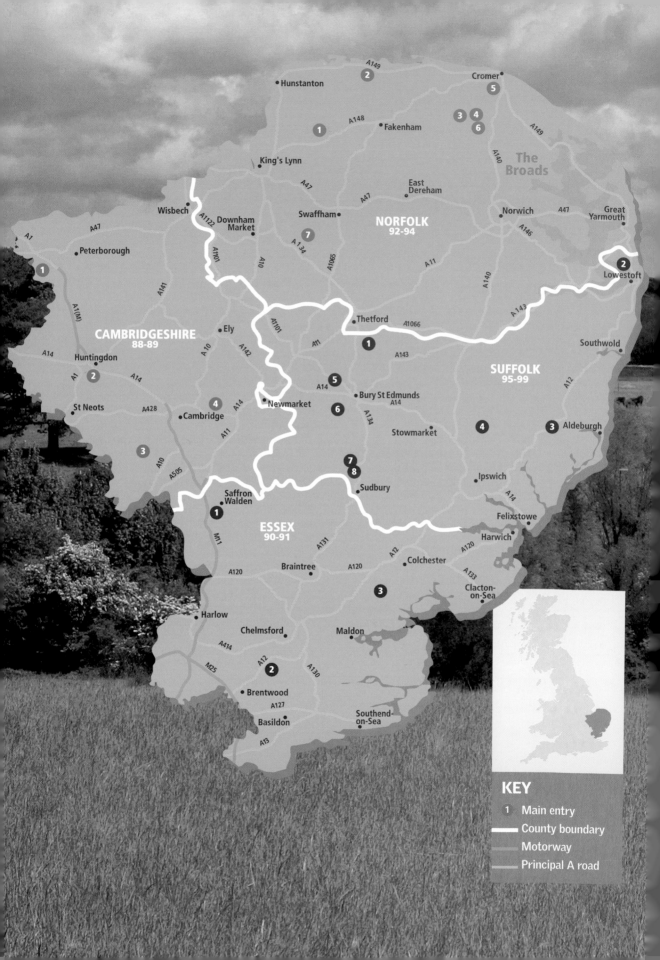

East Anglia

A patchwork landscape of forest and fenland levels
out under vast skies. Here sumptuous architecture,
lavish decoration and elegant interiors contrast
with the serenc beauty of isolated manors.

CAMBRIDGESHIRE

The ages merge here, medieval remnants blending with Tudor, Jacobean and Victorian architecture, and a Georgian mansion, all complemented by sublime gardens created in the 20th century.

❶ Elton Hall

The home of the Proby family since 1660, Elton Hall presents a romantic aspect amid its Edwardian gardens and parkland beside the River Nene. The house has grown up over centuries and, with its round and square towers, castellation and tall chimneys, appears part medieval castle, part Tudor manor, part Victorian Gothic revival.

Sir Thomas Proby bought the house from the Sapcote family in 1655 and pulled down most of it, retaining the 15th-century tower and chapel. Around these his brother John built a mansion. The chapel was converted to the drawing room in the 1760s. In 1860, Granville Proby, 3rd Earl of Carysfort, ordered substantial alterations. Henry Ashton created the Marble Hall and main staircase, and designed the dining room with three large Gothic windows modelled on those in the chapel's north wall. The 12,000 books that cram the shelves of the library have been accumulated since Sir Thomas's time. His portrait hangs in the Marble Hall. The meticulous accounts he kept are displayed in the inner library within the medieval tower.

The gardens are a 20th-century creation, begun in around 1913 when Colonel Proby laid them out to designs prepared by A.H. Hallam Murray, his daughter-in-law's father. The Gothic-style Orangery was built to mark the millennium.

▶ *PE8 6SH. 8 miles SW of Peterborough at junction of A605 and B671. Limited seasonal opening.*

❷ Island Hall

'This is the loveliest, dearest old house, I never was in such a one.' Octavia Hill, one of the founders of the National Trust, wrote thus of Island Hall to her sister in the 19th century. The situation of this elegant Georgian mansion, on the banks of the Great Ouse, in the small town of Godmanchester, is part of its tremendous appeal. It was built in the late 1740s of red brick with stone dressings, in the classical style, crowned with a pediment. The house appears entirely serene despite suffering slights and near catastrophe – it was given over to the WAAF and RAF in the Second World War, converted to flats afterwards, and damaged by fire in 1977. Restored by the Herrtage family, it was bought in 1983 by Christopher Vane Percy, a descendant of the Baumgartner family, who lived here for six generations. Island Hall is a family home, hung with portraits. Tours of house and grounds are conducted by family members, and visitors can take lunch in the stone-flagged hall, or enjoy afternoon tea and a game of croquet. What could be more civilised?

▶ *PE29 2BA. N of Godmanchester town centre, 1 mile S of Huntingdon. Group tours all year by prior arrangement.*

❸ Wimpole Hall

'A man that lives in might great fashion, with all things in a most extraordinary manner noble and rich about him, and eats in the French fashion …' Diarist Samuel Pepys so describes Thomas Chicheley, who began this enormous house – the largest in Cambridgeshire – in 1640, possibly to his own design. Chicheley was an ace tennis player, extravagant, and an ardent Royalist who lent generously to Charles I in the Civil War. Unfortunately for him, too much of the 'noble and rich' living left him short of money and he was forced to sell the Hall.

In the ensuing centuries a series of illustrious architects, designers, decorators and landscapers left their mark, principally James Gibbs, Sir James Thornhill, Charles Bridgeman, Henry Flitcroft, Sir John Soane, Capability Brown and Humphry Repton. The house's façade was nearly 90m (300ft) long, and it was approached by a broad, 2 mile drive. The voracious property nearly bankrupted more than one owner. Its last private chatelaine was Elsie Kipling, daughter of Rudyard. She and her husband, George Bambridge, bought the decaying building in 1938. George died just five years later, but Elsie was a woman who could meet with triumph and disaster and treat those two impostors just the same. She soldiered on for 30 years, working to bring the old pile back to life and recover its dispersed collections.

In 1976, Wimpole Hall and the Kipling archive passed to the National Trust. Visitors can see the Long Gallery, created by Flitcroft from three of Gibbs's rooms, libraries by Soane and Gibbs, Soane's Yellow Drawing Room, a wealth of period furniture and paintings and a park

ANGLESEY ABBEY

'naturalised' by Brown. They will not see a once-magnificent Victorian conservatory. Faced with what she considered an extortionate repair bill, Elsie flattened it, and then photographed the wreckage with her Box Brownie.

▶ *SG8 0BW. 9 miles SW of Cambridge on A603. NT. Seasonal opening of Hall (closed Fridays and most Thursdays); park open daily all year.*

❹ Anglesey Abbey, Garden and Lode Mill

The park surrounding a former Augustinian priory could be an 18th-century creation but, in fact, it was the work of American-born Huttleston Broughton in the 20th century. The priory was dissolved in Henry VIII's Reformation, and the house that replaced it in the early 1600s, built by Thomas Hobson, has been much altered, although some of the medieval arches remain. Hobson's approach to hiring out horses gave rise to the expression 'Hobson's choice', but the great character here is Huttleston Broughton. He and his brother Henry bought Anglesey Abbey in 1926. When Henry married, he turned the abbey over to Huttleston, who got down to work. He had the money and leisure to indulge his passions for art, history,

horse racing and garden design. He was created 1st Lord Fairhaven in 1929, and lived to see his great landscaping achievement marked by the publication in 1964 of Lanning Roper's book *The Gardens of Anglesey Abbey*. Great vision went into the planning of vistas, the planting of avenues, the placing of pool, rivers and temples, the Monks Garden, Daffodil Walk, Arboretum and Dahlia Garden. Coronation Avenue was planted to commemorate the crowning of George VI in 1937, alternating London plane and horse chestnut in four rows – a copy of an avenue in Windsor Great Park (Windsor Castle was a personal obsession).

Among the house's great treasures are works by Gainsborough and Constable, nudes by the Victorian artist William Etty, Bruges tapestries, Ming porcelain and a collection of rare clocks. The monks' old parlour served as the dining room. Visitors can buy flour from a working 18th-century watermill. Huttleston Broughton was a bachelor and he bequeathed the estate to the National Trust in 1966, so that house and garden might 'represent an age and way of life that was quickly passing'.

▶ *CB25 9EJ. 6 miles NE of Cambridge on B1102. NT. Seasonal opening of house; garden and mill open all year.*

EAST ANGLIA

ESSEX

Nothing is as originally intended – Audley End was once twice the size, Ingatestone Hall was four-sided, Layer Marney should have had an even bigger house to go with it – but all are fascinating and full of riches.

❶ Audley End House

Charles II liked a flutter on the horses, and bought this glorious edifice to be close to Newmarket. The house began life as Audley Inn, built by Sir Thomas Audley on the site of the dissolved Walden Abbey. His grandson, Thomas Howard, 1st Earl of Suffolk, built in its place a 'prodigy house' in which to entertain royalty. It was completed in the reign of James I – possibly at the king's expense. Thomas was James's Lord Treasurer. In 1619, he and his wife were sent to the Tower for suspected embezzlement.

John Evelyn wrote of Audley End in 1654: 'Without comparison it is one of the stateliest palaces in the kingdom … It shines without like a diadem, by the decorations of the cupolas and other ornaments on the pavilions.' It passed out of royal ownership in 1701 after Sir Christopher Wren warned William III that the cost of repairs would be ruinous. The king handed the house back to the Suffolks, who commissioned John Vanbrugh to demolish the greater part of it, although what remains is hardly a remnant. Sir John Griffin Griffin, 4th Baron Howard de Walden and later 1st Lord Braybrooke, engaged Capability Brown to landscape the parkland, and Robert Adam to create new reception rooms. In the 1820s to 1830s, the 3rd Lord Braybrooke swept away Adam's classical interiors and returned the house to its old Jacobean self. The Ministry of Works, in turn, restored some of Adam's work after it bought the house in 1948. It is ravishing, with many art treasures.
▶ *CB11 4JF. Just W of Saffron Walden, 4 miles S of Junction 9 of M11. EH. Seasonal opening.*

❷ Ingatestone Hall

When Sir William Petre bought the lands of the dissolved Barking Abbey, he found the old steward's house 'scarce mete for a fermor to dwell on'. He knocked it down and built a new house, with a courtyard enclosed on four sides. Mod cons included spring-fed flushing drains. Sir William was a secretary of state to Henry VIII, Edward VI, Mary I and Elizabeth I, who stayed here on her summer Progress in 1561. In the 18th century, a new wing was added, and a tower featuring a one-handed clock was set upon an arched Tudor outbuilding, displaying the family

motto, 'Sans Dieu Rien'. The west wing, which housed the Great Hall and dining chamber, was pulled down, leaving a U-shape that seems to welcome visitors with open arms. Rooms were remodelled, Georgian panelling installed, and mullioned casements replaced by fashionable sash windows. The family were recusant Catholics, and priest holes recall the days of religious persecution. Beneath the low ceiling of the Drawing Room, walls bristle with antlers and are hung with Tudor portraits and paintings by Stubbs. Family portraits in the Long Gallery, period furniture, tapestries and ornaments encourage an atmosphere of intimacy. Lord Petre's son and his family have an apartment in one wing.
▶ *CM4 9NR. Just S of Ingatestone town centre, 7 miles SW of Chelmsford off A12. Limited seasonal opening; guided tours for groups at other times by prior arrangement.*

❸ Layer Marney Tower

The ambitions of Henry Marney did not stop with this extraordinary structure, which was intended to be the gatehouse of a far grander house. Marney was Henry VIII's Lord Privy Seal and Captain of the Horse. Some of his master's grandiosity must have rubbed off on him, for in *c*.1520 he began to build a palace to rival Hampton Court (see page 83). When he died in 1523, and his son two years later, the work was not finished. What had been completed was a main range 90m (300ft) long, the stable block, a church and the soaring gatehouse, which dominates the surrounding countryside. Its four flanking turrets rise over seven and eight floors, higher than any preceding Tudor mansion. Although Gothic in outline, and in some details, its decoration is Renaissance. Perhaps Marney had the services of the king's craftsmen to produce fashionable terracotta and stucco work. Lord Marney's splendid tomb in the church's north aisle incorporates his effigy in black stone. A series of private owners have left their mark upon Layer Marney. In the early 1900s Walter de Zoete converted the stables into the Long Gallery for his collections of furniture and art. Nicholas and Sheila Charrington continue the restoration.
▶ *CO5 9US. 2 miles E of Tiptree off B1022. Limited seasonal opening; group visits all year by prior arrangement.*

LORD MARNEY'S TOMB. LAYER MARNEY

HOLKHAM HALL

NORFOLK

A famously haunted property and a moated manor share the limelight with the halls of the Walpoles and an abundance of Georgian elegance. Outside, the grounds of grand Holkham stretch down to the sea.

❶ Houghton Hall

Robert Walpole, 1st Earl of Orford, 'the fat old squire of Norfolk', was Britain's first prime minister in all but name. In 1700, aged 24, he inherited the modest Restoration house that was his place of birth. At the height of his power, in 1722, he engaged a series of architects to build a grand new mansion to display his art treasures. The house, which stands in a park grazed by white deer, is Colen Campbell's Palladian masterpiece, topped with baroque domes from James Gibbs's earlier design. The rectangular central block comprises ground floor, piano nobile, bedroom floor and attics. Colonnades connect it to flanking wings. The detached stable block was the work of William Kent, who was unleashed on the Hall interiors. The project cost £200,000, and upon his death in 1745, Walpole left such a heavy debt that, in 1779, his grandson, George, 3rd Earl, sold his precious art collection to Catherine the Great. Horace Walpole, Robert's youngest son (see Strawberry Hill House, page 78), lamented the estate reduced to 'destruction and desolation', and stepped in to save the furniture.

With what confidence does this great mansion rise above past troubles! The 7th Marquis of Cholmondeley has carried out major restoration. In the Stone Hall a bust of Sir Robert sits under a stucco ceiling by Giuseppe Atari, across which cherubs disport themselves around the Walpole coat of arms. The decorative splendour throughout is almost overwhelming.

▶ *PE31 6UE. 1 mile N of Harpley on A148 King's Lynn-Fakenham Road. Limited seasonal opening.*

❷ Holkham Hall

An Englishman's home, Sir Edward Coke so memorably declared, is his castle. Coke was Lord Chief Justice to James I. The home built by his descendant, Thomas Coke, 1st Earl of Leicester, from 1736, is more a palace. The house was designed around Coke's art collection, amassed on the Grand Tour. Coke designed it himself, with Richard Boyle, 3rd Earl of Burlington, and William Kent. It resembles a Roman villa, a single storey, with pavilions on each corner. Most of the interiors are Kent's work. This superb, pale golden Palladian mansion is so lavishly ornamented, furnished, gilded and swagged, it is like being inside a vast jewel box.

When Queen Mary slept here in the Green State Bedroom, the painting of Jupiter caressing Juno was considered too lewd and was removed to an attic. This is a house accustomed to receiving royalty. Princess Victoria, aged 16, stayed for two days, as her mother took her about to show her off to her subjects. Now Jupiter and Juno (by Gavin Hamilton, 1730–97) are back in their place, with the tapestries, the giant four-poster and antiques. Paintings by Rubens and Van Dyck hang in the Saloon. The Marble Hall is built of softer, more translucent Derbyshire alabaster. The Statue Gallery is lined with ancient Roman statuary. The Hall was used as a location for *The Duchess*, starring Keira Knightley. The grounds stretch down to pine woods and an unspoilt shoreline.

▶ *NR23 1AB. 2 miles W of Wells-next-the-Sea on A149. Limited seasonal opening of house; daily seasonal opening of museum, walled gardens and park.*

3 Mannington Hall Gardens

The Walpoles acquired this 15th-century moated manor house in the 1720s, but the first one to live here was Horatio William Walpole, 4th Earl of Orford (in the title's third creation), in 1860. He restored the ramshackle building and added a wing. The interior is not open to the casual visitor, but Lord and Lady Walpole make it available for charity events, weddings, concerts, exhibitions, drama and guided tours. The gardens within the moat are reached via a drawbridge and divided into 'rooms'. The Scented Garden is laid out to the design of the Drawing Room ceiling.

▶ *NR11 7BB. 10 miles SW of Cromer on minor roads off A140. Limited seasonal opening.*

4 Wolterton Hall

Here is Houghton Hall's self-effacing little brother. In the 1720s, while Sir Robert Walpole was overreaching himself with his grand mansion (see left), younger brother Horatio was exhibiting marked restraint in building this redbrick, pedimented house with rusticated stone basement. His architect was Thomas Ripley, who also oversaw the works at Houghton. Later generations altered and revived Wolterton, adding a wing and enclosing the park.

Horatio's great great grandson, Horatio William, 4th Earl of Orford, abandoned Wolterton when he moved to and restored Mannington (above). The present Lord and Lady Walpole also choose to live at the more romantic Mannington. They are still very much involved with Wolterton, though, and have been pursuing a programme of reorganisation, conservation and research into the history of the family and of house and park. It is a rich seam to mine. In the State Rooms on the first floor the walls are hung with family portraits. From the Saloon window there is a long view over to the lake.

▶ *NR11 7LY. 9 miles SW of Cromer on minor roads off A140. Seasonal opening of house; group tours all year by prior arrangement; park open all year.*

5 Felbrigg Hall

'A great mass of wings and courtyards, a confusion of roofs and twisted barley-sugar chimneys ...' In her book *Dry Rot and Daffodils*, Mary Mackie offers a bird's eye view of this isolated 17th-century country house, which is protected from scouring sea winds by woodlands of chestnut, oak, redwood and beech. Until 1990, Mary's husband, Christopher Mackie, was administrator, or 'houseman', here.

John Wyndham bought the estate in the 15th century. In 1620, Thomas Wyndham rebuilt the medieval house, looking to nearby Blickling Hall (below) for inspiration, since it was undergoing similar transformation. William Samwell added a wing in the 1680s. The rugged Jacobean exterior, a mix of brick, flint, stone and patchy cement render, with Dutch gables, is crowned by the exultation GLORIA DEO IN EXCELSIS. And – Glory be to God in Heaven! – inside the house lies splendid Georgian elegance, from the rococo Dining Room to the Rose Bedroom. A gallery is hung with paintings collected on the Grand Tour by William Wyndham. A Victorian pleasure garden is laid out around the 18th-century Orangery. Robert Wyndham Ketton-Cremer, who died in 1969, left the property to the National Trust, despite his repeated threat – or promise – that he would leave it to a cats' home.

▶ *NR11 8PR. 3 miles SW of Cromer off A148. NT. Seasonal opening.*

6 Blickling Hall

Blickling has two claims to fame. A former owner was the model for Shakespeare's comic Falstaff; and Anne Boleyn was born here. The first is undoubtedly true, the second is questionable, although Anne's father, Thomas Boleyn, once lived at Blickling. In any case, none of them would have known the fine Jacobean manor that stands here today. It was designed by Robert Lyminge for Sir Henry Hobart, Lord Chief Justice of the Common Pleas under James I, work continuing from 1616 to 1625.

The Hall richly repays a visit. The brick exterior has stone and stucco dressings and is topped with turrets and cupolas, tall chimneys and a 19th-century clock tower. The Print Room is papered with copies of Old Masters. Among the house's treasures are an exceptionally fine collection of rare books, Mortlake tapestries, antiques, works by Canaletto and Piranesi and a medieval fireplace from Caister Castle. A tapestry in the Peter the Great Room, which portrays Peter vanquishing the Swedes, was a gift from Catherine the Great.

Although Anne Boleyn's link with the house is tenuous, a statue of her stands in a niche above the oak staircase and she is said to be one of the resident ghosts at what is the National Trust's most haunted property. A fellow apparition is Sir John Fastolf of Caister, so unflatteringly portrayed in three of Shakespeare's plays. Sir John owned the 15th-century Hall, and his coat of arms is displayed in the 'new' house. Especially around May 19, the anniversary of her death,

susceptible visitors report seeing Anne, sitting with her head in her lap, in a coach driven by a headless coachman. The last private owner, the Marquis of Lothian, bequeathed the estate to the Trust in 1940.

▶ *NR11 6NF. 1 mile W of A140, 8 miles S of Cromer. NT. Seasonal opening (closed on Tuesdays and some Mondays).*

❼ Oxburgh Hall

This ancient manor house, standing within a square moat, has a serene air of permanence, and yet was so nearly swept away. It was built for Sir Edmund Bedingfeld, who, in 1482, was granted a licence to crenellate by Edward IV. It was to be of chalk and flint, but the aspirational Sir Edmund went for expensive brick, the choice of aristocrats. Fortifications, including an imposing gated entrance tower with arrow slits and drawbridge, were a show of status rather than defensive. The family were recusant Catholics and Royalists, and the house has a priest hole while visible repairs indicate damage suffered in the Civil War. For his loyalty to the king, Henry Bedingfeld was granted a baronetcy by Charles II.

The Great Hall was replaced by a saloon in the 1780s. Further alterations were made in Victorian times by the 6th Baronet, who used to give his address as 'The Ruin'. He included a secret passage for fun. The 9th Baronet sold the estate in 1951 but his mother, Sybil, Lady Bedingfeld, managed to buy it back. A local timber merchant had planned to demolish it and cut down the trees. Oxburgh was given to the National Trust in 1952. It contains beautifully wrought embroidery worked by Mary, Queen of Scots during the 19 years she spent as a prisoner of her cousin Elizabeth I.

▶ *PE33 9PS. 8 miles SW of Swaffham on minor roads. NT. Seasonal opening.*

BEHIND THE BOOKS LIES A HIDDEN WAY OUT OF THE LIBRARY

CONCEALED DOOR AT OXBURGH HALL

SUFFOLK

These beautiful houses were inhabited by an eclectic set of people from a licentious earl to Beatrix Potter. Their alluring stories are told through the artefacts, paintings and journals they left behind.

❶ Euston Hall

Diarist John Evelyn, a passionate gardener and noted landscaper, came to 'magnificent and commodious' Euston Hall with Charles II and his court in 1671. It was Evelyn who designed the walk through the pleasure grounds that visitors enjoy today. The wider park, laid out by William Kent and finished by Capability Brown, with watermill and folly, is among Kent's masterworks.

When Henry Bennet, Earl of Arlington, bought the Hall in 1666, it was a ruin, and he set out to create a grand house in the French style, around a courtyard, with a pavilion on each corner. He was Secretary of State to Charles II. When the king suggested that Arlington's daughter Isabella, aged five, might marry his illegitimate son, nine-year-old Henry, his servant blenched and said, ahem, he had hoped that she would marry a duke. No problem! Charles simply ennobled his son.

Henry and Isabella, Duke and Duchess of Grafton, inherited Euston Hall, and *c.*1750 their son Charles, the 2nd Duke, engaged Matthew Brettingham to remodel it, replacing domes with low pyramid roofs, and refacing parts of the exterior. A fire in 1902 destroyed two of the wings, and although they were rebuilt, the 10th Duke found the property unmanageable; the south and most of the west wing were demolished in 1952. The present duke's art collection, much of it brought together by Arlington, includes works by Stubbs, Van Dyck and Lely, and family portraits, among them a painting of Barbara Villiers, Charles II's mistress and Henry's mother. Henry died fighting for William of Orange against his uncle, James II.
▶ *IP24 2QP. 4 miles S of Thetford on A1088. Closed for restoration. Park and house are due to reopen to the public in summer 2013.*

❷ Somerleyton Hall

Samuel Morton Peto was a civil engineer. He managed the construction of the Palace of Westminster and Trafalgar Square. Then came the age of the train. A bust on Norwich Station commemorates Peto, a man who foresaw the importance of rail travel. In 1843 he engaged John Thomas, a protégé of Charles Barry's and Prince Albert's favourite architect, to rebuild a Jacobean house at Somerleyton that would become 'one of the most beautiful stately homes in Britain'. Thomas was also a sculptor with a 'wonderful facility of invention'. His masterpiece stands above the River Waveney, the original red brick dressed with pale Caen stone. To either side, the stables, topped with a cupola, and an Italianate tower seem to advance to greet the visitor. The entrance hall is clad in oak and has green-veined Devon marble pillars and patterned Minton floor tiles under a stained-glass dome. Two fierce bears rear up. The words 'no expense spared' come irresistibly to mind.

In 1855 Peto received a baronetcy for his creation of a rail link to the Crystal Palace for the Great Exhibition, but by 1863 he was bankrupt and was forced to sell his 'earthly paradise' to the Crossley family, who still own and occupy it today. In the walled garden is a greenhouse designed by Joseph Paxton, architect of the Crystal Palace. A yew-hedge maze was planted by William Nesfield in 1846. The Pleasure Gardens are a riot of rhododendrons and azaleas in season.
▶ *NR32 5QQ. 6 miles NE of Lowestoft on B1074. Limited seasonal opening.*

❸ Glemham Hall

Elihu Yale not only endowed the renowned American University that bears his name, but he splashed out to help make this house what it is today. It started out as a beautiful Elizabethan manor in early Renaissance style, built by the de Glemham family. Dudley North bought the estate in *c.*1709. He married Catherine Yale, one of Elihu's daughters, and her father lavished gifts upon the couple.

In 1722–7 the house was remodelled and given a Georgian façade. After that it passed down through the generations until the Cobbolds acquired it in 1923. The family appear to rejoice in it. They live in every part of it, and share it through all manner of activities, from walks and productions of Shakespeare in the park, house tours, art classes, musical soirées and wine-tastings. It can be hired for parties and weddings. The reception rooms are Georgian, but atmospheric Jacobean sections survive. In the walled rose garden are a summer house, lily ponds and classical urns.
▶ *IP13 0BT. 10 miles NE of Woodbridge on A12. On A12 Woodbridge-Saxmundham road*

EAST ANGLIA

VIBRANT
MIXED
BORDERS
FOR ALL
SEASONS

HELMINGHAM HALL GARDENS

❹ Helmingham Hall Gardens

The Tollemache family's romantic courtyard manor house, although not usually open to the public, provides a beautiful centrepiece to the gardens. It gazes dreamily down at its own reflection in the surrounding lake. Its two drawbridges are still raised every night, as they have been since 1510. The house is Tudor in origin but has undergone periods of updating from its half-timbered beginnings. The façade is clad in brick and tiles. Mullioned windows are faced with pale limestone; crow-stepped gables are topped with pinnacles.

In the fragrant Rose Garden, beds are interplanted with forget-me-nots, edged with catmint and lavender. A Knot Garden was created in 1982. There are borders of shrubs and of grasses, borders for spring, borders for summer. A second, smaller moat surrounds the garden. Beyond it is the orchard with drifts of wild flowers, and an Apple Tree Walk. Visitors signing up to a cookery day will be welcomed in the Great Hall and taken for a walk to the kitchen garden to pick seasonal produce for the day's menu before a lesson in the kitchen and a feast.
▶ *IP14 6EF. 2 miles S of A1120, 10 miles E of Stowmarket, off B1077. Limited seasonal opening.*

❺ Hengrave Hall

A cloth merchant named Thomas Kytson built this singular house in 1525, crowning it with ornate turrets, cupolas, castellation and pinnacles. It is distinguished by its superb High Gothic gatehouse, which has elements of the emerging Renaissance in its rich adornment. Kytson's son, also Thomas, was a Catholic but he survived the Reformation and was even knighted by Elizabeth I. In the French Revolution, the Gage family, to whom the estate had passed by marriage, loaned the house to nuns from Bruges. Much altered in the Victorian era, it became a convent once more in 1952 and a religious retreat in the 1970s. It has a lake, verdant lawns and a chapel, and today serves as a wedding venue.
▶ *IP28 6LZ. 4 miles NW of Bury St Edmunds on A1101.*

❻ Ickworth House

Frederick Augustus Hervey, 4th Earl of Bristol, planned to bring together here his twin passions for art and Italy. The earl became Bishop of Derry in 1768 – George III called him 'that wicked prelate'. He was licentious, unashamedly materialistic, clever and eccentric.

The earl-bishop, as he was known, made the Grand Tour in high style and on his return ordered the building of a neoclassical mansion, with a giant rotunda, to house his magnificent collection, which was waiting to be shipped over from Rome. The designs for his dream home were by Mario Asprucci, adapted by Francis and Joseph Sandys. The front of the house is more than 189m (600ft) long, the rotunda 30.5m (100ft) high. The building was begun in 1795, and was unfinished when Frederick died in 1803, in Italy. He had spent the years since 1796 trying to recover his precious collection of art treasures, which had been confiscated by Napoleon's troops and sold at auction.

The 5th Earl inherited a building site and no art but he oversaw the house's completion and bought pictures to hang in it. Visitors can see works by Velazquez, Titian, Poussin, Gainsborough, Reynolds and Hogarth, Georgian silver, Regency furniture and porcelain. The Herveys were legendary oddballs. Lady Mary Wortley Montague said of them: 'When God created the human race he made men, women and Herveys.' When Frederick Hervey commissioned Ickworth, he created something extraordinary, with Italianate gardens, set within a deer park. It came to the National Trust in 1956 and today the west wing is used for events and the east wing is a luxury hotel.

▶ *IP29 5QE. 2 miles SW of Bury St Edmunds, signposted from A143. Seasonal opening of house (closed Wednesdays and Thursdays); gardens and park open all year.*

❼ Kentwell Hall

Sir Simonds d'Ewes was a 17th-century antiquarian and politician, 'a thin high-flown character of eminent perfection and exactitude' according to Thomas Carlyle. Among other activities, he kept meticulous journals of the proceedings of Parliament. This lovely old moated manor house became his home when he married into the affluent Clopton family, who had built it between *c.*1500 and 1550. The property has passed through many hands since then, but no hand had been laid heavily upon it until Robert Hart Logan called in Thomas Hopper to restore the interiors in Tudor Gothic style, following a fire in 1826. This work was never completed. Hopper died suddenly, in debt. The exterior was unaltered.

Since the 1970s, Patrick and Judith Phillips have been tending and restoring Kentwell, and they insist that 'this is not a "stately home" but very much a lived-in and loved family home'.

MELFORD HALL

Visitors will think it stately enough, but the great attraction at Kentwell is the 're-creation of everyday Tudor life', which owes its authenticity in great part to d'Ewes, who collected the Cloptons' papers. These are now held at the British Museum. The Phillipses put on Tudor Days throughout the year, along with various other events. In the grounds they have reinstated the ice house, dove cote, byres, brew house and other outbuildings, and also run a rare breeds farm. Novel elements include a two-dimensional maze on a Tudor rose pattern, Pied Piper topiary, a dead yew sculpted as the Tower of Babel by Colin Wilbourne, and Baron Munchausen's Galleon, designed by Terry Gilliam for the film of the baron's adventures.

▶ *CO10 9BA. 5 miles N of Sudbury off A1092. Limited seasonal opening for casual visitors; events all year.*

⑧ Melford Hall

At this turreted, redbrick Tudor mansion on the village green, lawyer William Cordell entertained Elizabeth I in 1578 on one of her Progresses. Queen Mary granted the Manor of Melford to Cordell in 1554, in recognition of his 'past good, true, faithful and acceptable service'. He had married Mary Clopton, a cousin of the Clopton family of Kentwell Hall, and began building his house on the site of the former banqueting house of the Abbots of Bury St Edmunds. A contemporary observer, Thomas Churchyard recalled the reception laid on for Elizabeth and her household: 'As I heard there were 200 young gentlemen clad all in white velvet, and 300 of the graver sort apparelled in black velvet coats and with fair chains … a comely troop and a noble sight to behold.'

If the Cordells knew how to push the boat out, so did the Hyde Parkers, a naval family to whom Melford Hall passed, after many changes of ownership, in 1786. Sir Hyde Parker, 5th Baronet, was a vice-admiral. His reward of looted goods for capturing a Spanish ship in 1762, in the Seven Years War, can be seen in an upper room. Gifts from the emperor of China destined for the king of Spain thus ended up in Suffolk. In 1813, the family called in Thomas Hopper to remodel the interiors. There is a small display dedicated to Beatrix Potter, a cousin of Lady Hyde Parker and a frequent visitor, who wrote *The Tale of Squirrel Nutkin* at the Hall and painted a series of watercolours. The original Jemima Puddle-Duck was brought as a gift for the Hyde Parker children.

▶ *CO10 9AA. 4 miles N of Sudbury on B1064. NT. Seasonal opening*

EAST ANGLIA

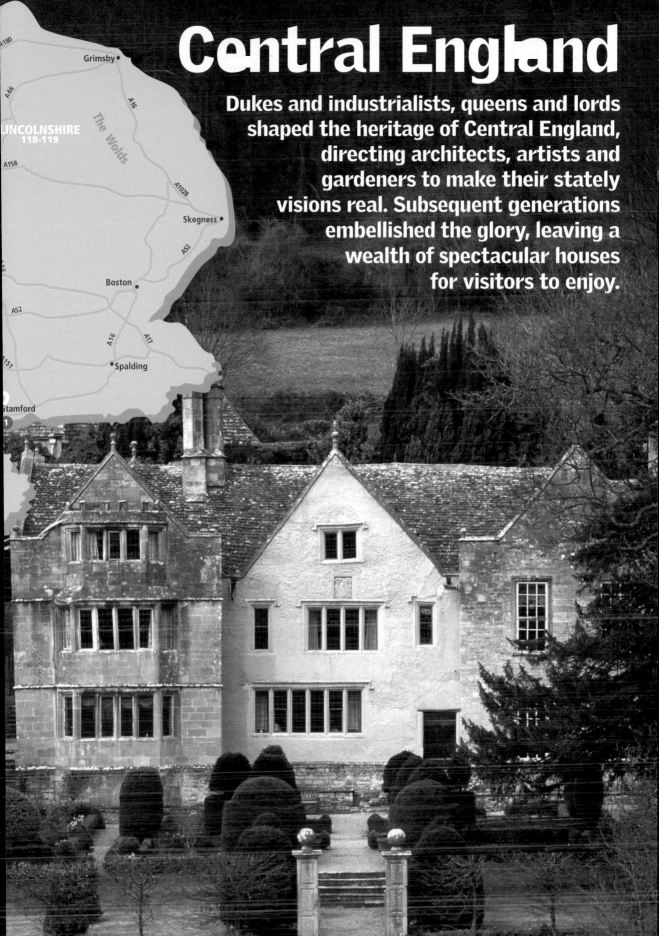

Central England

Dukes and industrialists, queens and lords shaped the heritage of Central England, directing architects, artists and gardeners to make their stately visions real. Subsequent generations embellished the glory, leaving a wealth of spectacular houses for visitors to enjoy.

LINCOLNSHIRE
118-119

The Wolds

Grimsby

Skegness

Boston

Spalding

Stamford

DERBYSHIRE

The grandeur of Chatsworth serves to emphasise the glorious individuality on show elsewhere – Calke Abbey, open for none of the usual reasons, the family home with a difference, and not least, quirky, steadfast Hardwick.

❶ Chatsworth

'It is indeed a palace for a prince, a most magnificent building.' Chatsworth stands on a valley slope beside the River Derwent, and Daniel Defoe, describing it in the 1720s, decided that the backdrop of rocky, wooded uplands serves 'to set off its beauty, and are, by the most exquisite decoration of the place, made to add to the lustre of the whole'.

Sir William Cavendish and his wife, Bess of Hardwick, began to build a splendid Elizabethan house at Chatsworth in 1553. With her fourth husband, the Earl of Shrewsbury, Bess had the task of guarding Mary, Queen of Scots here. Mary's rooms, above the Great Hall, are still known as the Queen of Scots Apartments, although Mary would not know the English baroque masterpiece of today. Sir William and Bess's son was made Earl of Devonshire in 1618, and starting in 1687, the 4th Earl (later 1st Duke) rebuilt the house completely. The south and east wings were designed by William Talman, the west front by Thomas Archer. In the 1760s Capability Brown landscaped the pastures and river. Joseph Paxton, who later designed London's Crystal Palace, installed greenhouses and a giant fountain for the 6th Duke. Jeffry Wyatville built the north wing with its Theatre, Sculpture Gallery, Grand Dining Room and Belvedere. 'Only with Chatsworth,' wrote architectural historian Nikolaus Pevsner, 'does Derbyshire appear on the truly national stage. The work of Talman then of Archer is among the essential document of the English style of *c*.1700.'

▶ *DE45 1PP. 8 miles N of Matlock off A6 Bakewell Road. Seasonal opening; park open all year.*

❷ Haddon Hall

Sir George Vernon was renowned for his love of entertaining, and hanging local men without trial. When Sir John Manners, son of the Duke of Rutland, had the temerity to court his younger daughter, Dorothy, Vernon dismissed him as 'this second son of an impoverished Earl'.

CHATSWORTH

Dorothy, however, was not deterred. In 1563 the ballroom at Haddon Hall was the scene of a party to celebrate the marriage of her elder sister, Margaret, to Sir Thomas Stanley. Slipping away unnoticed through a back door, Dorothy ran through the gardens, over the packhorse bridge across the River Wye, and into John's arms. The legend of the couple's elopement is as romantic as this medieval, mellow stone castle. Tucked in a valley and surrounded by forest, it was the seat of the Vernons from 1191, passing to the Manners family in 1565 by that triumph of love over daughterly obedience. The spectacular Elizabethan Long Gallery was built by John and Dorothy to mark the union of their two families.

Haddon Hall has survived without being gussied up by Georgians or Gothic-ised by Victorians. The worst it suffered was 200 years of neglect when the Manners clan favoured their seat at Belvoir (see page 116). It lay dormant until the 1920s, when the 9th Duke and Duchess of Rutland awoke the sleeping giant and made it a home once more. In the Banqueting Hall, which is spiked with antlers and overlooked by a minstrels' gallery, hangs a tapestry made for Henry VII. A manacle was designed to restrain any guest

'who did not drink fayre'. The gardens were laid out in Elizabethan times, with terraces stepping down to the Wye, in a style inspired by Italian hilltop villas. Roses, delphiniums, clematis, crumbling walls – the romance goes on and on.
▶ *DE45 1LA. 2 miles SE of Bakewell on A6. Seasonal afternoon opening.*

❸ Hardwick Hall

Bess of Hardwick was born at the now ruined Hardwick Old Hall and was around 70 years old when the foundation stone was laid for the 'new' hall in 1590. She may have been 'first lady of Chatsworth' (see page 102), but it is here that her personality finds most expression. Bess was a forceful character who made four strategic marriages to wealthy men, becoming the second richest woman in the kingdom, after the queen.

Hardwick Hall is an extraordinary survivor from the Tudor period. It is very much Bess's statement. In describing it, Nikolaus Pevsner could be describing Bess herself: 'There is nothing of surrounding nature either that could compete with its uncompromising, unnatural,

HARDWICK HALL

graceless, and indomitable self-assertiveness. It is an admirable piece of architectural expression: no fussing, no fumbling, nor indeed any flights of fancy.' In fact, this is a very special building of glowing golden stone. There is ego in the 'niggly strapwork frills on the tower balustrades which frame Bess's proud and ostentatious initials', but its windows were so many, so beautiful – and so conspicuously costly – that it was often said the hall was 'more glass than wall'. These were the trademark of the house's designer, Robert Smythson. The atmospheric interiors are hung with tapestries and embroideries. Portraits of the chatelaine show that Bess was no great beauty, but she has a kind of majesty. Her garden with its 'madly crenellated walls' and banqueting hall with 'crazy headgear' are an idiosyncratic delight.

▶ *S44 5QJ. 8 miles SE of Chesterfield on minor roads. NT. Limited seasonal opening of house and gardens.*

❹ Renishaw Hall

'With the Sitwells at Renishaw,' wrote Evelyn Waugh in his diary in August 1930. 'Sachie likes talking about sex. Osbert very shy. Edith wholly ignorant … She said that port was made with methylated spirit; she knew this for a fact because her charwoman told her.' This has been the Sitwells' home for almost 400 years. Edith, Osbert and Sacheverell Sitwell were poets and style setters. Their father, Sir George, laid out the Italianate gardens at Renishaw in 1895; he gave the low-built, mellow Jacobean manor a Gothic makeover. He was, his butler, Henry Moat, once said, 'the strangest old bugger you ever met'. His inventions included a musical toothbrush and a small revolver for killing wasps. He spent wantonly on acquiring works of art and building architectural follies, but would examine a bill in minute detail.

Renishaw brims with Sitwell art and memorabilia. The visitor sees portraits by Sargent and Copley, tapestries, murals by John Piper, Chippendale furniture. Some interiors are Jacobean. The Great Drawing Room and Ballroom are Regency. Today Alexandra Sitwell lives at Renishaw. It is a family home like no other.

▶ *S21 3WB. 9 miles SE of Sheffield on A6135. Limited seasonal opening; pre-booked guided tours only.*

❺ Sudbury Hall

Louis Laguerre's allegorical mural of *Industry* and *Idleness* at Sudbury portrays a winged Saturn, representing Time, rewarding Industry with a cornucopia; Idleness gets only thorns. A cornucopia, then, for George Vernon, who was

his own architect when he built this house in 1660. It was the year of the Restoration, but Vernon looked to the past. The E-plan façades north and south, with mullioned windows and stone dressings, appear Jacobean. Visitors, perhaps expecting dark oak panelling and faded tapestries, take a step back when confronted by such opulent interiors. The Great Staircase is Sudbury's *pièce de resistance*. It may also be to Vernon's own design, and is exuberantly decorative, with carving by Edward Pearce, an assistant to Christopher Wren, and plasterwork by James Pettifer. The motif of fruitful abundance is echoed in the Saloon. In the blindingly white and gilded Long Gallery hang family portraits as well as likenesses of Nell Gwyn and Barbara Villiers, mistresses of Charles II. The alabaster Queen's Room is where Queen Adelaide slept when she lived here for a time after the death of William IV. The servants wing houses a Museum of Childhood. Surrounding the house are extensive gardens, with terraces, a lake and an 18th-century Gothic Deercote.

▶ *DE6 5HT. 10 miles S of Ashbourne on A515. NT. Seasonal opening.*

❻ Calke Abbey

A handsome baroque mansion, built in 1701–4, Calke Abbey stands amid parkland, behind an Ionic portico, which was added a century later. The building is decayed, its paintwork flaking, its courtyards overgrown, its rooms stuffed with quirky junk. The National Trust acquired it from the last member of the Harpur-Crewe family in 1985, dusted it down, blew away the cobwebs, and today present it as an illustration of a period in the 20th century when many great country houses fell into decline.

Sir Vauncey Harpur-Crewe, 10th Baronet, who died in 1924, was a strange, reclusive man. He would have no electricity – the house made its first tentative connection with the national grid in the 1960s. In the Saloon glass cases of stuffed birds and animals surround a billiard table. The 'theme' continues in the Bird Lobby with an orgy of taxidermy. Deer heads lie in a tragicomic jumble on a bed. The one exhibit of real value turned up by chance in a packing case that had never before been opened. Bed hangings of Chinese silk, believed to be a gift from George II's daughter Princess Anne, have been framed and displayed as a pristine and exquisite example of 18th-century silk embroidery.

▶ *DE73 7LE. 10 miles S of Derby on A514. NT. Seasonal opening of house (closed on Thursdays and Fridays); park open all year.*

CENTRAL ENGLAND

SNOWSHILL MANOR

Riotous assembly

Displaying all the tenacity of hunter gatherers, avid collectors filled their homes with anything that took their fancy.

The Grand Tour of Europe was a rite of passage for young English aristocrats, from the late 1600s to the early 1800s. A young man might spend several years abroad, accompanied by a tutor, to return with 'a mind well furnished with classical ideas'. His stately home might then also be well furnished, with antiquities, sculpture and old masters collected along the way. This was not exploration but acquisitive cultural tourism. As well as paintings and objets d'art, travellers took ideas and inspiration from their host countries.

In Rome, Pompeo Batoni produced 200 standing portraits of English noblemen, posed in a manner to suggest that they all but owned the Eternal City. Batoni's portrait of Thomas Dundas, the future 1st Baron Dundas, which hangs at Aske Hall in Yorkshire, shows him gesturing airily towards a sleeping Ariadne, as if to say, 'Wrap her and deliver her to my door.' In this way, trunk-loads of casts, copies and genuine artefacts came to adorn English country houses.

Sometimes the tourist overreached himself. John Cecil, 5th Earl of Exeter (1648–1700), made four Grand Tours with his wife, Anne Cavendish, filled Burghley in Lincolnshire with splendid purchases and left the estate with 50 years of debt.

Scandalous big-spender

The most profligate and driven of the great collectors was William Beckford. He was author of *The History of the Caliph Vathek* (1786), portraying himself as the villainous caliph satiated with sensual pleasures. Forced into exile amid scandal, Beckford travelled with an entourage that included a harpsichordist, painter and personal physician. Such was his air of importance that he was once mistaken for the emperor of Austria. He had a taste for Italian 15th-century paintings and 18th-century French furniture. Back in England he so overspent on his fantastical home and lifestyle that the collection went to auction, but part of it can be seen at Brodick Castle in Ayrshire.

An oddball collector of a different kind, Sir George Reresby Sitwell (1862–1943) assembled at Renishaw Hall in Derbyshire enough books and papers to fill seven sitting rooms. He had his cows stencilled in blue and white willow pattern to make them easier on the eye, and hung a notice on his gate: 'I must ask anyone entering the house never to contradict me or differ from me in any way, as it interferes with the functioning of my gastric juices and prevents my sleeping at night.'

Sir Vauncey Harpur Crewe (1846–1924), a man of erratic temper, filled Calke Abbey in Derbyshire with stuffed birds and animals that numbered several thousand by the time he died.

Seventh heaven

Charles Paget Wade (1883–1956), an architect, artist and poet, spent his life from the age of seven amassing a collection of 22,000 objects from the everyday to the extraordinary, from small toys to an oak magician's chest, mechanical novelties and peculiar clocks. Then he restored Snowshill Manor in Gloucestershire to display them. They are presented as he intended, filling the house to the rafters. Had these objects been brought together by numerous hands, they would not have the same powerful impact. Chosen and fetishised by one man, they take on a personality and are charged with meaning. Wade enjoyed dressing up in costumes from the collection to receive visitors, among them John Betjeman, Virginia Woolf, J.B. Priestley and Graham Greene. He gave the rooms names – 'Dragon', 'Meridian', 'Seventh Heaven'. The 'Green Room' is home to 26 suits of Samurai armour.

In a similar but sadder way, the collections at Chiddingstone Castle in Kent tell the story of Denys Bower (1905–77). A bank clerk who lived with his parents until he was 34, he was disabled in a motorcycle accident in his youth. In 1955 he took a £6,000 loan from the bank and bought his castle to display another eclectic mixture of exhibits, from his top hat and binoculars to Japanese swords and Egyptian amulets. His deep preoccupation with the Stuarts and the Jacobite cause are revealed by Stuart documents, important paintings, medals and such relics as the heart, hair, blood and garter ribbon of James II. There is a drinks bill written to Charles Edward Stuart, Bonnie Prince Charlie, of whom it is said Bower believed himself to be a reincarnation.

After two failed marriages Bower went to prison in 1950 for attempted murder and suicide after he haplessly loosed a bullet at a girlfriend who had declined to be the third Mrs Bower, then, thinking he had killed her, turned the gun on himself. On his release after four years he commissioned Dame Laura Knight to paint the portrait that hangs at Chiddingstone. It portrays him reunited with one of his prized objects, a gilded bronze Tibetan Buddha, and apparently wearing a Jacobite ring, secret symbol of allegiance to that long-dead cause.

GLOUCESTERSHIRE

Superb examples of Arts and Crafts renovation exist side by side with atmospheric survivors from much longer ago. Innovative gardens are a main feature and Owlpen's topiary has to be seen to be believed.

❶ Dyrham Park

Visitors to the Drawing Room at Dyrham Park must have thought they were seeing double. For a time Murillo's *Urchin Mocking an Old Woman* hung in mirror image to a copy by an associate of Gainsborough's. The strange juxtaposition told a tale of fortunes won, lost, regained. This beautiful baroque Bath-stone mansion within a deer park was the realisation of the ambitions of William Blathwayt, who served both James II and William of Orange. In 1686 he married Mary Wynter, heiress to Dyrham, and began to rebuild the Tudor manor house, employing Huguenot architect Samuel Hauderoy to design a French-inspired west front with 15 bays. He engaged William Talman to create a suite of state rooms, and filled the interiors with Dutch pictures, furnishings and Delftware. The old Great Hall received a sprung dance floor of Flemish oak. Upon Mary's death, the Tapestry Bedchamber became a shrine to her. A bedroom prepared for Queen Anne waited in vain for her visit.

When Blathwayt's descendants fell on hard times, in 1765, the Murillo was sold, but a copy was made before the original was bought back. Dyrham will be familiar to fans of Merchant Ivory's film *The Remains of the Day,* in which it starred as Darlington Hall.
▶ *SN14 8ER. 8 miles N of Bath on A46. NT. Seasonal opening.*

❷ Newark Park

In 1790 James Wyatt effected a magical transformation of a 16th-century clifftop hunting lodge into an element of a Picturesque landscape. The original house was built for Nicholas Poyntz, Groom of the Privy Chamber to Henry VIII, and extended in the 17th century. Poyntz's house was distinguished by its early classical symmetry and grandeur. Its Renaissance detail suggests the work of court masons rather than local builders. When Wyatt was called in by the Reverend Lewis Clutterbuck, he exploited the drama of the house's lofty situation. While the east face, with a doorway of Renaissance design, remained untouched, Wyatt contrived a Gothic south entrance with embattled parapet, and created a lake in the valley.

Mrs Annie Poole King, a widow, moved in with her five children in 1898 and added servants' quarters. In 1949 the estate passed to the National Trust, but it was an American architect, Bob Parsons, who eventually took up residence and brought it back to life. The visitor sees original Tudor upper floors and Wyatt's restored interiors, Poyntz's attic bedroom and garderobe – and from this Cotswolds escarpment, glorious views of the Mendips.
▶ *GL12 7PZ. 1 mile E of Wotton-under-Edge, 6 miles E of M5 (Junction 14). NT. Limited seasonal opening.*

❸ Owlpen Manor

'Owlpen in Gloucestershire – ah, what a dream is there!' Vita Sackville-West was not alone in being enraptured by this stone manor in a Cotswold hamlet (population 35), sequestered deep in a valley, with a tall hill as a backdrop. The manor of Owlpen passed down through family from 1100, until Norman Jewson, a rising young architect in thrall to Arts and Crafts, bought the house in 1925. He loved its romantic situation and found in it 'symbols of the accumulated history of the past'. Local artisans were called in to restore it using local materials. It passed through several loving hands, and since 1974 Sir Nicholas and Lady Karin Mander have continued the restoration.

The manor was begun in 1450, with add-ons in 1720. Three 17th-century gables are unmatched. The asymmetrical south elevation moved James Lees-Milne of the National Trust to remark that it was 'illogically satisfactory'. Jewson's touches include a motif of plaster owls, although 'Owlpen' derives, not from a nocturnal bird of prey, but from the Saxon Olla, who enclosed the land in the 9th century. There are William Morris oak chests and a table by Sydney Barnsley of the Arts and Crafts Workshop. Queen Margaret's Room – in which Henry VI's queen, Margaret of Anjou, is said to have slept and which she apparently now haunts – is lined with hangings of painted cloth portraying the story of Joseph and the coat of many colours. The garden topiary is another of Owlpen's wonders, including the great yew 'ballroom'.
▶ *GL11 5BZ. Signposted from Uley village, S of Stroud on B4066. Seasonal opening.*

❹ Berkeley Castle

Over the fireplace of the Long Drawing Room at Berkeley hangs a portrait of a butcher's daughter who rose to be a countess. One of the finest examples of medieval domestic architecture in Britain, this castle was begun in 1076. The deposed Edward II met a terrible death here at the hands of Queen Isabella and her lover, Roger Mortimer. If, as Marlowe wrote, 'the shrieks of an agonising king' can still be heard, it is no wonder. And yet this pearly pink-grey edifice, steeped in history, is the happy home of the 24th generation of Berkeleys, a 'fairytale castle' in which they take great pride.

The Berkeleys are synonymous with the hunt. Sporting and hunting images form the centrepiece in the Picture Gallery, where Stubbs's *A Groom and Horses* is prominent. In the Dining Room are displays of Georgian silverware and portraits of the family in their hunting yellow. The 14th-century Great Hall is hung with Oudenarde tapestries; stained-glass windows celebrate family alliances. And the woman, painted by John Hoppner, who looks down upon the Long Drawing Room? This was Mary Cole, mistress of the 5th Earl of Berkeley and, from 1796, his wife. She had borne him five children; their legitimate son, Thomas Moreton, was born the year they wed. The couple forged parish records to suggest that they had married previously in secret, to legitimise their offspring. In 1811 the Berkeley peerage case resulted in the earldom passing to Thomas, while his eldest sibling, William Fitzharding, received the title Earl Fitzhardinge.

▶ *GL13 9PJ (for satnav). 1 mile W of A38, 16 miles SW of Gloucester. Limited seasonal opening.*

❺ Woodchester Mansion

There are finer houses than this Victorian Gothic masterpiece, but few more intriguing: why was it never completed? It stands in a valley on a deer park enclosed by the Huntleys in *c.*1612. The Ducie family landscaped the park with a chain of lakes. The house was begun for William Leigh, in 1850. The servants' wing was built by Charles Hansom, but a young architect, Benjamin Bucknall, then took over. He and Leigh were both Catholic converts and admirers of the French architect Eugène Viollet-le-Duc. Bucknall's designs may have been based on earlier ones by Augustus Pugin, as well as on the work of Viollet-le-Duc. Ground-floor rooms have vaulted ceilings. Gargoyles on the glazed south front symbolise the hunt. Of the principal rooms, only the Drawing Room was completed at the time of Leigh's death in 1873. There are colourful tales of ghosts and curses, but the truth is that Leigh's heirs could not afford to see the project through. The mansion remains as it was when builders, masons and carpenters downed tools. Some of the carvings are among the finest of their kind anywhere.

▶ *GL10 3TS. 4 miles SW of Stroud near Nympsfield. Seasonal opening.*

❻ Bibury Court

William Morris thought the Cotswold village of Bibury, on the River Coln, 'surely the most beautiful in England'. Throngs of tourists are drawn to its chocolate-box charms, so the time to visit is in winter, with the prospect of a fireside tea at this Grade I listed mansion. Its roots are Elizabethan, but Bibury Court really took shape from 1633 for Sir Thomas Sackville, Knight and Gentleman-Usher in Dailie Waiting of the King to James I. With the death of the last male heir it passed through the female line to the Cresswells. Years of litigation over a disputed will provided Dickens with the material for the interminable court case in *Bleak House*, Jarndyce and Jarndyce. The building had fallen into disrepair when the Clark family bought it in 1922. Their legacy is the Art Deco wallpaper in the bar. Bibury Court has been a hotel since 1968.

▶ *GL7 5NT. 8 miles NE of Cirencester on B4425.*

❼ Chavenage House

The Cromwell and Ireton bedrooms at this Elizabethan hall recall the events of Christmas 1648, when Nathaniel Stephens was lord of the manor. He was a colonel for Parliament against Charles I, but a wise, moderate man who would have urged a treaty on the king. Among the guests, however, was General Henry Ireton, son-in-law of Oliver Cromwell. He pressed Stephens to quit the revelry and come to Parliament to support a vote for Charles's execution. Nathaniel's daughter Abigail, on learning after New Year that he had done so, put a curse on her father. The legend of Chavenage has it that, soon afterwards, he fell sick and died. Mourners at his deathbed saw a hearse draw up at the door, drawn by plumed black horses and driven by a headless man. The colonel rose, paid his respects to the coachman, and entered the hearse to be borne away. From that day until the family line became extinct, so the story goes, on the death of each lord of the manor, the same phantom would appear to carry him away.

History begs to differ but the tale takes a hold here. Almost unchanged in 400 years, Chavenage remains deeply atmospheric. The rooms slept in by Cromwell and Ireton are hung with 17th-century tapestries, and there are Civil War relics – a hat, horse tackle, swords and pikes. The house contains a contemporary copy of Lely's portrait of Cromwell. An extension added by Arts and Crafts architect John Micklethwaite in 1904 houses a ballroom.

▶ *GL8 8XP. 1 mile NW of Tetbury on minor roads, off B4014. Limited seasonal opening; group tours at other times by prior arrangement.*

❽ Rodmarton Manor

When William Morris turned his back on mechanisation, he withdrew to the Cotswolds, living out an idyll in a half-imagined pre-industrial England. In the 1890s, three young architects, Ernest and Sidney Barnsley, and Ernest Grimson, followed his example and settled near Cirencester, seeking a simpler life and to nurture endangered crafts. Rodmarton – one of the last country houses to be built in the traditional style, using Cotswold stone and local timber, the local smithy and skilled local artisans – was designed by Ernest Barnsley. He was 'a big, handsome, jolly type of man, fond of good company, good food and good cheer of every sort', and the interiors reflect his personality, although the limestone exterior speaks more of the owners' austere religious faith.

The manor was begun for the Hon. Claud and Margaret Biddulph in 1909, and the stitching, painting, sawing, planing, hammering, metalworking and gardening were the work of 20 years, in which the Barnsley-Grimson circle grew, and more skilled hands were pressed into service. Here are furniture and pottery painted by Alfred and Louise Powell, lead and brass work to the designs of Norman Jewson from Owlpen Manor (see page 108) and appliqué wall hangings worked by the Women's Guild. Although she considered Rodmarton 'a fake', even Vita Sackville-West admired the gardens created by Margaret Biddulph.

▶ *GL7 6PF. 8 miles SW of Cirencester off A433. Limited seasonal opening.*

❾ Sudeley Castle

Visited by Henry VIII and Anne Boleyn, home to both Jane Seymour and Catherine Parr, graced by Elizabeth I on her summer Progress, this castle has so many claims to history. In the Civil War the Lords Chandos declared for the king. Sudeley sheltered Charles I, and was all but demolished by Cromwell's men. For 200 years it remained a picturesque ruin. Today it appears intact in all its 16th-century majesty thanks to rescue by the Worcester glove-makers John and William Dent, who began restoration in 1837. By 1840 the Elizabethan ranges of the outer courtyard were complete. In 1842 the Dents took advantage of the 'great sale' at Strawberry Hill House (see page 78). The 7th Earl Waldegrave, owner of Strawberry Hill House, having been sent to prison by the Twickenham Bench for 'riotous behaviour', determined to take it out on the town by offloading Horace Walpole's collection and letting his house go to rack and ruin. The Dent brothers snapped up Tudor treasures to add to other Gothic furniture and fittings at Sudeley. In 1854 they engaged George Gilbert Scott to restore the chapel and to build the stable block.

On the death of the brothers, the castle passed to their nephew John Coucher, whose wife, Emma, as chatelaine, left a wealth of memorabilia to be exhibited here. Correspondence with Charles Dickens, Charles Darwin and Florence Nightingale, scrapbooks and diaries all came to light in a chest in the Long Room some years ago. Emma devoted 50 years to the castle and the superb gardens, and her touch is in evidence everywhere. Much of the furnishing is by William Morris. An apartment at Sudeley is home to Elizabeth Dent-Brocklehurst, Lady Ashcombe and her family.

▶ *GL54 5JD. Winchcombe, 7 miles NE of Cheltenham on B4632. Seasonal opening.*

❿ Stanway House

'The atmosphere of Stanway closed around me once again – that charged atmosphere haunted not by ghosts but by the persisting past … familiar things seemed to enfold me like wings.' In *Remember and be Glad*, Cynthia Asquith brings to life the family home that she loved 'as one loves a human being'. The visitor will understand. Built of 'Guiting yellow' Cotswold stone that glows in the sunset, it is a Jacobean manor with an Elizabethan entrance and Great Hall. It is approached through an exquisite gatehouse crowned with Dutch gables.

The Stanway estate was owned by Tewkesbury Abbey for 800 years. It was acquired by the Tracy family after Henry VIII's Dissolution of the Monasteries, passing down through their descendants, the Earls of Wemyss. Stanway was restored in 1900 by Cynthia's father, Lord Elcho, one of a group of intellectuals known as the

AT ONE TIME MORE THAN 100 PEOPLE LIVED HERE
SUDELEY CASTLE

'Souls'. H.G. Wells and J.M. Barrie both visited. The house is filled with oak furniture, antlers, tapestries and Pre-Raphaelite family portraits, and is home to Lord and Lady Neidpath. Among its wonders is the 18th-century water garden, with the second-tallest single-jet fountain in Europe, rising over 90m (300ft), and the Cascade, the longest in Britain.

▶ GL54 5PQ. 12 miles NE of Cheltenham on B4632. Seasonal opening.

⑪ Sezincote

When the covetous Prince Regent visited Moghul-style Sezincote in 1812, he was so taken with it that he commissioned one like it – only bigger (see Brighton Pavilion, page 66). In 1795, Colonel John Cockerell, who was descended from Samuel Pepys, had returned from Bengal and acquired the estate of 'See-zin-kt'. On

his death in 1798, he bequeathed it to his youngest brother, Charles, who had worked with him for the East India Company. Another brother, Samuel Pepys Cockerell, built him a house in the Indian manner, with help from Thomas and William Daniell, painters of Indian landscapes and buildings. Samuel's son, architect C.R. Cockerell, added lodges to the drive.

The Cockerells sold the house to the Dugdales in 1884. Poet John Betjeman used to visit Colonel and Mrs Arthur Dugdale here. In 'Summoned by Bells' he wrote of 'The bridge, the waterfall, the Temple Pool', of 'onion domes', of 'chajjhas and chattris made of amber stone'. At the end of the Paradise Garden are two sculpted elephants. Sir Cyril and Lady Kleinwort bought the house in 1944 and set about much-needed restoration with the help of John Fowler, co-founder of Colefax and Fowler The Regency interiors were jazzed up in the 1960s when

Fowler commissioned George Oakes to paint wallpaper of Indian scenes. Today Sezincote is home to the Kleinworts' grandson and his wife, Edward and Camilla Peake. What could be more unexpected in the very English picture-postcard Cotswolds than an evocation of Rajasthan?

▶ *GL56 9AW. 4 miles NW of Stow-on-the-Wold on A424. Limited seasonal opening.*

⑫ Kiftsgate Court Gardens

The creamy white rambler *Rosa felipes Kiftsgate* romps in a garden created in the 1920s by Heather Muir. The Georgian portico of the house at its centre once graced Mickleton Hall in the valley. Mickleton's owner, Sydney Graves Hamilton, was a can-do sort of chap. In 1887, deciding that he would prefer a hilltop situation, he built a railway and transported the house front and portico to a new abode here. In creating the garden, Heather Muir was assisted by Lawrence Johnston from Hidcote (opposite), but resisted imposing strict design, preferring it to take shape organically, with colour-themed planting. The result is a very 'feminine garden', with steps, terraces, and a fountain. From the 1950s Muir's daughter Diany Binny tended the gardens. She redesigned the white sunken garden to incorporate a pool and fountain. Today, Kiftsgate is run by Diany's daughter Anne Chambers, with her husband.

▶ *GL55 6LN. 3 miles NE of Chipping Campden on minor roads. Limited seasonal opening; groups by arrangement.*

⑬ Hidcote Manor Gardens

In the late flowering of the Arts and Crafts movement, a wealthy American, Mrs Gertrude Winthrop, bought this traditional Cotswold manor for her son, Major Lawrence Johnston. Not much is known of Johnston, other than that he fought for Britain in the Boer War, and from 1907, created here on the hill a garden to rival Sissinghurst (see page 46). As was the emerging fashion, he conceived the design as a series of 'rooms', using lawns and hedging for the 'walls'. Hidcote is famous for spectacular plantings, its rare trees and shrubs. Johnston gave advice to Heather Muir when she was creating Kiftsgate's garden across the way, making the dissimilarity between the two all the more to be enjoyed.

▶ *GL55 6LR. 3 miles NE of Chipping Campden on minor roads. NT. Open for most of the year (not every day).*

HEREFORDSHIRE

The mansions of rural Herefordshire have mostly been restored or revamped in fashionable 19th-century style, but echoes of a more distant past still reverberate through the polished halls and courts.

❶ Burton Court

A 14th-century manor, extended and remodelled in Regency and Victorian times, was completed in 1912 when Clough Williams-Ellis (renowned architect of Portmeirion Italianate model village in Wales) added a Tudor revival front. Commander Robert Simpson and his wife, Helen, bought this 'typical squire's house' in the 1960s and established a soft-fruit farm to pay for the upkeep. The Simpsons conduct group guided tours of the house, affording the opportunity to see the Great Hall and a collection of costumes, militaria, paraphernalia, natural history exhibits, model ships and just about everything but the kitchen sink. The Edwardian gardens were laid out at the same time as Williams-Ellis was refacing the house, and are being brought back to life with the aid of old photographs.

▶ *HR6 9DN. 6 miles W of Leominster on A44.*

❷ Hampton Court

A riverside, castellated Gothic castle was begun here 80 years before Hampton Court Palace (see page 83), but the present house is largely a 19th-century re-creation. The land was granted by Henry IV to Sir Rowland Lenthall, his Master of the Wardrobe, on Sir Rowland's marriage to Margaret Fitzalan, and in 1427 the new landowner built a quadrangular manor of local pink and yellow-grey sandstone. Sir Rowland had fought at Agincourt and the castle was said to be furnished with the spoils of war.

In 1510 it was sold to Sir Humphrey Coningsby, and passed down through inheritance until 1817 when it was acquired by Richard Arkwright, whose father made a fortune from inventions for the cotton industry. Arkwright paid £226,535 for castle and park, then rebuilt Lenthall's already much-altered stronghold, tricking it out in the full Gothic style. His architect was the amateur Charles Hanbury Tracy, a future Lord Sudeley. The two did not get along. Arkwright worried constantly over the expense, and declared he wished Tracy had 'never touched a stone'. Arkwright's son was left 'penniless'. Hampton Court struggled on under various disaffected owners until 1994, when Americans Robert and Judith van Kampen came to the rescue, commissioning a complete restoration of the interiors. Within garden walls a sublime new flower garden has been created, divided by canals, pleached avenues and pavilions. Organic produce is supplied to the Orangery Café, which is located in a conservatory by Joseph Paxton. The pastoral situation, beside the River Lugg, is wonderfully romantic.

▶ *HR6 0PN. Hope under Dinmore, 5 miles S of Leominster on A417 off A49. Seasonal opening.*

❸ Croft Castle

A sturdy quadrangular manor house, with giant chess-piece round towers at each corner, was begun here in the late 1300s and became home to the Croft family. In the Civil War they fought for Charles I, and afterwards the castle was slighted to prevent further military use. In 1746 the impoverished family moved out and the castle was bought by ironmaster Richard Knight. In 1760, Thomas Farnolls Pritchard of Shrewsbury, a specialist in chimneypieces and funerary monuments, was engaged to refurbish the interiors in Gothic style.

The Crofts had sold a medieval castle, and in 1923 they bought back a castellated Georgian manor house with Victorian and Edwardian alterations. The Blue Room is lined with Jacobean panelling and has one of Pritchard's rococo chimneypieces with a portrait by Gainsborough framed by the overmantel. The 'Georgian' dining room dates from 1913. In the Oak Room is another rococo fireplace, exquisite in its detail. The hallway has Jacobean furniture and is lined with Croft portraits. In the surrounding parkland there are giant veteran trees, notably avenues of Spanish chestnut, oak and beech.

▶ *HR6 9PW. 6 miles NW of Leominster on B4362. NT. Seasonal opening.*

❹ Berrington Hall

Frederick Cawley made his fortune from patent black dye, which was much in demand upon the death of Queen Victoria in 1901 when a nation was in mourning. With his new wealth he bought this rust-red, neoclassical Georgian mansion, which had been built for Thomas Harley by Henry Holland in the 1770s. The surrounding landscape was created by Holland's father-in-law, Capability Brown.

CENTRAL ENGLAND

113

Harley's daughter Anne married George Rodney, the son of Admiral Lord Rodney – paintings of naval battles commemorating two of his victories hang in the Dining Room. The Hall passed through generations of Rodneys until George, 7th Lord Rodney, gambled away his inheritance, forcing the sale of the property to the Cawleys. Lady Cawley lived here until her death in 1978, aged 100; a small sitting room is known as Lady Cawley's Room.

The somewhat austere Palladian front that the house presents gives little hint of interiors that show Robert Adam influences, with a delicate French accent. Holland's Staircase Hall is spectacular, with marbled columns, niches and statues. The Drawing Room ceiling is attributed to Biagio Rebecca. There are fine paintings and furniture, a Georgian dairy, Victorian laundry and Edwardian nursery. A display of military uniforms might give the visitor pause to reflect on a bitter irony. Frederick Cawley, who so profited from the fashion for black crêpe, and who was made a baronet in 1906, was to lose three of his four sons in the First World War.

▶ *HR6 0DW. 3 miles N of Leominster on A49. NT. Open all year.*

❺ Hellens

'It is a part of virtue to abstain / from what we love if it will prove our bain.' What is such a cryptic couplet doing etched on an upper windowpane of this Jacobean manor house? Allegedly, the words were scratched with a diamond ring by Hetty Walwyn in the 18th century. Her father kept her locked up there for 30 years, until her suicide, after she tried to elope with a stable hand. Hellens is full of ghosts and shadows, with interiors of dark carved wood and worn flagstones. Sunlight streams through leaded windows and pools on faded carpets. Panelled walls are hung with numerous portraits, including Lely's study of Anne Hyde, first wife of James II, and Benedetto Genari's of Mary Modena, his second.

The house acquired its name when it was leased to Walter de Helyon in the 14th century. The estate was handed down through the family until the 1950s, when it passed to Major Malcolm Munthe. He was the son of Axel Munthe, author of *The Story of San Michele*, a memoir of building a dream villa on Capri. Malcolm's dream, no less romantic, was of a bygone England, and he shaped his home accordingly. Many claims are made on history and royalty – a room with a four-poster bed is laid out for Mary Tudor; the Black Prince's crest appears on the fireplace in the Stone Hall. The manor was rented by one of the Black Prince's comrades for a pair of silver spurs. It is now run as a family trust and hosts educational and cultural events, but retains a genuine atmosphere of home.

▶ *HR8 2LY. 4 miles SW of Ledbury on A449. Seasonal opening.*

❻ Eastnor Castle

The scale of the ambition of John Cocks, 1st Earl Somers, in building this castle is astonishing. In 1810, with a banking fortune and a legacy from a former Lord Chancellor, Cocks engaged Robert Smirke to build a Norman revival castle worthy of his wealth and status. For more than six years, 250 men laboured night and day. In the first 18 months, mule trains carried 4,000 tonnes of sandstone quarried in the Forest of Dean. The fantasy castle, with cloverleaf towers at each corner, took ten years to complete and cost £86,000. There was not the money for lavish decoration, and Smirke had, anyway, planned simple interiors, to reflect the medieval style of the exterior. In 1849, the 2nd Earl called in Augustus Pugin, who had recently remodelled the House of Lords, to redesign the Drawing Room in high Gothic style.

For some time the family continued to prosper, but such juggernaut estates so often roll over later generations. In 1989, James Hervey-Bathurst and his then wife, Sarah, took on the restoration of a near ruin, depleted of contents, and rose to the challenge of restoration with panache. The Drawing Room, executed by John Crace, is among Pugin's finest interiors, hung with tapestries, lit by a vast chandelier. The Red Hall contains a fantastic collection of medieval armour. Eastnor's arboretum has grown tall from seeds garnered by the 2nd and 3rd Earls on their travels. Deer graze in the park.

▶ *HR8 1ES. 2½ miles from Ledbury, on A438, off A449 between Ledbury and Malvern. Limited seasonal opening.*

❼ Kentchurch Court

Jan Lucas-Scudamore was overseeing the preparation of Kentchurch for filming *The Regency House Party* **when a cache of** treasures came to light. It included a pair of Queen Victoria's cream silk stockings, a eulogy by Winston Churchill on the death of Leonie Leslie, and letters and cards from Robert Baden-Powell. The ancestral home of the Scudamore family has stood since the 14th century, although the family has far deeper roots on the estate. This is an historically important house. In a room in the tower at Kentchurch, it is said, Owain Glyndwr, the last true prince of Wales – Shakespeare's Owen Glendower, 'he of Wales' who 'swore the devil his true liege-man' – took refuge after his failed rebellion against the English. Glyndwr's daughter Alice married John Scudamore. Sir James Scudamore, a courtier of Elizabeth I's and a champion jouster, was the inspiration for the knight in Edmund Spenser's *The Faerie Queene*. Kentchurch stands on 2,020ha (5,000 acres) of land. In 1795 Colonel John Scudamore engaged John Nash to 'modernise' the house in the Gothic style. After the colonel's death, the renovation was deferred until the 1820s, when Thomas Tudor came in to complete the work, adding the hall with barrel-vaulted ceiling. Portraits date from the 16th century. Grinling Gibbons carvings are to be seen in the Dining Room and Terrace Room. This is a family home, but house and grounds are occasionally open to the public.

▶ *HR2 0DB. 12 miles SW of Hereford off A465. Limited seasonal opening for pre-booked tours.*

EASTNOR CASTLE

LEICESTERSHIRE & RUTLAND

Snapshots of history enliven these dignified houses, from the origins of afternoon tea to the untimely end of an aviation pioneer. Probably the most far-reaching legacy is one duchess's acclaimed garden design.

❶ Belvoir Castle

Here at Belvoir Castle was born the civilised English tradition of afternoon tea. Queen Victoria was aged 24 when she and Prince Albert visited. The bed in which they slept can be seen in a room hung with hand-painted Chinese wallpaper. One of Victoria's ladies-in-waiting, Anna Maria Russell (née Stanhope), Duchess of Bedford, finding that she suffered 'a sinking feeling' at around 4pm, would have her servants bring her a pot of tea and a little something to tide her over until supper. Friends began to join her for sandwiches and fancies, and the practice caught on with society hostesses.

Belvoir was begun in Norman times. It suffered damage in the Wars of the Roses and destruction in the Civil War. In 1799 James Wyatt began to rebuild it in Regency Gothic style for the 5th Duke of Rutland. A fire in 1816 consumed most of the 17th-century fabric and priceless old masters. Nevertheless, Belvoir's interiors are spectacular, with styles ranging from oriental to Louis XIV and Georgian. Gobelin tapestries depict the adventures of Don Quixote. Despite the conflagration, a fantastic art collection remains, including paintings by Gainsborough, Reynolds, Holbein and Poussin, as well as antique furniture, porcelain, silks and tapestries.

In the Elizabeth Saloon there is a sculpture of the 5th Duchess who, as Wyatt worked on the building, designed the gardens and park, framing views of the Vale of Belvoir. Statues terraced into the hillside include work by Charles II's sculptor Caius Cibber. Belvoir is home to the 11th Duke and Duchess of Rutland and their five children.
▶ *NG32 1PE. 8 miles W of Grantham. Limited seasonal opening.*

BEAUTIFUL VIEWS EXTEND OVER THE VALLEY
BELVOIR CASTLE

❷ Stapleford Park

Owned by the Sherards, later Earls of Harborough, for nearly five centuries, this house stands in grounds landscaped by Capability Brown. The Sherards bought the property in 1402 and rebuilt it in 1500. The surviving wing of that house was redecorated in 1633 and the visitor sees it adorned with Dutch gables and Gothic niches, some showing Sherard ancestors. Although William Sherard's name is carved in stone, this was probably the creation of his wife, Abigail. In 1894 the house was bought by Lord Gretton, a brewer with ambitions to join the horsy hunting set. He added a series of reception rooms and more bedrooms. Stapleford Park has been a hotel since it was acquired in 1988 by the ebullient American restaurateur, the late Bob Payton.

▶ *LE14 2EF. 4 miles E of Melton Mowbray on minor roads off B676.*

❸ Staunton Harold Hall

Beside a beautifully situated mansion in a valley, by a lake, stands one of the few churches to be built between the Civil War and the Restoration of the Monarchy. Royalist Sir Robert Shirley, 1st Earl Ferrers, extensively rebuilt an earlier house that stood on the site and added the church. An inscription over the west door reads: 'In the year 1653, when all things sacred were throughout ye Nation either demolished or profaned, Sir Robert Shirley,

Baronet, founded this church, whose singular praise it is to have done the best things in ye worst times and hoped them in the most calamitous. The righteous shall have everlasting remembrance.' In the puritan days of Cromwell's rule, this was an audacious thing to do, and the baronet was to die in the Tower of London.

The house has had a mixed history. It was remodelled in the 18th century in Palladian style, to which was added a Georgian front of brick with a stone-faced, pedimented centre surmounted by figures of Minerva, Apollo and Ceres. It has been earmarked for demolition, served as a Cheshire Home and later became a hospice. Today it is a family home, paying for itself through various endeavours. Events and weddings are held here, and the grounds are open to the public. Craft workshops are housed in the converted Georgian stables.

▶ *LE65 1RT. 5 miles N of Ashby-de-la-Zouch. NT (church only). Group visits by prior arrangement.*

❹ Stanford Hall

Lieutenant Percy Pilcher, an aviation pioneer, built some of his hang-gliders here in the 1890s and flew, birdlike, over the estate. He was planning a flight with a motor-powered hang glider, but was mortally injured when the tail of his glider, The Hawk, snapped and he crashed. A replica of the tragically flimsy craft – in which he broke the world distance record – can be seen in the stable-block museum of this glorious William and Mary house.

The ancestral home of the Cave family, Stanford Hall was rebuilt for Sir Roger Cave in the 1690s by William Smith of Warwick, and remains home to his descendants. In 1745, the east front received a Georgian makeover and became the entrance, while the original entrance was transformed into the pink and gilded ballroom. The interiors are superlative, elegant but lived-in. The panelled library contains important historical documents and a family Bible embroidered in silk in the 17th century. A collection of Stuart portraits was acquired by Sarah Otway-Cave, 3rd Baroness Braye, in 1842, in Rome, where the Stuarts held their court in exile. In the Dining Room is a collection of family costumes. Public events and open days are held in the house, as well as private functions. There is a walled rose garden beside the River Avon, which runs through the park. A weir upstream causes the waters to pool into a romantic lake.

▶ *LE17 6DH. 5 miles S of Lutterworth, N of Stanford on-Avon, E of M1 (Junction 19).*

LINCOLNSHIRE

A visit from royalty was an accolade devoutly to be wished, and at least two of these country houses were built with that aim firmly in mind. Lord Burghley probably knew he could count on it.

❶ Burghley House

Burghley provided a backdrop for the filming of *Elizabeth: The Golden Age* – and it is indeed one of the greatest houses from the golden age of Elizabethan architecture. When Daniel Defoe saw this 'noble palace' in the 1720s, he recorded that 'the towers and the pinnacles so high, and placed at such a distance from one another, look like so many distant parish churches in a great town, and a large spire cover'd with lead, over the great clock in the centre, looks like a cathedral'.

It was built for William Cecil, Lord Burghley. Cecil was for 40 years the trusted servant of Elizabeth I, holding almost every high office, and this very grand edifice proclaims his status as one of the most powerful figures of his day. There are 35 major rooms on the ground and first floors, and more than 80 less grand rooms, halls and corridors, all under 0.3ha (¾ acre) of lead roof topped with a wealth of beautiful ornament. Cecil brought to bear his talents for art and architecture in his stately home. The exterior of beautiful and hardwearing limestone is little changed since the 16th century, but the interiors have been altered by successive generations. The state rooms were transformed in the 17th and 18th centuries, from Tudor mansion to treasure house for spectacular art collections. The landscaping is largely by Capability Brown. In accordance with the will of the 6th Marquis, access to the park is free.

▶ *PE9 3JY. 1 mile SE of Stamford. Seasonal opening.*

❷ Belton House

'Young' Sir John Brownlow, High Sheriff of Lincolnshire, enriched by an inheritance, set about building a fine Restoration house in the style of a French mansion, and enclosing a deer park. The architect of this serene, honey-coloured stately home – approached through the Lion Gates – was once thought to have been Sir Christopher Wren, although Belton is more probably the work of William Winde and William Stanton. Sir John and Lady Brownlow took up residence in November 1688, and became known for their lavish entertaining, playing host to William III. The Queen's Room was redecorated in 1841 when William IV's widow,

Queen Adelaide, stayed, sleeping in a rococo-style canopied bed embroidered with her monogram. The Windsor Bedroom was used by Edward VIII and his future wife, Wallis Simpson, and contains photographs of the couple. The interiors were refurbished by Sir Jeffry Wyatville in the early 1800s. Mortlake tapestries depict scenes from the life of Diogenes. Among more than 200 pictures are portraits by Lely and Reynolds, as well as porcelain, silver and Regency furniture. Very little survives of the original garden, but Wyatville's grand plans included the Italian Garden, Fountain and Orangery. The house featured in the BBC's

1995 adaptation of *Pride and Prejudice*. Mr Darcy had the Blue Bedroom. The visitor can follow the route that Lady Catherine and her party took to see the parish church, which contains memorials to Brownlow family members.

▶ *NG32 2LS. 2 miles NW of Grantham on A607. NT. Seasonal opening.*

❸ Doddington Hall

The visitor descending the Grand Staircase at Doddington is met by Reynolds's portrait of Sir Francis Blake Delaval, who led the charge in the burning of St Malo in 1758. An unlikely daredevil, the MP Sir Francis hung out with dissolute actors, he womanised, gambled, caroused. To evade his creditors he joined the Grenadier Guards, and found himself bound for France. Leaping from the boat he swam ashore

to storm the undefended town, and became an accidental war hero. He celebrated in true Delaval style by getting drunk – and was created a Knight of the Bath by George III.

An Elizabethan prodigy house, designed to receive royalty, the Hall was built for Sir Thomas Tailor in 1595, and has passed down through generations of Husseys and Delavals. It displays architect Robert Smythson's fascination with symmetry, and with huge grids of windows. The fabric is brick with stone quoins, rising to three storeys, topped with belvedere cupolas, yet it is just a single room deep. The Georgian interiors, remodelled for Sir John Hussey Delaval in the 1760s, come as a surprise. Another great Reynolds picture graces the upper Long Gallery, which runs the length of the house.

▶ *LN6 4RU. 7 miles W of Lincoln on B1190 off A46. Limited seasonal opening.*

BELTON HOUSE

NORTHAMPTONSHIRE

An annual garden fair and a literary festival highlight the way historic country houses slot into present-day life. Fabulous art and mixed architectural styles add to the attraction, plus a preserved horse's head!

❶ Canons Ashby

Sir Henry Dryden was known as 'the Antiquary'. In the 81 years that he lived in this Elizabethan house he altered nothing.
In 1551, using stones from the dissolved Augustinian priory on the estate, his ancestor John Dryden constructed a staircase tower and H-shaped mansion. In the 17th and 18th centuries, later Drydens ordered some remodelling but when the property passed to Sir Henry in 1837, time stood still. He was a noted archaeologist and draughtsman, beloved of his tenants, a friend to tramps, being sometimes taken for one himself. His instinct was to consolidate, not to modernise. A single tap and earth closet met the needs of Dryden, his wife and his daughter, Alice.

When the National Trust took on Canons Ashby in 1980, it was in a parlous state. Today it is as it should be. The Great Hall is on a modest scale, with antlers, weaponry and armour on the walls. The panelled Dining Room is hung with family portraits. The Winter Parlour is adorned with crests and emblems. In Henry's 'Book Room' shelves groan under the weight of words. Canons Ashby qualifies as 'stately' for its quiet dignity and venerability rather than for opulence or grandeur.
▶ *NN11 3SD. 15 miles SW of Northampton on minor roads. Seasonal opening.*

❷ Althorp

The ancestral home of the Spencers since the 16th century will be forever associated with one woman, the late Diana Spencer, Princess of Wales. She spent her teenage years at Althorp. It was here that she first met her future husband, Prince Charles, when he came to shoot in November 1977 – and it was to Althorp that 'England's rose' was brought from Westminster Abbey on September 6, 1997, for burial on an island in the lake. An exhibition in the Italianate stables celebrates her life and work. A famous

CANONS ASHBY

forebear, Georgiana, Duchess of Devonshire, sister of the 2nd Earl Spencer, was an 18th-century feminist and socialite who courted scandal and cultivated a salon of literary and political figures. In April 1992, Diana's brother, Charles, Viscount Althorp, became the 9th Earl.

The first house at Althorp was a moated medieval manor of local orange stone. It was rebuilt in Tudor redbrick, improved and added to over generations, and refaced in white brick and tiling by Henry Holland in 1790. Within, the visitor can see an impressive art collection and numerous family portraits, including works by Kneller, Orpen and Augustus John, with the present earl and his lamented sister given pride of place in the Saloon. Every summer 'All-trup' hosts a literary festival. Georgiana would approve.

▶ *NN7 4HQ. 5 miles NW of Northampton on A428. Open in July and August.*

❸ Holdenby House

The favour of Elizabeth I was a mixed blessing. She was fond of visiting her noblemen, and many were impoverished by building houses to receive her. Sir Christopher Hatton, Lord Chancellor, built a mansion to rival Hampton Court Palace as a 'shrine' to the 'holy Saint' Elizabeth, and he determined not to see it before she visited. Lord Burghley, splurging on his Lincolnshire seat (see page 118), wrote with fellow feeling, 'God send us long to enjoy Her for whom we are both meant to exceed our purses.'

Holdenby House was designed around two courtyards, with 123 glass windows as evidence of Sir Christopher's wealth. 'The dancing chancellor' did not live long to enjoy it. The spring went out of his step, he died bankrupt, without heir, and it seems the queen never did visit. James I bought the house in 1607. Charles I was confined here for five months in 1647 after the Civil War, and soon afterwards Holdenby was sold to Adam Baynes, a Parliamentarian who reduced the building to a single wing.

In 1709 it was bought by the Duke of Marlborough, passing to his relatives the Clifdens and down to the Lowthers, who own it today. The surviving house, based around the original kitchen wing, was restored and extended in the 1800s for Lady Clifden by architect Richard Carpenter. Although Hatton's creation was eight times the size, Holdenby is a beautiful Victorian house in the Elizabethan revival style, abundantly adorned with family portraits.

▶ *NN6 8DJ. 8 miles NW of Northampton on minor roads between A428 and A5199. Very limited seasonal opening; group tours can be arranged.*

❹ Cottesbrooke Hall

This supremely elegant Queen Anne mansion of rose-coloured brick may have been Jane Austen's model for Mansfield Park. Here can be seen Sir James Buchanan, Lord Woolavington's collection of sporting and equestrian art, brought together in the 19th and early 20th centuries, including works by Munnings and Stubbs. Whisky magnate Sir James was the Canadian-born son of Scottish parents and a breeder and trainer of champion racehorses.

The park was landscaped in the 1700s, with vistas, lakes and specimen trees. The gardens were created in the 20th century by Robert Weir Schultz, Sir Geoffrey Jellicoe and Dame Sylvia Crowe, and continue to evolve. Cottesbrooke hosts an annual Garden Fair in June.

▶ *NN6 8PF. 9 miles N of Northampton off A5199. Limited seasonal opening.*

❺ Kelmarsh Hall

'How lucky I've been to live in such beautiful places and able to make them as I dreamed ... I've adored my houses more than my friends (or husbands).' Nancy Lancaster was an American who set the trend for the romantic, patrician, uncluttered 20th-century country-house style and became a partner in Colefax and Fowler. She first came to Kelmarsh Hall as a tenant in 1927, with her husband Ronald Tree, first American Master of Fox Hounds. In lieu of rent they were to redecorate. In 1933 the Trees moved to Ditchley Park (see page 52). They split up in 1947, and Nancy returned to Kelmarsh to marry her former landlord and lover, Claude Lancaster – the marriage lasted five years.

'A perfect, extremely reticent design, done in impeccable taste,' was architectural historian Nikolaus Pevsner's verdict on this house, designed by James Gibbs in the 1730s. It was built by Francis Smith in red brick, and is Palladian in style, with a pediment. The first owner was antiquarian William Hanbury. Smith called in the Atari brothers to create the fabulous plasterwork in the hall. When the Trees arrived, this was painted 'a dark, rather sad green'. Nancy had it repainted in 'an Italian pink, a light terracotta', copied from Lady Islington. 'Kelmarsh pink' was much admired and in turn copied by the Trees' neighbours. The Chinese Room has rare 18th-century wallpaper. Nancy also laid out the flower gardens around an 18th-century lake, with the help of Norah Lindsay and Geoffrey Jellicoe.

▶ *NN6 9LY. 12 miles N of Northampton at junction of A508 and A14. Seasonal opening.*

BOUGHTON HOUSE

❻ Lamport Hall

Sir Gyles Isham, 12th Baronet, was a star of stage and screen, and played opposite Greta Garbo in *Anna Karenina*. The first house was built here by his forebear John Isham, a wealthy merchant, in the 16th century. In 1655 John's great-grandson, Justinian, engaged John Webb to add a five-bay Renaissance-style extension that is the garden front. Justinian's son Thomas, as a schoolboy, kept a diary in Latin, providing insights into 17th-century country life. December 16, 1671: 'Tom a'Bedlam paid us a visit, and said that his only son had been eaten by a sow, that his wife was home consumed with grief and that he had become melancholy.' December 20, 1671: 'Today we challenged the Maidwell men to a cock fight. Two oxen were killed for Christmas.'

In 1676 Thomas embarked on the Grand Tour and brought back paintings that still hang here. Lamport's collection contains works by Van Dyck, Kneller and Lely. In 1732–40, Francis Smith of Warwick added flanking wings to Webb's building. The last remnant of the old house were swept away in 1819 when a new dining room went up on the site of the Tudor Great Hall. On Sir Gyles death in 1976 the house passed to a trust.

▶ *NN6 9EZ (satnav to main entrance); otherwise NN6 9HD. 9 miles N of Northampton on A508. Limited seasonal opening.*

❼ Boughton House

'The English Versailles' does indeed have the outward appearance of a French château. The north façade is of pale limestone with tall first-floor sash windows, an entrance loggia, mansard roof and dormers. Five state rooms have ceilings by Louis Chéron depicting scenes from Greek mythology. Beyond all this magnificent show, however, Boughton is a Tudor house, built around charming courtyards. Ralph, 1st Duke of Montagu, was sent by Charles II as an ambassador to the court of Louis XIV from 1669 to 1678, and on his return, his admiration for French architecture, decoration and landscaping found expression at his ancestral home.

'Bout'n' remains the family home of the Duke of Buccleuch ('Buck-loo') and Queensberry. The fabulous art collection includes family portraits by Van Dyck, and works by Murillo and El Greco. Displays of porcelain, weaponry, armour, textiles and curiosities fill the huge and labyrinthine house. In the Grade I listed park are avenues of lime trees, sweeping lawns and waterscapes.

▶ *NN14 1BJ. 4 miles N of Northampton on A508. Limited seasonal opening.*

❽ Rockingham Castle

Charles Dickens used to visit Rockingham, and drew inspiration from it for *Bleak House*. There has been a castle here since Norman times, on a high bluff above the Welland Valley. A treasure chest in the Great Hall is said to have been left by King John. Henry VIII granted the castle to Edmund Watson, who turned the medieval stronghold into a Tudor house. A Royalist stronghold in the Civil War, the castle was seized for Parliament then besieged by the king's men. In the 19th-century Anthony Salvin reversed earlier updating, crenellating the old gatehouse, adding a flag tower, extending and remodelling. The visitor passing between flanking drum towers comes upon a cluster of honey-coloured buildings from different periods. The interior is replete with art treasures and antiques. From a terrace created on the old fortified wall, views extend over five counties.

▶ *LE16 8TH. 1 mile N of Corby, off A6003. Limited seasonal opening.*

❾ Deene Park

Half a league, half a league, half a league onward from Rockingham is the historic seat of the Brudenells. Behind the portraits on show lie fascinating tales. Here is Sir Edmund Brudenell, twice High Sheriff of Nottinghamshire, whose diary in the library records a visit by Elizabeth I in 1566. Here is Charles II's mistress Louise de Kerouaille, later mother-in-law of the Hon. Anne Brudenell. But Deene's most celebrated son was James Brudenell, 7th Lord Cardigan, who can be seen in a painting in the Dining Room, leading the gallant 600 in the Charge of the Light Brigade. Adeline Horsey de Horsey, a sylph-like brunette, was Cardigan's mistress. On the death of Lady Cardigan, James and Adeline left under a cloud to marry in Gibraltar. She was 33, he 60, but, as she recalled in her racy memoir, he was 'singularly handsome, fair and tall, with a fine figure and most fascinating manner'. He died of a stroke, falling from his horse, and lay in state at Deene for 12 days, while 6,000 admirers filed by.

The house is predominantly Elizabethan with Jacobean and Georgian additions and alterations. The Victorians added battlements. The Great Hall has an impressive carved hammerbeam roof. The old Great Chamber is a tapestry room. Displayed in the White Hall is the preserved head of Ronald, Cardigan's beloved horse, who survived the fateful charge and lived on for 18 years at Deene.

▶ *NN17 3EW. 5 miles NE of Corby, off A43. Limited seasonal opening.*

NOTTINGHAMSHIRE

Time has mellowed the former abbey home of Lord Byron, who was no respecter of ancestral property, while for some decades an Elizabethan mansion built by a coal-mining tycoon has housed a nature museum.

1 Newstead Abbey

'The Gothic Babel of a thousand years ... /
Still older mansion; of a rich and rare /
Mix'd Gothic, such as artists all allow /
Few specimens yet left us can compare …' Lord Byron made occasional use of his ancestral home from 1808 to 1814. A bear and a wolf prowled the corridors. He dug up the floor of the north cloister in a vain search for monastic gold. Newstead had suffered wilful damage and neglect when it came to the great romantic poet from his uncle, William, 5th Baron Byron, in 1798. The mansion was created from the cloisters and domestic quarters of a 12th-century abbey that had been dissolved in the Reformation. The 'mad, bad, dangerous to know' Byron redecorated, but his only building work was a marble monument to his Newfoundland dog, Boatswain, who died of rabies. He was in debt when, in 1818, he sold the property to a friend, Thomas Wildman, heir to a Jamaican sugar plantation. Wildman appointed John Shaw to rebuild in neo-Gothic style. William Webb, an explorer and friend of Dr Livingstone's, bought the abbey from Wildman's widow in 1861. In 1931 it was presented to Nottingham City Council. The visitor sees Victorian interiors, as well as furniture

NEWSTEAD ABBEY

and some of Byron's possessions, portraits of his family and friends, the giltwood bed he slept in and the pistol with which he practised shooting in the Great Hall. Other bedrooms are named after English monarchs. The mansion is adjoined by the picturesque ruin of the west front of the church and surrounded by fascinating gardens and parkland with lakes, ponds and waterfalls. The gardens include a Japanese, American and French garden, rose and sub-tropical gardens. The French garden was described by the Victorian novelist Edward Bulwer Lytton as 'Mrs Wildman's embroidery garden'. A stump is all that survives of an oak planted by Byron.

▶ *NG15 8GE. 1 mile W of A60, 12 miles N of Nottingham. House tours on Sunday afternoons; gardens open all year.*

❷ Wollaton Hall

The industrialist Francis Willoughby mined coal on his estate at Wollaton and used his fortune to build an Elizabethan mansion in the English Renaissance style. It was designed by Robert Smythson, architect of Hardwick Hall (see page 106), Longleat (see page 104) and Doddington Hall (see page 119). A soaring central section is surrounded by four towers that glint with Smythson's profligate use of window glass 'like some evocation of a house out of *The Faerie Queene*'. Sir Jeffry Wyatville remodelled the interiors between 1801 and 1830. In the gallery of the main hall is Nottinghamshire's oldest pipe organ. Like Newstead Abbey, Wollaton is owned by Nottingham council. It has been home to a natural history museum since the 1920s. Tours take the visitor to the Tudor kitchens, Regency dining room, Bird Room and up to the Prospect Room, which affords panoramic views across the deer park and city.

▶ *NG8 2AE. 2 miles W of Nottingham city centre. Open all year.*

❸ Holme Pierrepont Hall

'There were many amongst them, as exactly proportioned as ever any goddess was drawn by the pencil of Guido or Titian – and most of their skins shiningly white, only adorned by their beautiful hair …' Lady Mary Wortley Montagu, née Pierrepont, was writing of a visit to a Turkish bath in Adrianople in April 1717, where the women were 'in a state of nature, that is, in plain English, stark naked'. A pioneer of smallpox inoculation, Lady Mary is celebrated for the letters she penned on her travels, especially from Turkey, where her husband was ambassador. She was an exceptional woman from an exceptional family whose exploits would fill a book – indeed they do. *From Domesday to Dukedom and Beyond: the History of the Pierrepont Family* runs to 464 pages of text and illustrations.

Holme Pierrepont today is the surviving part of a Tudor house beside the River Trent that was commissioned by Sir William Pierrepont in c.1500. It was the first in the county to be built of brick. The mix of architectural styles runs from medieval to Victorian. The visitor can see many family portraits. The Grade II listed courtyard garden was laid out in the 1870s, with a knot garden. The formal 17th-century East Garden has been reclaimed within the past 50 years.

▶ *NG12 2LD. 5 miles E of Nottingham on A52. Limited opening February–April; groups all year by appointment.*

SHROPSHIRE

Rescue and recovery seem to be the bywords here – grand houses brought back from the brink of ruin, a castle renovated and a family seat regained – but one aged manor house has survived intact, betokening another life.

❶ Shrewsbury Castle

Standing on a hill in a bend of the River Severn, overlooking the town, this red sandstone castle had been knocked about by history when Thomas Telford rose to the challenge in about 1790. The great engineer converted it to a Gothic-style private residence and constituency home for Lord Pulteney, MP for Shrewsbury. Telford lived in the castle as he worked on it, and ran his architectural practice from it. William Pulteney had become his patron, and over ten years a close friendship developed between the men. Telford was nicknamed 'Young Pulteney'.

The Corporation of Shrewsbury acquired the castle in 1924, began restoration, and opened it to the public two years later. It now passes muster as home to the Shropshire Regimental Museum. Civil ceremonies are held in the Thomas Telford room, and the grounds play host to theatrical events in summer.

▶ *SY1 2AT. Access Shrewsbury from A5, castle in town centre. Seasonal opening of castle, museum and grounds.*

❷ Attingham Park

In 1778 Noel Hill MP was given the family seat of Tern Hall, which stood in the serene setting of a deer park beside the River Severn. It can't have quite come up to spec for a gentleman of his standing. Four years later he commissioned George Steuart to build a showy classical mansion in front of the old house for himself and his wife Anna, 1st Lord and Lady Berwick, and their six children. His son Thomas was 19 when he inherited both the estate and the title. Thomas set off on the Grand Tour, returned with paintings and engaged John Nash to build a picture gallery with domed glass roof, while Humphry Repton landscaped the park. In his late thirties, Thomas met Sophia Dubochet, a courtesan aged 17, and lost both heart and head. Like a bower bird he continued embellishing his mansion.

THE DRAWING ROOM, ATTINGHAM PARK

Sophia consented to marry him, and encouraged him in wild overspending. He went bankrupt. His younger brother William, ambassador to Italy, returned to save the day, refurbished the mansion and filled it with Italian furniture and French porcelain. The intensely feminine drawing room, with Italian furniture and a palette of eau de nil and gold, is hung with fine paintings and an elegant crystal chandelier.

A bibulous third brother, Richard, became the 4th Lord Berwick aged 68. His son, Richard II, inherited in 1848 and brought the estate up to date, building a model farm and new kitchen, and establishing a herd of Hereford cattle. Attingham is a showpiece house with a soaring portico and pediment. In a harsh urban setting it, too, would look harsh, but its parkland situation among grazing cows has a softening effect upon it.
▶ *SY4 4TP. 4 miles SE of Shrewsbury on B4380. NT. Seasonal opening of house; gardens open all year.*

❸ Benthall Hall

George Maw was a polymath, potter, painter, plant hunter and much more. This Elizabethan house was built for the Benthall family in 1535, and is home to Benthalls today, but the family lost ownership between 1720 and 1934 – a long hiatus in which Maw was among several occupants to leave their mark.

In 1850, George and his younger brother Arthur bought a struggling tile-making business, which for a time they ran from the house, using it as a showroom by laying tiled floors here. One of those was recently discovered under an oak floor in the grand entrance hall. In 1871 Maw accompanied plant hunter Sir Joseph Dalton on a foray to Morocco and the Atlas Mountains. A distinguished botanist, he became an expert on the genus *Crocus* and produced a monograph with watercolours in 1886, which, according to John Ruskin, was 'most exquisite … quite beyond criticism'. Rare plants from around the world grow in Benthall's gardens thanks to Maw's industry. The crocuses burst into life in spring and autumn.

The house stands on a plateau above the Severn Gorge. It is built of stone with mullioned, transomed bay windows. A carved oak Jacobean staircase built in 1618 impresses. The Benthalls were recusant Catholics, as attested by a priest hole above the porch. The place was restored, and is maintained by, the National Trust, to whom it was given in 1958, but it feels lived in, and the family's collections of pottery are on display.
▶ *TF12 5RX. 1 mile W of Ironbridge. Limited seasonal opening of house and gardens.*

❹ Upton Cressett Hall

Shakespeare's *Much Ado about Nothing* was staged here in August 2011 to celebrate the Hall's readiness for opening to the public. *A Midsummer Night's Dream* would have been more appropriate – or, given the nature of this remote enclave, *Hamlet*.

The first thing Bill and Biddy Cash saw of Upton Cressett was the enchanting gatehouse. In 1971 the MP and his wife were walking off the beaten track when they came upon this Tudor brick building with twin octagonal turrets. Behind it lay the ancient seat of the Cressett family. At its heart the manor is a 14th-century Great Hall. In the 16th century Richard Cressett built upon and around it, adding enormous chimneys. His son Edward was a prominent Royalist and the gatehouse basks in the romantic tale of the dashing cavalier Prince Rupert of the Rhine, nephew of Charles I, sheltering here. Linen tapestries depicting *The Four Seasons of Prince Rupert* hang in the panelled bedroom where he slept. Edward Cressett died fighting Cromwell's troops at Bridgnorth. His son, Sir Francis, took part in a bid to rescue the imprisoned king from Carisbrooke Castle on the Isle of Wight in 1648. The manor was in a state of neglect when Bill and Biddy moved in and began four decades of renovation. It is today home to their son William, who for two years put heart and soul into completing the restoration. Love's labours were not lost.
▶ *WV16 6UH. 4 miles W of Bridgnorth on minor roads off A458. Limited seasonal opening.*

❺ Dudmaston Hall

Charles Babbage, mathematician, philosopher, 'father of the computer', lived at this 17th-century country house, even installing central heating. The estate was in the ownership of the Wolryches from the reign of Henry I until the 20th century. The lakeside house, believed to be the work of Francis Smith of Warwick, was begun for Sir Thomas Wolryche in 1695. It passed to the Whitmores, distant relatives who, on inheriting Dudmaston, took the name Wolryche-Whitmore. In 1814, Babbage married Georgiana Whitmore and came to Dudmaston.

The house is an historic showcase for a significant collection of contemporary and modern art brought together by the diplomat Sir George Labouchere and his wife, Rachel Wolryche-Whitmore, to whom the estate passed in 1966. Rachel was the last of a line stretching back 850 years. Her taste for botanical pieces is in particular evidence. In the library, Dutch flower paintings by Jan van Os and Jan van Huysum hang with works by Modigliani and Augustus John. The formal garden is filled with modern sculptures. Through the wooded 'Dingle' winding paths lead past waterfalls and bridges. In 1978 the property was presented to the National Trust, and the Picturesque landscape is being restored.

▶ *WV15 6QN. 3 miles SE of Bridgnorth on A442. NT. Limited seasonal opening.*

❻ Mawley Hall

The beauty of this stately mansion is matched by its situation. It stands in parkland, commanding views of the Malvern and Clee hills and the Brecon National Park. Mawley was built for Sir Edward Blount in about 1730, probably by Francis Smith of Warwick, of red brick with sandstone ashlar dressings. Three storeys rise above a basement. Around a slate roof, urns and statues adorn the parapet. This is the embodiment of Georgian grace, a vision of perfection that has been brought back from the derelict state into which it had fallen by the 1950s. The interiors are richly decorated. The plasterwork is by one or more of the great Italian stuccotori – Francesco Vassalli or the Atari brothers, or Giovanni Bagutti, perhaps. Whoever executed the work, they did so *con brio*.

The razzle-dazzle starts with the entrance hall, from which ascends a freestanding staircase with an extraordinary serpentine mahogany handrail – a sinuous snake with its head at the lower newel end, a sphere in its jaws – and carvings of 'The Pursuits of Man'. Visitors see four of the grand ground-floor reception rooms, including the Dining Room, decorated in the Adam style in 1770. Mature oaks, beech and cedars spread their sheltering boughs over gardens laid out in the 1960s, with lawns and parterres, and walks down to the River Rea.

▶ *DY14 8PN. 10 miles W of Kidderminster on A4117. Open on selected days by arrangement.*

❼ Stokesay Castle

The ochre-coloured Jacobean gatehouse to this 'castle', with its showy timber frame, is the very model for the gingerbread house in *Hansel and Gretel*. Stokesay is, according to English Heritage, 'quite simply the finest and best-preserved fortified manor in England'.

An affluent wool merchant, Lawrence of Ludlow commissioned a residence 'builded like a castle', close to the Welsh border, in 1281. The Great Hall is a yawning space with an impressive timber roof, Gothic windows, open hearth fire with no chimney, and a staircase with treads cut from whole tree trunks. Lawrence's Withdrawing Chamber, with huge lancet windows, was remodelled in the 17th century with oak panelling and an intricately carved Flemish overmantel. The gatehouse was added by the Craven family in about 1620. They declared for the king in the Civil War – and kept their fingers crossed. When they came under siege by Roundheads they surrendered without a fight, and the curtain wall was demolished, but the manor survived to tell us something of 13th-century life on the borders at a time when the strife between England and Wales was approaching its end.

▶ *SY7 9AH. 7 miles NW of Ludlow off A49. EH. Seasonal opening (daily).*

❽ Stokesay Court

It is touching to imagine Sir Philip Magnus and his wife Jewell living in a few rooms of this great Victorian pile after the Second World War, he penning his biographies of Lord Kitchener and Edward VII, she tending her prize carnations, as Stokesay Court quietly mouldered. In its heyday it had employed an army of retainers, but now there was no money for that.

The house was built for John Derby-Allcroft, a philanthropic entrepreneur whose father had worked hand in glove with J. and W. Dent (see Sudeley Castle, page 110). It was designed by Thomas Harris and completed in 1892. Harris had worked on industrial buildings, and drew on his experience to incorporate such modern luxuries as integral electric lighting, and underfloor heating for the Great Hall. There was nothing industrial about the beautiful exterior with its gables and roof balustrade, gateposts, towers and pinnacles, however. Magnificent interiors include a gentlemen's wing, ladies' wing and service wing laid out around a central block. Derby-Allcroft had just six months to enjoy it.

Stokesay Court came through the wars, but was very much in the wars when it passed to a niece of Derby-Allcroft's granddaughter. Until she opened a letter from the solicitors, she had no idea that she was in line to inherit a 90 room house in acres of parkland, yet she has risen to the challenge of renovation, and the visitor can see a near-perfect example of a grand Victorian home, by guided tour – or by watching a DVD of *Atonement*.

▶ *SY7 9BD. 5 miles NW of Ludlow off A49. Tours by prior arrangement.*

129

Past glories reclaimed

Crumbling mansions are being brought back to life so the visitor can marvel anew at the strange way things once were.

Evelyn Waugh's Lt Hooper, a chippy platoon commander, ruminates on the fictional stately home of Brideshead Castle: 'It doesn't seem to make any sense – one family in a place this size. What's the use of it?' Waugh wrote *Brideshead Revisited* in 1943 in a mood of pessimism over the fate of Britain's grand country houses. Many stately homes had been requisitioned for barracks, military hospitals and to hold prisoners of war. The abuse of disaffected servicemen made an already dire situation far worse.

In his 1937 spoof of Felicia Heman's poem, Noel Coward had already spelled out a litany of woes faced by the owners of the stately homes of England, which 'had gone to seed', were 'on the blink', 'had to be rebuilt', were 'mortgaged to the hilt', were fire risks, collapsing, freezing, with outmoded plumbing. It seemed they had had their day.

Yet what a day they had had! At their height they had been a focal point of a community. Their owners had lived – however luxuriously – in a state of mutual

ATTINGHAM PARK

touring the country, visiting impoverished nobles in their mouldering piles, who had no hope of keeping up appearances. At Stourhead in Wiltshire Lady Hoare apologised for the absence of a housemaid, before observing, with a glint, 'The Duchess of Somerset at Maiden Bradley has to do all her own cooking.' There is always someone worse off than oneself! Stourhead was turned over to the Trust in 1946.

With later grants, tax concessions, the efforts of the National Trust, English Heritage, charitable trusts, Lottery funding and private wealth, a great many buildings and their contents have not only been saved but are subject to painstaking restoration.

An entire industry has grown up around this heritage revival, with traditional skills called into service, as specialist painters refresh faded murals, stucco artists repair plasterwork, joiners plane and saw, gardeners plant. At Attingham Park in Shropshire, the National Trust is bringing the house and grounds back to life and offers the visitor an opportunity to see 'conservation in action'.

Forensic re-creation

Everything is underpinned by meticulous research. When 17th-century Uppark in West Sussex was gutted by fire in 1989, the Trust embarked on a £20 million rebuilding programme. Nigel Seeley used skills honed as a Home Office forensic scientist to trace scraps of wallpaper back to the original French manufacturer and the art of remodelling rococo plasterwork was rediscovered. Redecoration was contrived to mimic the fading effect of sunlight, and over all was laid a patina of age.

A few committed individuals take on such challenges. When William Cash inherited Upton Cressett Hall in Shropshire in 2007, it was barely habitable. He might simply have updated it but, discovering fragments of 16th-century wall paintings and friezes – realising 'the weight of history' – he knew he had a duty to return it to its Tudor glory. As part of the programme he employed the artist Adam Dant, who used only Elizabethan materials to renew the paintings – including sheep's urine and soot.

Gardens, too, are being recovered from their weed-choked ignominy. Wrest Park in Berkshire had suffered years of neglect when English Heritage took it on in 2006 and made a commitment to spend tens of millions of pounds over 20 years to revive 'one of the finest surviving 18th-century landscapes in Britain'.

Public demand drives this regeneration as the British people rediscover their shared heritage. It must have been with a mix of chagrin and relief that Waugh looked back upon his magnum opus as a 'panegyric preached over an empty coffin'.

dependence with local people. They had been employers and providers, but by the time of the Great War, that way of life was all but history. Death duties were exorbitant, the cost of repairs and maintenance crippling. The young, fit male workers were gone for soldiers, every one. Sons and heirs – if they survived – would inherit unsustainable burdens. A common feeling, expressed by the Marquess of Hertford at Ragley Hall in Warwickshire in 1951, was that a great estate was 'a life sentence'.

From the introduction of the Country House Scheme of 1937, however, some owners had begun to find their sentences reduced. They were spared inheritance tax if they passed their properties to the National Trust with an endowment, and they could even stay on if they opened to the public. Even as Waugh was writing *Brideshead*, James Lees-Milne, Secretary of the Country Houses Committee, was

STAFFORDSHIRE

Among these treasure-filled estates, rumours of ghostly happenings and intriguing tales of exotic animals, Spanish gold and the Holy Grail vie with the idea of a 17th-century lady becoming her own architect.

CHILLINGTON HALL

1 Weston Park

'You will find Weston beautiful. I marvel whether I shall ever see the like of it again!' Benjamin Disraeli expressed this sentiment in 1878. He was not the only prime minister to be impressed. Tony Blair was also attracted to this 17th-century house, built for Lady Elizabeth Wilbraham. It is probable that she designed it herself, making reference to Palladio's *First Book of Architecture*, which she heavily annotated. The park was landscaped by Capability Brown.

Weston passed through the female line to the Bridgeman family and was placed in a charitable trust in 1986. In 1998 it hosted the G8 summit. An important art collection includes works by Van Dyck, Holbein the Younger, Gainsborough, Reynolds and Stubbs. Also on display are Chippendale furniture, Gobelin tapestries, Chinese and Japanese porcelain and ceramics by Derby, Worcester, Wedgwood and Coalport.

▶ *TF11 8PX (satnav for house);TF11 8LE (satnav for art gallery). 8 miles E of Telford on A5. Limited seasonal opening.*

2 Shugborough

George Anson was just 14 when he joined the navy, and began working his way up to become First Lord of the Admiralty. In 1740–4 he circumnavigated the globe or, as Disraeli wrote, 'that stupid Lord Anson, after beating about for three years, found himself back in Greenwich' and thereby 'the illimitable was annihilated & a fatal blow dealt to all imagination'. Anson brought back with him wares from China that can be seen here today. His great coup, however, was the capture of a Spanish treasure galleon, which enriched him by £400,000. With this bounty he paid for his elder brother, Thomas, to transform a modest William and Mary country house into a Georgian mansion. The architect Thomas Wright oversaw the work between 1745 and 1748, adding flanking pavilions and filling it with Vassalli plasterwork. The building was again remodelled by Samuel Wyatt in 1790–1806 for Viscount Anson. Wyatt rebuilt on the horizontal, clad the façade with dressed slate and added a colonnade.

The house and its treasures are impressive, but it is the parkland that most distinguishes Shugborough. Thomas Anson had made the Grand Tour. He was a founder member of the Dilettanti Society, established for the promotion of Greek classical art, and commissioned his friend James 'Athenian' Stuart to build eight monuments for his parkland, including the Chinese House, a neoclassical arch, Doric Temple and Tower of the Winds. An inscription on the Shepherd's Monument is said to hold a clue to the whereabouts of the Holy Grail.

▶ *ST17 0XB. 6 miles E of Stafford, off A513. NT. Seasonal opening.*

3 Chillington Hall

The ancestral home of the Giffards is approached by a mile-long drive through a park landscaped by Capability Brown, with buildings, bridges and urns by James Paine, and a lakeside Grecian Temple, perhaps by Robert Adam. The house, which began as a medieval manor, was rebuilt in Tudor times and again in the 1720s, possibly by Francis Smith of Warwick. In 1786 Sir John Soane added a portico to the redbrick façade, built an additional wing and made over the interiors in spectacular fashion. Light floods through a glass ceiling dome upon a Saloon in the former Great Hall. The eau-de-nil walls perfectly offset delicate plasterwork. In the Morning Room, a roundel in the stucco ceiling depicts the goddess of architecture. The recurrent motif of a panther derives from the family crest ('Panther's head couped full-faced spotted various with flames issuing from his mouth') and recalls the day in the reign of Henry VIII when Sir John Giffard took his bow and arrow and felled a panther that had escaped from his menagerie and was stalking a mother and child.

▶ *WV8 1RE. 7 miles NW of Wolverhampton on minor roads. Limited seasonal opening of house and grounds.*

4 Whitmore Hall

For 900 years the manor of Whitmore passed down through family, always inherited, never sold. An original medieval, timber-framed E-plan house was rebuilt as a Restoration mansion in the 1670s in deep-red brick, nine bays wide, with a pediment and huge chimneys. A porch is one of a number of Victorian additions. The Hall stands at the end of an avenue of limes that leads from the parish church. Family portraits date from 1624 to the present. Elizabethan stables are fitted with 17th-century carved oak stalls, divided by Doric columns topped with ornamental arches. A Victorian summerhouse stands in the landscaped gardens. The ghostly sounds of a clavichord have been heard in the house, and there have been reported sightings of the spectre of a groom.

▶ *ST5 5HW. 4 miles SW of Newcastle-under-Lyme on A53. Limited seasonal opening.*

WARWICKSHIRE

Historic houses abound in the heart of England, masterful re-creations and makeovers exerting their own charm among enduring originals. Internationally renowned art shines among the mementoes on show.

❶ Ragley Hall

When the family trust proposed bulldozing the ancestral home of the Conway Seymours, Marquises of Hertford, the 8th Marquis fired off rude postcards to each trustee. In 1958 he opened the doors to the paying public for an entrance fee of half a crown. The visitors got their money's worth and Ragley was reprieved.

The house was begun in 1680 by Robert Hooke, an associate of Sir Christopher Wren's, and completed in the mid 1700s to designs by James Gibbs and James Wyatt. The interiors are a marvel. Visitors, passing under Wyatt's portico, enter Gibbs's two-storey Great Hall, which has a ceiling centrepiece of Minerva, and the figures of War and Peace over the fireplaces. After Gibbs's death, the Atari brothers, stucco artists, executed the baroque plasterwork to his design. If they have plasterwork in heaven, it probably looks something like this. In the Drawing Room are portraits of Seymours by Sir Joshua Reynolds. A more recent work, a *trompe l'oeil* mural in the south staircase hall, was painted by Graham Rust between 1969 and 1983. It is a work so entrancing it would repay hours of study, and amusingly includes Seymours in modern dress. The parkland was laid out by Capability Brown.

▶ *B48 5NJ. 2 miles SW of Alcester close to junction of A46, A435 and A422. Limited seasonal opening.*

❷ Coughton Court

The history of 'Coaton' is inextricably linked to the history of the Throckmorton family, recusant Catholics in the time of the Tudors and Stuarts. The house was at the centre of the Throckmorton Plot, a failed bid to assassinate Elizabeth I in 1583. Sir Francis Throckmorton was a key conspirator. Then, in the reign of James I, Throckmortons were implicated in the Gunpowder Plot to blow up parliament.

The centrepiece of Coughton's façade is a Henrician gatehouse with hexagonal turrets and oriel windows in the English Renaissance style. Crenellated side wings are Strawberry Hill Gothic (see page 78). These were built by John Carter, who, in the 1770s, declared himself a 'zealous admirer of Gothic architecture ... for these few years past fallen greatly under the censure of immodest admirers of Grecian architecture'. Ancient Greece would have no place here; Gothic perfectly reflects the Throckmortons' religious sensibility. Interiors are a mix of styles, and visitors will see all manner of relics and curios, including the chemise in which Mary, Queen of Scots was beheaded (displayed, without apparent irony, on a headless form), a bishop's cope worked on by Catherine of Aragon and wood from the bed in which Richard III slept before the Battle of Bosworth Field. A wall in the Tapestry Dressing Room is devoted to *The Rape of the Sabine Women*.

To the rear, timbered Tudor wings reach out into gardens designed by Christina Williams, daughter of Coughton's owner, Clare McLaren-Throckmorton. A walled garden, bog garden, vegetable garden, orchard and riverside walks are there to explore along with formal lawns. A collection of rare, late-flowering daffodils commemorates the late Dr Tom Dercum Throckmorton of Des Moines, Iowa, creator of the daffodil colour-coding system.

▶ *B49 5JA. 6 miles SE of Redditch on A435. NT. Seasonal opening.*

❸ Compton Verney

'If any one has a right to be proud of his shire, surely it is a Warwickshire man. Shakespeare's own Warwickshire, in the very heart of England.' The man so proud of his shire was Richard Greville Verney, 19th Baron Willoughby de Broke, the last of the Verneys to

THE COURTYARD IS LAID OUT AS A KNOT GARDEN
COUGHTON COURT

live at Compton Verney, the family seat for 500 years. A diehard Tory peer, 'no more than two hundred years behind his time', he wrote a paean to fox-hunting, and a memoir, *The Passing Years*.

After his death in 1923, Compton Verney endured a period of decline, and was suffering serious neglect when it was bought by Sir Peter Moores in 1993. House and outbuildings have been restored and live again as an art gallery of international standing. The permanent collections include Neopolitan art from the 17th to 19th centuries, Northern European medieval art, British portraits, Chinese bronzes from the neolithic and Shang periods, British folk art and 20th-century textiles. Four sphinxes guard a bridge built by Robert Adam, who redesigned this Georgian mansion. The grounds were landscaped by Capability Brown.

▶ *CV35 9HZ. 9 miles S of Warwick at junction of B4455 and B4086. Seasonal opening.*

❹ Charlecote Park

'I allude ... to Charlecote Park, whose innumerable acres, stretching away, in the early evening, to vaguely seen Tudor walls, lie there like the backward years melting into a mighty date.' The redbrick house of which Henry James was writing was Elizabethan in origin, built by Sir Thomas Lucy in 1558. The gatehouse survives intact from that era. The Lucy family, who arrived with William the Conqueror, have owned the estate since 1247. Charlecote was known to Shakespeare, who was caught poaching in the grounds. Elizabeth I stayed a night or two in 1572; her arms are displayed over the porch.

In outline, the building is Tudor. It had been modified over generations, but in the 19th century, George Hammond Lucy returned it to its original style. Thomas Willement, 'the father of Victorian stained glass', designed everything – carpets, wallpaper, bookcases. A fine collection of family portraits hangs in the Great Hall under a barrel-vaulted ceiling. In the dining room is 'the Warwickshire sideboard', by Willcox of Warwick, which has been called both 'a masterpiece of craftsmanship' and 'a monster of inelegance'. It was shown with pride to Queen Victoria when she came by. In the park, landscaped by Capability Brown, Jacob sheep crop the grasses, as they have since 1756 – 'poetic, historic, romantic sheep ...' wrote James, 'they were there for their presence and their compositional value; and they visibly knew it.' The River Avon runs through.

▶ *CV35 9ER. 5 miles E of Stratford-upon-Avon off B4086. NT. Seasonal opening of house; gardens and park open all year.*

⑤ Packwood House

The National Trust suggests that visitors might walk from here to Baddesley Clinton. Both houses are Tudor in origin, but the 16th-century interiors at Packwood are a 20th-century creation. In 1556–60, John Fetherston built a timber-framed farmhouse, which passed down through his family until the line became extinct in 1876. The house was a ruin when it was bought by Alfred Ash, a Birmingham industrialist, in 1905. From 1925, his son, Graham Baron Ash, spent 20 years obsessively creating a Tudor home, authentic in every detail (Ash was very big on detail). He bought tapestries and furniture from Baddesley Clinton, and invested in architectural salvage including flooring, fireplaces and panelling. There is a Great Hall and a Long Gallery. 'Ireton's Room' was allegedly where the Parliamentarian colonel slept on that chill night before the first pitched battle of the Civil War, at Edgehill.

Packworth, furthermore, has one of England's great topiary gardens, begun in the mid 17th century. Clipped yews are said to represent the Sermon on the Mount, with twelve 'Apostles', four 'Evangelists', smaller specimens called 'The Multitude' (planted in the mid 19th century), and, at the top of a hummock, approached by a spiral path, 'The Master'. Some of the yews are 15m (50ft) high. The painting of the Forth Bridge was officially completed in December 2011. At Packwood the clipping never ends.
▶ *B94 6AT. 9 miles NW of Warwick on B4439. NT. Seasonal opening of house and garden; park open all year.*

⑥ Baddesley Clinton

When priest-hunters came hammering at the door of this moated manor in 1591, they found no Papists within. A secret conference of priests had broken up the night before, and when the 'pursuivants' staged their dawn raid,

PACKWOOD HOUSE

only six remained. They spent 4 hours crouched uncomfortably in a sewer beneath the house to evade discovery.

There was no fear of religious persecution when another staunch Catholic, Rebecca Dulcibella Orpen, came to live here in 1867 as wife of the squire, Marmion Ferrers. Her self-portrait, *The Artist at her Easel*, was executed in 1885, the year she married her second husband, Edward Dering. An element of farce pervades this tale. Rebecca was living in County Cork with her 53-year-old spinster aunt, Lady Chatterton, when Dering approached the good lady to ask if he might marry Rebecca. Being hard of hearing, Lady Chatterton thought she had been proposed to. Upon her acceptance, Dering gallantly married her, and Rebecca instead married Ferrers. She brought her aunt and Dering to her marital home. The 'Baddesley Quartet' were a devoted foursome, talking philosophy and reading Tennyson to each other. On the deaths of their two spouses, Rebecca and Edward finally wed.

Although the house looks and feels authentically old, part Tudor, part Jacobean, it was Rebecca who turned the clock back with a late-Victorian makeover. Many of the pictures that hang here were painted by her, including one of her apparently rather beautiful aunt. Wisteria grows in the courtyard garden, and there are views to what remains of the Forest of Arden.

▶ *B93 0DQ. 5 miles S of Solihull, off A4141. NT. Open most of the year (closed on Mondays).*

❼ Arbury Hall

George Eliot was born Mary Ann Evans, in 1819, at South Farm on the Arbury Estate. In her book *Scenes of Clerical Life* she used Arbury as her model for Cheveral Manor, while Sir Christopher Cheveral was based on Arbury's owner, Sir Roger Newdigate, an MP, collector of antiques and founder of the Newdigate Prize for poetry. He died 13 years before the author was born, but he must have lived in her imagination.

When she wrote of Cheveral Manor 'growing from ugliness into beauty', she was describing how Sir Roger had transformed an Elizabethan mansion at Arbury into a masterpiece of the Gothic revival. He spent half a century making over the ancestral home and, although he lived to 87, did not see it completed. It is interesting that, despite having made sketches on the Grand Tour, he did not favour the Classical style. The house exterior was encased in stone, presenting four distinct aspects, with battlements, pinnacles and other headgear. Inside, visitors' necks crick and their jaws drop at the sight of fan-vaulted ceilings with pendants and the filigree tracery described by George Eliot's father as 'petrified lace'. Arbury was built on the ruins of a monastery confiscated by Henry VIII. It remains home to the Newdigates, Viscounts Daventry. The gardens are also mostly Sir Roger's legacy, laid out in the Picturesque manner, with a natural lake.

▶ *CV10 7PT. 2 miles SW of Nuneaton. Seasonal opening of house and gardens on bank holiday weekends; weekday group visits by prior arrangement.*

❽ Stoneleigh Abbey

Jane Austen briefly visited this house in 1806 and was intrigued. She wove it into *Mansfield Park* as Sotherton. For 400 years, Stoneleigh was home to Austen's relatives the Leighs. Originally a Cistercian abbey, founded in the reign of Henry II and dissolved by Henry VIII, the property was acquired in 1561 by Sir Thomas Leigh. The building had been repaired and improved over time when, after his return from the Grand Tour, Sir Edward Leigh called in Francis Smith of Warwick in 1720 to remodel it. Smith added a palatial four-storey, 15-bay west wing with a range of state apartments. Humphry Repton landscaped the park in 1809, altering the course of the River Avon to create a lake. A classical bridge by John Rennie was added in 1814. In the 19th century, Charles Samuel Smith built a Gothic revival stables and riding school. To the house he added the Long Corridor, with stained glass by Thomas Willement.

Traces of the original monastic buildings, including the 14th-century gatehouse, have outlasted Smith's masterpiece. In 1960 the upper storey of the house was devoured by fire, but restoration was begun in 1996, the property having been handed over to a charitable trust, and it is open to the public for guided tours. The rescue plan was devised by architect Kit Martin, who has made a career of converting imperilled stately homes. He suggested creating separate houses and apartments from parts of the buildings,

and the gabled east range has been divided into four houses. It is to Smith's baroque wing what chalk is to cheese — and there is nothing wrong with chalk.

▶ *CV8 2LF. 2 miles E of Kenilworth. Limited seasonal opening of house and grounds (house for guided tours only).*

❾ Warwick Castle

Begun by William the Conqueror, Warwick Castle is straight out of a fairytale, and today is a showcase for drama and playful fantasy. It is run by Tussauds, and visitors are invited to explore the castle's long evolution, from medieval fortress, through 17th-century palace to 19th-century residence.

Among its many formidable inhabitants was Richard Neville, 16th Earl of Warwick. Known as 'Kingmaker', Warwick was one of the main protagonists in the Wars of the Roses. Sir Fulke Greville, one of the Barons de Willoughby, a poet, dramatist and statesman during the reigns of Elizabeth I and James I, was granted the castle in 1604 and made substantial improvements. He was stabbed to death by a servant who believed that Sir Fulke had cheated him. Greville is said to haunt the tower that had been furnished for him in Jacobean style.

In the Great Hall there is a formidable display of armour. Queen Anne's bedroom, hung with tapestries, was prepared for a visit that never occurred. When Victoria and Albert came to lunch in 1858, they were entertained in the state dining room, where an equestrian portrait of Charles I by Van Dyck hangs. Afterwards they toured the ramparts and planted trees in the garden. A tableau of an Edwardian 'royal weekend party' includes waxworks of the Prince of Wales, Lord Curzon, and the Dukes of Devonshire and Marlborough. A visit to Warwick Castle is nothing less than an entertaining roller-coaster journey through history.

▶ *CV34 4QU. Warwick town centre, off A46, 2 miles from M40 (Junction 15). Open all year.*

❿ Upton House

Walter Samuel, 2nd Viscount Bearsted, was a passionate art collector with wide-ranging tastes. He brought together diverse works by Hogarth, Stubbs, Canaletto, Brueghel, El Greco, Tintoretto and Hieronymus Bosch; portraits by Reynolds, Raeburn and Romney; tapestries and porcelain. They adorn the house he inherited from his father, the 1st Viscount and founder of Shell, and line the walls of a picture

gallery converted from a squash court in the 1930s. The treasure trove was given to the National Trust in 1948, and it is this, above all, that attracts visitors to Upton. The house itself is low built, of local sandstone. It was begun in the late 17th century, in the Carolean style. The 1st Viscount bought it in 1927 and engaged architect Morley Horder to extend it. The gardens have been restored to their 1930s charm, with a sweep of lawn, terraces, herbaceous borders, kitchen garden, water garden and brilliant spring plantings.

▶ *OX15 8HT. 7 miles NW of Banbury on A422. NT. Seasonal opening.*

⑪ Farnborough Hall

England would look very different today if all those wealthy young men had not made the Grand Tour. Exposed to the cultural legacy of classical antiquity and the Renaissance, they came back laden with treasures, visions, ideas.

In 1720 William Holbech returned with a huge haul of Roman busts, as well as works by Canaletto and Panini. In 1745 he ordered the remodelling of his family's mellow Hornton 'gingerbread' stone house to create a showcase for his treasures. The architect was either Holbech's friend and near neighbour Sanderson Miller, or William Jones. The makeover included Palladian façades, sash windows, pedimented doorways and a balustrade to the roofline of the west front. Lavish rococo plasterwork was executed by William Perritt. Niches were created in the Italianate Hall to receive all those busts.

Farnborough Hall has been the home of the Holbech family since 1684, although it is now under the auspices of the National Trust. Today, the Canalettos and Paninis are copies, but the gardens still slope down to a lake and a terrace walk leads past an Ionic temple and oval pavilion to an obelisk.

▶ *OX17 1DU. 6 miles N of Banbury off A423. NT. Limited seasonal opening.*

WORCESTERSHIRE

Size and exuberance matter here – vast houses show off elaborate decoration, huge murals and one great fountain, but across the reedy moat of a more modest Tudor manor, priest holes tell a darker story.

❶ Madresfield Court

Evelyn Waugh visited Madresfield often, and used it as his model for the great house in *Brideshead Revisited*. He had befriended Hugo Lygon at Oxford, and based characters on the Lygon family, the Earls Beauchamp. Anyone recalling the BBC's serialisation in the 1980s must banish the image of that baroque palace – Castle Howard (see page 172) was TV's Brideshead. Madresfield, a moated redbrick house, standing against a backdrop of the Malvern Hills, has passed down since the 1100s through 28 generations. It began as a 12th-century Great Hall, evolving over centuries.

In 1865, Frederick Lygon, 6th Earl, commissioned Philip Hardwick to remodel the house to his Tudorbethan ideal. The result was a sprawling building with 160 rooms. Tudor brickwork, crow-step and neo-Gothic gables mix and match with barley sugar-twist chimneys, mullioned windows, ironwork banners and gargoyles. The makeover was completed for William Lygon, 7th Earl, who was an Arts and Crafts enthusiast, and the work of the movement finds full expression here. C.R. Ashbee was commissioned to create a library that holds 8,000 books, some pre-dating the printing press. Carvings were executed by members of the Guild of Handicrafts. In the adjoining chapel, Henry Payne's delicately coloured fresco paintings depict the seven children of the family in a bower.

The 7th Earl was himself an artist; the flame-stitch embroidery covering a set of chairs is his work. The former Great Hall, which serves as a dining room and is hung with royal portraits, was done out by Hardwick with minstrels' gallery and hammerbeam roof. The staircase hall is vast, lit by three glass cupolas. The house is approached by a mile-long drive from the Gloucester Gate.
► *WR13 5AH. 2 miles NE of Great Malvern. Closed for renovation in 2012. Open for seasonal visits by appointment from 2013.*

❷ Hanbury Hall

If the Painted Hall at Greenwich Hospital is Sir James Thornhill's great masterpiece, his paintings on the staircase at Hanbury have no less brilliance. The house was built for chancery lawyer and Whig MP Thomas Vernon in the early 1700s, in William and Mary style, of red brick with pitched roof, dormer windows and a cupola. Thornhill created the murals of Greek deities and mythological figures for him in *c.*1710, at the same time as he was at work at Greenwich. Approached from a dark, panelled hall hung with gilt-framed portraits, they are a revelation. Side panels in *trompe l'oeil* architectural frames explore the life of Achilles. Olympian gods look down from on high. The unfortunate figure being cast to the Furies is the Reverend Henry Sacheverell, a Tory propagandist who was charged with sedition by the Whig government. There is more of Thornhill's work in the Dining Room, which looks out onto a restored 18th-century parterre. The property passed to the National Trust in 1953, although Doris, Lady Vernon stayed on, living here until her death in 1962.

HANBURY HALL

The artistic team who, over ten years, brought the cracked, flaking, faded paintings back to life, received a Pilgrim's Trust Award in December 2010 for 're-establishing the unity of this historic painted space'.

▶ *WR9 7EA. 4 miles E of Droitwich Spa off B4090. NT. Seasonal opening of house and gardens.*

❸ Harvington Hall

The visitor to Harvington Hall, seeing its priest holes, can only imagine the terror and claustrophobia experienced by those who took refuge within them. A moated medieval and Elizabethan manor, Harvington is testament to an age of religious persecution. No house in England has a more impressive series of such concealed spaces – above a bread oven, within walls, in the rafters. Four of them, around the Great Staircase, were almost certainly the work of master carpenter Nicholas Owen, who met his wretched fate elsewhere, after being starved out of one of his own hiding places.

From 1580, Harvington was owned by the Pakington family, recusant Catholics. A marriage in 1696 joined them with the Throckmortons of Coughton Court (see page 134), to which many of the interior fittings were removed. This house was derelict in 1923, its moat choked with weeds, when a benefactor granted it to the Archdiocese of Birmingham for restoration. In 1936 it yielded more of its secrets, when the removal of whitewash revealed wall paintings, including arabesque graffiti in the Mermaid Passage and back staircase, and the figures of the Nine Worthies on the second floor. Owen was fiendishly cunning and incredibly discreet. He told no one outside the household where his poky refuges were. He was tortured but took his secrets to his grave, so it is possible that more of his refuges will even now come to light.

▶ *DY10 4LR. 3 miles SE of Kidderminster on A448. Limited seasonal opening.*

❹ Hagley Hall

'I can't describe the enchanting scenes of the park ... broke into all manner of beauty; such lawns, such wood, such rills, cascades ... I wore out my eyes with gazing, my feet with climbing and my tongue … with commending.' Horace Walpole visited George, 1st Lord Lyttelton, at his new house in 1753, and was thrilled by the landscaping of the park.

Lyttelton was private secretary to Frederick, Prince of Wales, and briefly Chancellor of the Exchequer. Hagley was largely his creation.

Architect Sanderson Miller built for him the 'last of the great Palladian houses', with corner pavilions and pyramid roofs. Lyttelton had made the Grand Tour, and Italy left the deepest impression on him. Figures of Bacchus, Mercury, Venus and a Dancing Faun, in niches in the White Hall, are copies of those in the Pitti Palace in Florence. Two marble busts of Roman emperors travelled back with him. A bas relief over the chimneypiece is the work of Francesco Vassalli. More of Vassalli's brilliance can be seen in the Saloon, where plasterwork festoons frame family portraits. A chinoiserie motif runs through rococo plasterwork in the Long Gallery, which occupies the full length of the east front. Ho-ho birds and a pagoda feature in the carving on the chimneypiece.

A portrait of the satirical poet Alexander Pope, with his Great Dane, Bounce, hangs in a library that is home to a wealth of rare books. Many were lost in a fire on Christmas Eve 1925. The house was restored by the 9th Viscount Cobham and his wife. Hagley is today home to the present Viscount, and a wedding and events venue.

▶ *DY9 9LG (satnav). Otherwise DY9 9LQ. 7 miles NE of Kidderminster on A456. Closed until January 2013.*

❺ Witley Court

Here is a house of music and silence, a mirage, a dream, a vast shell of a palatial home in which Edward Elgar once gave recitals. A Jacobean brick manor house was built on this site for the Russell family, and sold to Thomas Foley, an ironmaster, in 1655. He added towers on the north side, and his grandson, the 1st Lord Foley, added wings that enclose the entrance courtyard, and a new parish church for which, in 1747, James Gibbs created a fantastic baroque interior. In the late 18th century, the entire village of Great Witley was relocated to clear the way for a landscaped park.

In 1805 the 3rd Lord Foley commissioned John Nash to carry out ambitious rebuilding, including the addition of vast Ionic porticoes to the north and south. When fire tore through the building in 1937, it left Witley Court a spectacular ruin, open to the skies. Under the care of English Heritage, the park created by William Andrews Nesfield (his 'monster work') has been under restoration – and the massive Perseus and Andromeda fountain in the south parterre garden once again roars like an express train.

▶ *WR6 6JT. 10 miles NW of Worcester on A443. EH. Open all year (weekends only in winter).*

Northwest England

While Mr Darcy graced the lake at Lyme Park with his fictional presence, other houses of the Northwest lay claim to older heroes, from the mythical Sir Gawain of Arthurian legend to William Shakespeare.

CUMBRIA
148-150

Carlisle

Workington

Keswick

Whitehaven

The Pennines

Penrith

Brough

Lake District National Park

Windermere

Kendal

Yorkshire Dales Nat. Park

Barrow-in-Furness

Lancaster

LANCASHIRE, Liverpool and Manchester
151-155

Clitheroe

Blackpool

Burnley

Preston

Blackburn

Southport

Bury

Rochdale

Bolton

Oldham

Wigan

St Helens

Salford

Manchester

Liverpool

Warrington

Stockport

Birkenhead

Runcorn

Wilmslow

Ellesmere Port

Macclesfield

Chester

CHESHIRE and The Wirral
144-147

Crewe

KEY

1 Main entry

━━━ County boundary

━━━ Motorway

━━━ Principal A road

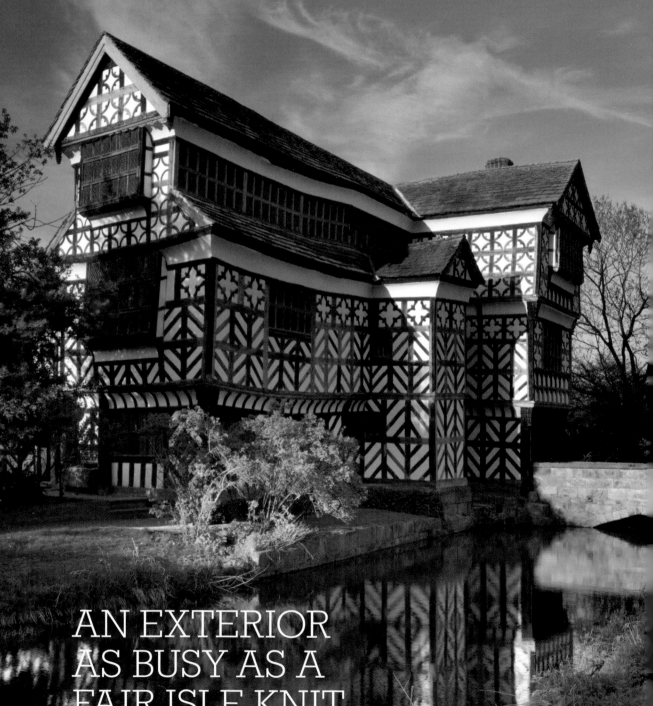

CHESHIRE & THE WIRRAL

From an extraordinary Tudor manor to a romantic former abbey, these country estates have stood the test of time. Even if altered, extended, transformed, they still exude the heady scent of the past.

AN EXTERIOR AS BUSY AS A FAIR ISLE KNIT

LITTLE MORETON HALL

❶ Little Moreton Hall

With a black and white exterior as busy as a fair isle knit, wonky walls and squiffy rooflines, Little Moreton looks like someone's mad imagining of a Tudor house – and yet it is the real thing. In fact, it is in part pre-Tudor. If it looks somewhat cobbled together, that's because it was. The Great Hall was built in 1450 for Sir Richard de Moreton. The gatehouse, bay windows and Long Gallery are Elizabethan. The imposition of the Long Gallery caused the south wing to bend and bow in protest. The diagonal and quatrefoil studding is decorative and was an anachronism in that age. Richard Dale, carpenter, worked here in the 1550s; his inscription is above a window. The interior is unfurnished.
▶ *CW12 4SD. 4 miles S of Congleton on A34. NT. Seasonal opening.*

❷ Arley Hall

For couples who marry at this stately home the story of a former Arley housekeeper, Elizabeth Raffald, is the icing on the cake. Arley has not always smiled on newlyweds. When Elizabeth Whittaker married one of the gardeners, John Raffald, both were dismissed. The resilient Elizabeth wrote a book, *The Experienced English Housekeeper*, and dedicated it to her former employer, Lady Warburton. It was a bestseller. In it she gave a recipe for a 'Bride Cake' that went on to become the traditional English wedding cake.

Forebears of the Warburtons lived at Arley from the late 11th century, and the Warburton Flower family, Viscounts Ashbrook, still do. A medieval timber house, remodelled in the Georgian era, passed from Sir Peter Warburton in 1813 to his great nephew Rowland, aged eight. In 1826, upon coming of age, Rowland Egerton-Warburton determined to rebuild the run-down property in a manner that reflected its antiquity. He engaged George Latham to build in the 'Queen Elizabethan' style, faithful in every detail to that period. Latham quoted £6,000. By 1841 the project had cost £30,000. That would be approaching £2.5 million today – but Rowland had his money's worth. This is a bravura Jacobethan house with diapered brickwork, stone windows, Dutch gables and tall chimneys. There are fine ceilings and fireplaces in panelled interiors. A room is dedicated to Rowland, a keen huntsman and poet.

The gardens have developed over the past 250 years and contain another possible first – the earliest herbaceous border of its kind planted in England. When Rowland lost his sight in later life, he continued to walk around the grounds, breathing the scent of flowers, led on a leather strap by his gardener.
▶ *CW9 6NA. 7 miles SE of Warrington on minor roads off B5356. Limited seasonal opening, house by guided tour only.*

❸ Tatton Park

'Green velvet lawns, bathed in sunshine, stretched away on every side into the finely wooded park ... the melting away of exquisite cultivation into the wilderness had an inexplicable charm to her.' Elizabeth Gaskell grew up in Knutsford and knew Tatton Park. In her novel *Wives and Daughters*, she used it as a model for Cumnor Towers. Built by John Egerton, the house was completed in 1716, and remodelled in neoclassical style after 1780 by Samuel Wyatt and his nephew Lewis. A two-storey Palladian villa with portico, it stands within extensive gardens and parkland.

In 1958 the 4th Baron Egerton gave the estate, the mansion and its valuable contents to the National Trust. The cluttered library contains 8,000 books, globes, card tables, chess tables and reading chairs. Important works of art, acquired by Wilbraham Egerton in the Victorian era, include paintings by Van Dyck, Poussin, Chardin, Carraci and Guercino. Visitors see Gillow furniture commissioned especially for the house, antiques and porcelain, as well as servants' quarters and domestic offices. There is a kitchen garden, a Japanese garden, a conservatory by Joseph Paxton, glasshouses and a maze. Deer roam the grounds. Tatton is presented as the home it once was, but these days it is a museum and social space, hosting 100 events every year, from an RHS Flower Show and concerts with the Hallé Orchestra to antiques fairs. Tatton has always been hospitable. Wilbraham threw great house parties; he entertained the Prince and Princess of Wales, the Shah of Persia and the Crown Prince of Siam.
▶ *WA16 6QN. 2 miles N of Knutsford, 2 miles NE of Junction 19 of M6. NT. Seasonal opening.*

❹ Capesthorne Hall

Edward Davies Davenport made the Grand Tour later than most, and took in Elba. He was granted an interview with the exiled Napoleon, who impressed him with his 'candour, naiveté and wonderful knowledge of the world'. In 1837 Davenport commissioned the extensive remodelling of his 18th-century home as a neo-Jacobean mansion to house his antiquities.

The architect was Edward Blore, who would later take on Buckingham Palace. The design, with huge façades, is variously described as 'imposing' and 'provocative'. Lenette Bromley-Davenport, mother of the present owner, wrote that it 'can repel violently or attract irrevocably … To many the exotic towers, domes and pinnacles are grotesque and ugly …' But, 'Great and mysterious, [Capesthorne] carries within its heart the secrets and dreams of many families.' Interiors are by Anthony Salvin, who was called in after a fire in 1861, but the colour palette is Lenette's. The saffron-yellow Entrance Hall, with stained glass by Thomas Willement, contains paintings, marble sculptures and antiques. In the Sculpture Gallery and Saloon are more paintings, marbles, family portraits and porcelain. On the staircase a balustrade detail shows Gladstone as a felon with a noose around his neck. Despite his 'wit, literature and polished manners', Edward Davies Davenport was a 'splentic, gloomy soul'. His despondency with parliament expressed itself in his poem 'The Golden Age', a jeremiad ostensibly written by one J. Jobson LLD of Slutchby in the Fens. Woodland, park and gardens surround the hall.
▶ *SK11 9JY. 6 miles W of Macclesfield on A34. Limited seasonal opening.*

❺ Adlington Hall

'As many Leighs as Fleas / Massies as asses, / Crewes as crows / And Davenports as dogs' tails.' In this old Cheshire saying, the Davenports of Capesthorne and the Masseys of Dunham Massey are joined by another local dynasty, the Leghs. The manor of Adlington became home to the family in the reign of Edward II. A Great Hall was built of timber between 1480 and 1505, and later refaced with brick and stone. After the Civil War the house was confiscated from Colonel Thomas Legh. When he recovered it in 1656, it was battle-scarred and neglected. Following the Restoration, the north front was given a gabled façade. Charles Legh, who inherited Adlington in 1739, was responsible for the transformation of a fairly modest Tudor dwelling into a fine part-Georgian manor with a ballroom running the length of the first floor and a towering portico. Legh may have been his own architect as well as planning and designing the gardens, woodland and parkland. Further changes were made in 1928, designed by Sir Hubert Worthington.

This is, then, a house of many periods. Wings have been built, pulled down, extended, abbreviated. Under the hammerbeam roof of the Great Hall are wall paintings, a baroque gallery,

and, stealing the show, an ornate 17th-century organ flanked by murals of saints playing instruments. Above, under a carved canopy, gilded cherubs play a fanfare on their trumpets. George Frederic Handel was a friend of the Leghs. He stayed at Adlington in 1741 on his way to Dublin for a performance of the *Messiah*. He would have pulled out all the stops.
▶ *SK10 4LF. 5 miles N of Macclesfield on A523. Limited seasonal opening.*

❻ Lyme Park

It was from the lake at Lyme Park that Mr Darcy emerged in the BBC's 1995 adaptation of *Pride and Prejudice* when Lyme Park stood in for Pemberley. The 'wet shirt scene' so affected one Mrs Leffman that she bequeathed £100,000 to the National Trust. Viewed from this aspect, the largest house in Cheshire is a Palladian colossus, the work of Giacomo Leoni for the Legh family in the 1720s.

LAVISH INTERIORS RECORD A WAY OF LIFE LONG GONE

LYME PARK

Visitors see first, however, what architectural historian Nikolaus Pevsner described as 'the craziest Elizabethan frontispiece', with Minerva buoyed up on a four-tier archway of Doric columns, niches and pediment. Beyond is an Italian Renaissance courtyard with a piano nobile supported on rusticated colonnades.

Lyme was home to the Leghs for 600 years. Originally built in the Elizabethan era in the deer park by Sir Piers Legh, over generations the house has been altered, improved, neglected, refurbished and finally made over in its present magnificent form. In Leoni's entrance hall is a Georgian portrait of the Black Prince, who first granted the estate to the Leghs who saved his skin at Crècy. The prince's portrait can be swung back to reveal a Jacobean drawing room – the old Great Chamber – with medieval stained glass. In the Stag Parlour the Jacobite Cheshire Club met and prudently decided not to join the rebellion. William John Legh was created the 1st Lord Newton in 1892. He commissioned the sunken Dutch garden with pond and fountain, and a new stable block.

Such a weight of history proved too much for the 3rd Lord and Lady Newton, who handed Lyme to the National Trust in 1946. 'Poor people …' reflected the Trust's James Lees-Milne, 'their day was done and life as they had known it was gone for ever.'

▶ SK12 2NR. 9 miles SE of Stockport off A6. NT. Seasonal opening

❼ Rode Hall

While Lyme Park proved too much for the Leghs, the Wilbrahams are going nowhere any time soon: 'It is our intention that the family should continue to live here for many years to come,' say Sir Richard and Lady Baker Wilbraham. Rode Hall is not one but two abutting houses. A two-storey Queen Anne house was built by Randle Wilbraham, son of Roger Wilbraham, who bought the estate in 1669. Its Venetian and small oval *oeil de boeuf* (ox-eye) windows and cupola are later additions. The second house was completed in 1752 for Randle Wilbraham II, a lawyer and politician. Mid Georgian in style, it is of the same red brick

as the first one, with white stone architraves. The portico was added in *c.*1820. Randle supported Josiah Wedgwood's initiative to build the nearby Trent and Mersey Canal. Wedgwood dined with Randle's son and daughter-in-law, Richard and Mary, at Rode Hall, in 1771.

The present Sir Richard has a superb collection of china and porcelain. The classical dining room is by Lewis Wyatt. Family portraits bring a pictorial record right up to the present. From Rode Hall can be seen, on a distant hilltop, a fragment of a castle. The remains of a medieval fortress? No, this is Mow Cop Castle, built in 1754 to enhance the Wilbrahams' view. They used it as a summerhouse and had picnics there. In the early 1800s a Miss Wilbraham wrote, 'We were accustomed to boil a kettle and have tea in it on calm days.'

▶ ST7 3QP. 5 miles SW of Congleton off A34. Limited seasonal opening.

❽ Combermere Abbey

'Thursday 21st July: At evening we came to Combermere, so called from a wide lake … It stands on the site of an old abbey of Benedictine monks … The library, which is forty feet by twenty-seven, is supposed to have been the refectory.' Writer and lexicographer Samuel Johnson came here in 1774 and tells the familiar tale of a monastery dissolved in the Reformation in 1539 and passing into private hands. It was granted to Sir George Cotton, who demolished most of it and converted the west range into a half-timbered Tudor house.

In 1814 it was remodelled in fashionable pointed Gothic style, and in 1820 a ballroom was added for a visit from the Duke of Wellington. In its long evolution, Combermere has received many important guests, including Charles II and William III. To Elizabeth, Empress of Austria, it was 'picturesque, wild and romantic'. Romantic it certainly is, seen across the lake, and today it is offered as a wedding venue. Visitors can take a guided tour of the Walled Gardens and the Geometric Garden, explore the fruit-tree maze and see the restored glasshouses.

▶ SY13 4AJ. 4 miles NE of Whitchurch on A525. Limited seasonal opening by pre-booked guided tour only.

CUMBRIA

A continuous thread through the centuries is provided by cherished ancestral homes with fine, antique-filled interiors, and gardens full of aged trees and topiary. Modern festivals bring them right up to date.

❶ Conishead Priory

A 12th-century Augustinian priory has been reincarnated as a Buddhist retreat. In 1537 the priory was confiscated by Henry VIII's agents, and the building was dismantled. The estate passed through the Phillipson and Dodding families, and came by marriage to John Braddyll in 1638. The 'tolerable gentleman's house' that passed to Colonel Thomas Braddyll in 1818 was too run down for repair, so he called in Philip Wyatt, youngest son of James Wyatt and nephew of Samuel, to rebuild it on a grand scale. All did not go well. Wyatt was dismissed and ended up in debtors' prison. The project was completed by George Webster of Kendal in a quaint mix of styles described as blending 'imitations of a fortified house with ecclesiastical structure and modern ideas of convenience'.

The entrance, between two soaring turrets, leads to a large hall like a medieval chapel. A traceried window depicts St Augustine with priory benefactors. Stained-glass windows by Thomas Willement depict scenes from the life of Christ. When the house was completed, the rooms were lavishly furnished and hung with old masters – then Braddyll, too, went bust. Since then Conishead has been a hydropathic hotel, a military hospital and a convalescent home for Durham miners. In 1976 it was sold to an organisation of Tibetan Buddhists, who set about restoring it. Today it is the Manjushri Kadampa Meditation Centre and is open to visitors.
▶ *LA12 9QQ. 2 miles S of Ulverston on A5087.*

❷ Holker Hall

'The record reveals that for 400 years my ancestors felt that, for them, Holker was more desirable, more favoured by Providence and more enhanced with natural beauty than any other place on earth.' Lord and Lady Cavendish take intense pride in their ancestral home. Holker has been in the ownership of the Preston, Lowther and Cavendish families since the 17th century, never bought or sold, but subject to alteration, refurbishment, ornamentation and, in the wake of a fire in 1871, partial rebuilding. In that event, providence favoured one 1830s Jacobethan wing

HOLKER HALL

by George Webster, but the west wing was lost. Paintings, statues, rare books and antiques were consumed by flames. The 7th Duke of Devonshire employed the Lancashire pioneer architects Edward Graham Paley and Hubert Austin to carry out an ambitious rebuilding plan. Architectural historian Nikolaus Pevsner deemed the work 'the grandest of its date in Lancashire' – as it then was – 'by the best architects living in the county … It is their outstanding work, red sandstone in the Elizabethan style.'

The bedroom where Queen Mary, consort of George V, slept in 1937 appears just as she would have seen it – William Morris fabrics, George I gilded armchairs, a Minton washstand, Venetian glass candlesticks (adapted for electricity) and a 19th-century armoire from Normandy. In the silk-lined Drawing Room on a Chippendale silver table is the book on Buckingham Palace that was her gift to the family after her visit. The gardens and parkland are ravishing.
▶ *LA11 7PL. 4 miles W of Grange-over-Sands on B5278. Seasonal opening.*

③ Levens Hall

'Along a wide extent of terraced walks and walls, eagles of holly and peacocks of yew will find with each returning summer their wings clipped and their talons pared.' Lord Stanhope was writing in the 1700s of a marvel created at Levens a century before. A gentleman's residence structured around a medieval pele tower by James Bellingham, from 1580, overlooks an extraordinary array of topiary, some of the world's oldest. It has evolved since Stanhope saw it. Strange, looming, anthropomorphic forms of box and yew, blobs, bulbs, mushrooms, pyramids consort with one another. In daylight they are larky and meaningless; at dusk they take on a more mysterious aura.

Levens passed on to James Bellingham's great grandson Alan, 'an ingenious but unhappy young man who consumed a vast estate'. Gilt hearts on some of the lead downspouts are taken to mean that the property was lost on the turn of a card. It was acquired in 1688 by Colonel James Grahme, a descendant of a 'fractious and naughty' clan of border rievers. He had made a career in the court of James II, and brought with him to Levens Guillaume Beaumont, a young Frenchman, who was to create for him these living sculptures.

The visitor steps directly into the Great Hall of a 'genial' Elizabethan home, its rooms panelled in oak, its ceilings elaborately plastered. Levens contains fine furniture, works of art, Spanish leather wall coverings, clocks, miniatures and

some of the earliest English patchwork, created by Grahme's daughters. James Bellingham's admiration for Elizabeth I is expressed in a repeated motif of her coat of arms.
▶ *LA8 0PD. 6 miles S of Kendal off A590. Seasonal opening.*

④ Sizergh Castle

Catherine Parr lived here after the death of her first husband in 1533. Widowed again, she had the good fortune to outlive her third husband, Henry VIII. Like Catherine, this castle is a survivor. A Tudor house, extended in the Elizabethan age, with some Georgian remodelling, was built around a medieval pele tower – one of a line of defences along the Scottish border. The Stricklands have been at Sizergh since the 13th century, and today are tenants of the National Trust. The old Great Chamber, now a dining room, is hung with Stuart portraits that recall the family's loyalty to that banished dynasty.

The superb Inlaid Chamber contains elaborate panelling, a 16th-century four-poster bed and fine porcelain. Elizabethan pendants hang from the ornate plasterwork ceiling; there is armorial glass in the window. This great setpiece of a room is here courtesy of the V&A. The museum bought the contents and fittings in the 19th century and has loaned them back. A Georgian drawing room stands in complete contrast to the heavy Elizabethan rooms, with a frivolous palette of sky blue and pink, high ceiling and wall niches. In the gardens are a pond, a lake, a national collection of hardy ferns, and a limestone rock garden.
▶ *LA8 8DZ. 4 miles S of Kendal on A591. NT. Seasonal opening.*

⑤ Wray Castle

A weird agglomeration of towers and turrets, with battlements and arrow slits, this 'castle' was built for James Dawson with his wife's inheritance. It impressed William Wordsworth, who in 1845 planted a mulberry tree here. It did not impress Dawson's wife, who refused to live in it. He was a retired Liverpool surgeon; she was heir to a gin fortune. Alcohol plays more than one part in the story. The architect, H.P. Horner, drank himself to death. Perhaps he was drunk when he designed Wray Castle. Nevertheless, the soaring grand staircase is masterly. The Potter family used to spend holidays at Wray when their daughter Helen Beatrix was small. She fell in love with the Lake District, and later made her home in Ambleside.

She bought Hill Top, a 17th-century cottage now owned by the National Trust, with the proceeds from her first book, *The Tale of Peter Rabbit*.

The grounds of Wray Castle overlook Lake Windermere, and as well as Wordsworth's mulberry, there are specimen trees including Wellingtonia, redwood and ginkgo.

▶ *LA22 0JA. 3 miles S of Ambleside off B5286. NT. Seasonal daily opening of house; grounds open all year.*

❻ Muncaster Castle

The ancestral home of the Pennington-Ramsdens is a personable and eccentric place, an authentic 13th-century castle, enlarged over the centuries, but still a low-built, rugged fortress overlooking the River Esk. The Drawing Room with barrel-vaulted ceiling was created by Anthony Salvin from the courtyard in 1862. His octagonal Library rises over two storeys, with portraits of Penningtons looking down from the gallery.

In 1983 the castle, 'with all its beauties and liabilities', was handed over by Sir William Pennington-Ramsden to his daughter Phyllida Gordon-Duff-Pennington and her family. The 'liabilities' include a number of ghosts, among them Tom Skelton, nicknamed Tom Fool, castle jester in the 16th century, who still indulges his sick sense of humour. A child is heard crying, a woman sings to comfort a sick infant, doors open inexplicably. The Tapestry Room is the spookiest, with sombre paintings and devil's-head iron firedogs. Thrill-seekers can spend a night. In the grounds is Muncaster's great visitor attraction, the World Owl Centre, home to a wide variety of species. It is no rose garden – but, then, they never promised us a rose garden.

▶ *CA18 1RD (satnav for main car park); otherwise CA18 1RQ. 2 miles E of Ravenglass on A595. Seasonal opening.*

❼ Dalemain

Over a Tudor fireplace at Dalemain hangs a portrait of the tenacious Lady Anne Clifford, who spent most of her life fighting for her birthright. She married two earls, petitioned James I to support her cause, was a patron of the arts, became High Sheriff of Westmorland, and is an all-round local heroine. Edward Hassell was her 'chiefe officer' until her death in 1676, aged 86. He acquired Dalemain three years later, and her last diary and other mementoes are here. The Tudor house that Hassell bought – still home to his descendants – incorporated a 14th-century

manor hall and 13th-century fortified pele tower. What visitors see first is a symmetrical Georgian façade of grey-pink ashlar, topped with a balustrade, looking out across gardens to the northernmost tip of Ullswater. This was built in 1744 to enclose a central courtyard between new and old parts of the house. Among the grand public rooms is the Chinese Room, still wearing its 18th-century hand-painted wallpaper. The Tudor parts are a warren of passageways and stairs. As well as antiques, there are paintings by Van Dyck, Zoffany and Davis, Hassell family portraits, ceramics, and displays of dolls' houses and old toys. In the pele tower is a museum dedicated to the Westmorland and Cumberland Yeomanry, traditionally led by Hassells. Dalemain hosts many events, including an annual marmalade festival. In the park are more than 100 old roses, ancient walnut trees, and a 200-year-old tulip tree.

▶ *CA11 0HB. 3 miles SW of Penrith on A592. Seasonal opening.*

❽ Hutton-in-the-Forest

'Perhaps the story of the house begins with the Arthurian legend of Sir Gawain and the Greene Knight, in which Sir Gawain rode into a deep forest that was wonderfully wild …' With this stretch of the imagination the Fletcher Vane family, Lords Inglewood, introduce their ancestral seat. In fact, it is not one but a series of buildings, incorporating a 14th-century pele tower and medieval hall, a 17th-century Renaissance gallery, a rococo east front topped with urns, and a riot of medieval flourishes that were the work of Anthony Salvin in the Victorian era. The quirky Gladstone Tower was the last addition, a late 1800s 'gift to the old house' from Margaret Gladstone, Lady Vane. Pink and red sandstone unify the diverse parts and lend the whole a roseate warmth.

The Fletcher Vanes have been here since 1605. Entry to their home is beneath the pele tower, through the barrel-vaulted Stone Hall. A chill space, its walls adorned with weaponry and antlers, the hall belies the warmth and richness of the varied interiors, which are crammed with antiques, paintings, and oak panelling. Family portraits hang in the gallery. A Mortlake tapestry greets visitors ascending the 17th-century Cupid Staircase. In walled gardens created in the 1730s are terraces with Victorian topiary. There is a lake and cascade and 17th-century dovecote. The annual Potfest in the Park, showcase for creative potters, is a popular summer event.

▶ *CA11 9TH. 7 miles NW of Penrith on B5305. Limited seasonal opening.*

LANCASHIRE, LIVERPOOL & MANCHESTER

A haunted tower, an impressive timber-framed mansion and a showcase of Edwardian life are enhanced by eminent literary connections, a food buff and the story of a circus girl and an earl – this region has it all.

❶ Leighton Hall

'Whitehall, December 10th. Yesterday the Principal Rebels taken at Preston, with their Servants, were brought to London, & committed Prisoners to the Tower, the Marshalsea, New Gate, & the Fleet.' On a list of Jacobite rebels captured by government troops in 1715 appears the name of 'Albert Hodgson of Leighton, Papist'. His property was seized, his house was sacked and burned. When it came up for auction, a friend, Mr Winkley, bought it and, upon his release from prison, Hodgson returned to a ruin. By good fortune his daughter Mary married George Towneley of Towneley Hall (see page 157), who ordered a rebuilding in the Adam style. The woods were replanted and the park was laid out much as it is today.

In 1822, Leighton was bought by Richard Gillow, grandson of the founder of the Lancashire furniture makers, who had the house refaced in the then fashionable Gothic style. A further wing was added in 1870 by pioneer architects Edward Paley and Hubert Austin. The exterior carries through into the hall, a great example of the early Gothic revival, with pointed-arch doorways and a curved stone, cantilevered 'flying staircase'. Other interiors are Regency. The Dining Room affords an opportunity to appreciate Gillow style, with dining chairs at once elegant and practical. This is still a Catholic family home. The altar in the chapel has a Gillow front. In the Music Room there is a Steinway grand piano and a painting of St Jerome. Shouldn't he be in the library?

▶ *LA5 9ST. 3 miles N of Carnforth on minor roads. Seasonal daily opening; group guided tours all year by prior arrangement.*

❷ Rufford Old Hall

Local lore holds that a young William Shakespeare stayed and even performed here. He was almost certainly known to Sir Thomas Hesketh, to whose care he was commended in Alexander Hoghton's will in 1581 (see Hoghton Tower, page 152). Rufford Old Hall was home to the Hesketh family for 500 years, passing to the National Trust in 1936. Shakespeare would have staged his drama in the Great Hall, a Tudor half-timbered building, somewhat altered in the reign of Queen Victoria. With its soaring hammerbeam roof carved with angels, and its quatrefoil adornments, it must have made a fine auditorium. A movable screen carved with heraldry and topped with long, decorative finials, is a unique and audacious piece of work. The adjacent gabled redbrick wing dates from 1662.

The Trust presents the house with authentic Victorian interiors. There are paintings of various Heskeths, but the portrait that most repays consideration is that of Kenelm Digby, a courtier and supporter of Charles I, a diplomat, natural philosopher, 'magazine of all arts'. He collected recipes that provide a fascinating insight into food and drink of that era. Digby was a family friend, and perhaps shared with Heskeths the secrets of making cock-ale, nourishing hachy, pith puddings and excellent good collops. There is pleasing topiary in Victorian and Edwardian gardens.

▶ *L40 1SG. 5 miles N of Ormskirk on A59. NT. Seasonal opening.*

❸ Croxteth Hall

William Molyneux, 2nd Earl of Sefton, was a sportsman, gambler and friend of the self-indulgent Prince Regent. He helped to establish Aintree racecourse, and was a principal sponsor of the Grand National. In London he acquired the nickname Lord Dashalong, because of his habit of racing through the streets with a carriage and four horses. The beautiful eleven-bay Queen Anne range at Croxteth, of red brick with stone dressings, was built for the Molyneux family in 1702, and no doubt Lord Dashalong enjoyed life on what was once a great country estate. A west range was rebuilt in 1902, and Liverpool City Council invites visitors to explore life above and below stairs in the Edwardian era. The original kitchens and domestic offices, the public rooms and parlours, bedrooms and boudoirs are fully furnished and maintained, and peopled by wax effigies. The public also dash along to enjoy the walled garden and country park.

▶ *L11 1EH satnav to free car park; otherwise L12 0HB. 5 miles NE of Liverpool city centre.*

SPEKE HALL

4 Speke Hall

Frederick Richards Leyland was a ship owner, art collector and patron of the Pre-Raphaelites. In 1867 he rented this jewel of a Tudor mansion. Speke Hall was built for the Norris family between 1530 and 1598. Today it is Grade I listed, and yet by the time Richard Watt bought it in 1795 it was not fit for human habitation, and was occupied by livestock. Using a fortune made from Jamaican sugar plantations, Watt restored one of Britain's finest 16th-century half-timbered residences. The moated house encloses a courtyard in which grow two very ancient yews nicknamed Adam and Eve. The exterior is highly decorative, with herringbone and quatrefoil timbering. Inside, Speke's secrets recall days of religious persecution. There is a priest hole and, in a bedroom, an observation hole for occupants to watch for approaching pursuivants bent on routing 'the Scarlet Woman', Catholicism. A hole under the eaves – an 'eavesdrop' – enabled servants to listen in on anyone waiting at the front door. Leyland's 19th-century legacy includes de Morgan tiles, Pre-Raphaelite pictures, William Morris wallpaper and fireplaces. The Great Hall, with deep, leaded bay windows, is, with the Great Parlour, the oldest part of the house. The Tudor home of a Victorian medievalist today stands in pleasant gardens on the River Mersey – right by Liverpool John Lennon Airport. Imagine!
▶ *L24 1XD. 8 miles SE of Liverpool city centre off A561. NT. Seasonal opening.*

5 Hoghton Tower

Rumours of a young William Shakespeare in Lancashire continue here. In 1581, Alexander Hoghton, a scion of the Hoghton family, entrusted 'William Shakeshafte' to the care of Thomas Hesketh, and it is suggested that the budding playwright stayed here before moving on to Rufford Old Hall (see page 151). This hilltop Elizabethan manor has been home to the de Hoghton family since its rebuilding in 1565. In 1617 Sir Richard Hoghton rolled out the red carpet for James I – all the way down the three-quarter mile drive. At the banquet laid on for him, the king was so impressed by the loin of beef that he took a sword and knighted it Sir Loin ('sirloin'). Family loyalties were divided in the Civil War, and Hoghton Tower came under siege by Parliament in 1643. Famous guests who have been entertained here include J.M.W. Turner and Charles Dickens, although when Dickens came in 1854 the house was in disrepair. He had

152

Hoghton in mind when he wrote, in his story *George Silverman's Explanation*, of: 'A house centuries old, deserted and falling to pieces … the ancient rooms … with their floors and ceilings falling, and beams and rafters hanging dangerously down … the oaken panels stripped away, the windows half walled up …'

Restoration began in 1870 after a century of neglect and today Hoghton is Grade I listed, and run by a charitable trust. The visitor can see the suite in which James I slept, and the menu for the memorable banquet, displayed in the Great Hall. Ghost tours explore 'the third most haunted house in Britain'. From the ramparts the views of Lancashire, the Lake District and North Wales are spectacular. Beneath are dungeons and a Tudor well house.

▶ *PR5 0SH. 7 miles SE of Preston on A675. Seasonal opening; groups all year by prior arrangement.*

❻ Gawthorpe Hall

'A drive of about three miles brought us to the gates of Gawthorpe … There towered the hall – grey, antique, castellated and stately, before me. It is 250 years old, and, within as without, a model of old English architecture.' Charlotte Brontë came here as the guest of Sir James and Lady Janet Kay-Shuttleworth in March 1850. A social reformer and 'father of popular education in England', Sir James had read the radical novel *Shirley*, and had been avid to meet its author, 'Currer Bell'. Currer, of course, turned out to be the diminutive Charlotte, who, although she was somewhat daunted by her aristocratic hosts, was enchanted by Gawthorpe, which brought to mind the works of her hero, Sir Walter Scott.

The house was built by Robert Smythson, and is constantly referred to as a 'gem'. It stands amid woodlands in a landscaped park with terraces stepping down to the River Calder. The central tower was probably a free-standing pele tower. The façade displays Smythson's love of glass – so expensive, so swanky in the Elizabethan age – with three storeys of mullioned windows. In 1849, Sir Charles Barry, architect of the Houses of Parliament, remodelled the interiors but the dining room is still overlooked by its original minstrels' gallery. Sir James's granddaughter, Rachel Kay-Shuttleworth, shared his social ideals, and passionately believed that crafts enhanced the quality of life. Her large collection of embroidery, lacework and textiles is displayed to advantage in grand period rooms.

▶ *BB12 8UA. 3 miles NW of Burnley off A671. NT. Seasonal opening for house; grounds open all year.*

'South Dreſsing ROOM GROUND FLOOR.

SOUTH WEST Dreſsing Room GROUND FLOOR

BLUE DRESSING ROOM.

LORD GREYS ROOM.

❼ Browsholme Hall

Thomas Lister Parker was an antiquary, High Sheriff of Lancashire, Bowbearer to the Forest of Bowland and Trumpeter to the Queen in the reign of George III. It was, however, one suspects, to blow his own trumpet that he called in Jeffry Wyatt (later Sir Jeffry Wyatville) in 1804 to extend and remodel 'Brusom' as a showcase for his paintings and antiquities, many acquired on the Grand Tour. He was a patron of Turner and Romney, Opie and Northcote, moved in high circles and gained the notice of the Prince Regent. He lost himself in admiration for a young actor, William Berry, followed him around and showered him with lavish gifts. Sadly, he overreached himself and was forced to sell his home to a cousin, at least keeping it in the family.

Browsholme Hall was begun in 1507. An H-plan house, it was refaced in pink sandstone a century later and received a Queen Anne wing 100 years after that. The original Hall is no soaring cathedral but a relatively warm and intimate space. There are stags' heads and guns on the walls, suits of armour, boots, shields, and such curiosities as a Civil War coat worn at the Battle of Newbury. A skull is said to be that of a martyr from the Pilgrimage of Grace. The Library, created from part of the Hall, has Jacobean panelling, its diamond pattern, say the Parkers,

BELOW STAIRS LIFE IN A BIG COUNTRY HOUSE

DUNHAM MASSEY

'only paralleled locally by the dining room at Towneley Hall'. Wyatt's Drawing Room has Regency furniture and is hung with numerous paintings, including works by Romney and Lely. In the Dining Room, which served as a gallery for Lister Parker's art treasures, is an affectionate portrait of Robert Shaw, last Keeper of the Forest of Bowland – one of 13 works by James Northcote at Browsholme. The forest situation of the house, overlooking the Hodder Valley, provides a spectacular stage set.

▶ *BB7 3DE. 5 miles NW of Clitheroe on minor roads. Limited seasonal opening; groups all year by prior arrangement.*

8 Towneley Hall and Park

'This part of Lancashire seems rather remarkable for its houses of ancient race. The Towneleys, who live near, go back to the Conquest.' Charlotte Brontë wrote thus to a friend on her visit to Gawthorpe Hall (see page 153). Indeed, the Towneleys trace their ancestry back to the Norman invasion, and the present house was their home for 500 years. Traces remain of an earlier building begun in 1400. A priest hole below a floor reveals that the family, like most of Lancashire's gentry, were recusant Catholics, living in fear of priest-hunters. John Towneley, a lawyer, was imprisoned for his faith in the reign of Elizabeth I. The most celebrated family member was the antiquarian Charles Towneley, renowned for his collection of classical statuary, sold to the British Museum.

The slightly dour Gothic exterior of the building does not prepare the visitor for the baroque grandeur and elegance of the Great Hall, remodelled in 1725, with fluted pilasters, classical statues and a ceiling by that supremely gifted Italian stucco artist Francesco Vassalli. The grand Regency reception rooms in the left-hand range, the work of Jeffry Wyatt, are equally unexpected. In 1844, more than 130 portraits hung in Towneley Hall but it was almost empty when it was sold to Burnley Corporation in 1901. It is now an art gallery and museum owned by the council, displaying collections of oil paintings, early English watercolours, regional period furniture, glassware and textiles, natural history, Egyptology and recovered Towneley portraits. The grounds, landscaped in the late 1700s, are today Burnley's largest and most popular public park.
▶ *BB11 3RQ. 2 miles SE of Burnley town centre. Open all year (Hall closed on Fridays).*

9 Dunham Massey

Kitty Cocks was a circus bareback rider and a woman of dubious repute. When she married George Harry Grey, 7th Earl of Stamford, in 1855, she was snubbed by Victorian Cheshire society, so the couple abandoned the family seat, taking precious silver and other treasures with them. They left behind a house begun in 1616 by Sir George Booth, and remodelled in the Georgian era. The Booths succeeded the Massey family, who originally came from Normandy and acquired the manor of Dunham after the Conquest. The Greys, in turn, succeeded the Booths. William 'Good Will' Grey, 9th Earl, ordered a makeover, but died in 1910 before it was complete. Roger Grey, 10th Earl, was 13 when the house passed to him. He devoted himself to buying back artworks and recovering the family silver. He made few alterations to the house, and died childless in 1976, bequeathing the estate, the house and contents to the National Trust.

Visitors see the collections in the context of a splendid redbrick Georgian mansion, set in a deer park, with Edwardian and Georgian interiors. In the study the 10th Earl is a palpable presence; the room is filled with magazines, books and local newspapers over which he pored. A solid mahogany staircase is hung with family portraits. The Great Gallery contains 18th-century bird's-eye-view paintings of the Dunham landscape, and Guercino's *Allegory with Venus, Mars, Cupid and Time*. The fitted oak bookcases in the library are packed with antique books. The carving above the fireplace is by Grinling Gibbons. In the Queen Anne Room is the canopied bed in which the queen slept – albeit not at Dunham Massey. It had languished in packing cases from the death of the 9th Earl until the National Trust uncovered it. The service wing is no less fascinating.
▶ *WA14 4SJ. 2 miles W of Altrincham off B5160. NT. Seasonal opening of house (closed on Thursdays and Fridays); gardens open all year.*

10 Bramall Hall

When Charles Nevill wanted to improve his grand half-timbered Tudor manor house in 1883, he dressed up the façade and called in Herbert Schmaltz. Schmaltz's painting of Viking meeting Saxon in the 'timber-effect' Banqueting Hall represents the joint heritage of the English race, and is as schmaltzy as one could wish.

The Davenport family lived at Bramall until 1881, in a house that had been transformed from an earlier hall house during the reign of Elizabeth I, at the behest of William and Dorothy Davenport. The number of shimmering glass windows in its black-and-white front must have shouted of wealth.

Bramall is 'one of the four best timber-framed mansions of England', in the judgment of architectural historian Nikolaus Pevsner. It passed to Stockport council in 1935 and guided tours take in the Great Hall, Banqueting Room, Chapel, servants' quarters and Victorian kitchen. The park has been landscaped in the style of Capability Brown. The hall is used for weddings and other functions.
▶ *SK7 3NX. 3 miles S of Stockport on A5102. Open all year for guided tours (weekends only in winter; closed on Mondays).*

NORTHWEST ENGLAND

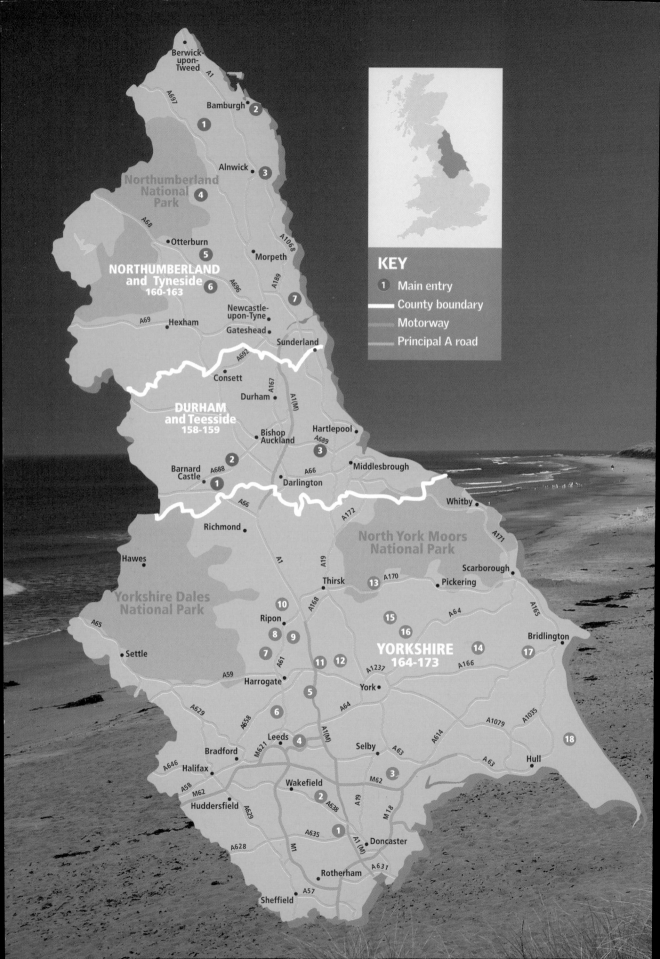

Berwick-upon-Tweed

A1

A697

Bamburgh ②

①

Alnwick ③

Northumberland National Park

④

A68

Otterburn

⑤

Morpeth

A1068

NORTHUMBERLAND and Tyneside
160-163

⑥

A696

A189

⑦

A69   Hexham

Newcastle-upon-Tyne

Gateshead

Sunderland

A692

Consett

A167

Durham

A1(M)

DURHAM and Teesside
158-159

Bishop Auckland

Hartlepool

A689

③

②

Barnard Castle

A688

Middlesbrough

①

A66   Darlington

A66

Whitby

Richmond

A172

A171

North York Moors National Park

Hawes

A1

A19

Thirsk

⑬ A170

Scarborough

Pickering

Yorkshire Dales National Park

⑩

Ripon

A168

⑮

A64

A165

A65

⑧ ⑨

⑯

Bridlington

Settle

⑦

A61

YORKSHIRE
164-173

⑭

⑰

A59

⑪ ⑫

A1237

Harrogate

A166

⑤

York

A64

A629

⑥

A1079

A1035

A658

Leeds ④

A1(M)

Selby

A63

⑱

Bradford

M621

A614

A63   Hull

A646   Halifax

A58

Wakefield

M62

③

M62

②

A638

A79

M18

Huddersfield

A629

①

Doncaster

A628

M1

A635

A1(M)

Rotherham

A631

Sheffield   A57

KEY
① Main entry
━━ County boundary
── Motorway
── Principal A road

Northeast England

Estates great and small have weathered history's storm in this unyielding territory. Traces of medieval rebellion are still in evidence, together with superb examples of Victorian ingenuity and wonderful collections amassed on the Grand Tour.

DURHAM & TEESSIDE

Venus brought fame to Rokeby, and the in-crowd of the day flocked to the dazzling residence of a young marchioness, bent on making her mark, but one Gothic pile had already taken its place in history.

❶ Rokeby Park

'I have been all morning pulling about my pictures and hanging them in new positions to make more room for my fine picture of Venus's backside by Velasquez.' In September 1820, John Bacon Sawrey Morritt wrote thus to his good friend Sir Walter Scott. Scott loved the wild landscape around Rokeby and dedicated his epic verse of that name to Morritt.

The house was built in 1725, by and for Sir Thomas Robinson, in an early variant of the Palladian style, described as 'a particularly erudite conception' by architectural historian Giles Worsley. Robinson was a gifted amateur architect and had the freedom to improve and extend. In the end, he over-extended himself. In 1769, to clear his debts, he sold the five-bay villa with recessed flanking wings, stables and outbuildings, in parkland, to J.S. Morritt. John Carr was then commissioned to add the neoclassical Dining Room. J.B.S. Morritt inherited the property in 1791, aged 20, and three years later embarked on the Grand Tour. Among his art treasures was *The Toilet of Venus* – acquired by the National Gallery in 1906 and thereafter known as 'The Rokeby Venus'. A copy hangs in the Saloon here.

Rokeby is still home to the Morritt family. A remarkable series of intricate needlework 'paintings' created by J.B.S.'s maiden aunt, Anne Eliza Morritt, is on display. Robert Southey visited in 1812, and afterwards wrote that 'the art cost her her life though at an advanced age; it brought on a dead palsy … Her last picture is hardly finished; the needle, Mr M says, literally dropt from her hands – death had been creeping on her for twelve years.' Visitors can only wonder at her flair and dedication.
▶ *DL12 9RZ. On A66, 3 miles SE of Barnard Castle. Limited seasonal opening.*

❷ Raby Castle

In the Middle Ages this formidable edifice was one of the great powerhouses of the north. Towers, turrets, battlements loom against the sky. The surrounding parkland is serene, with lakes and grazing deer, but Raby has lived through turbulent times. King Cnut (Canute) legendarily had a manor here, but it was as the stronghold of the Nevilles that Raby Castle stormed into history. Richard Neville, 16th Earl of Warwick, was known as 'Kingmaker' for making – and breaking – two kings in the Wars of the Roses. The castle was confiscated by the Crown, in retribution for Charles Neville, 6th Earl of Westmorland's role in the failed Rising of the North of 1569. Visitors can stand in the Baron's Hall and recall that, as Wordsworth relates, 'Seven hundred Knights, Retainers all / Of Neville, at their Master's call / Had sate together in Raby Hall!' Stout Catholics all, they had sworn to overthrow the Protestant Elizabeth I and bring Mary, Queen of Scots to the throne.

The place was bought in 1626 by Sir Henry Vane, an MP and member of Charles I's household, and is today home to John Vane, 11th Baron Barnard. Nevilles and Vanes look down from crimson walls in a theatrical space, made over in 1840 by William Burn, as part of Victorian remodelling. A window and the minstrels' gallery survive from the Nevilles' time. Earlier alterations were the work of James Paine and John Carr in the 18th century, when they created a luxurious suite of family rooms. The 'medieval' vaulted Entrance Hall, the work of Carr in the 1780s, has been described as 'the first truly dramatic interior of the Gothic revival'.
▶ *DL2 3AH. 7 miles SW of Bishop Auckland on A688. Seasonal opening.*

❸ Wynyard Hall

'I never left London with such a sense of relief and such anticipation of happiness.' Benjamin Disraeli reflected on his visits to Wynyard Hall, built by Benjamin and Philip Wyatt in the 1820s. This was the country house of the Vane-Tempest-Stewart family, Marquises of Londonderry, until the 1980s. Its exterior is impressive, with a massive Corinthian portico. Interiors are opulent, reflecting the taste and aspirations of Lady Frances Anne Vane-Tempest. Heiress to a coal fortune, Lady Frances was given away at her wedding, aged 19, by the Duke of Wellington. She entertained royalty, bigwigs, artists and writers at Wynyard. 'The most splendid 19th-century mansion in the country', in the words of architectural historian Nikolaus Pevsner, is today a hotel.
▶ *TS22 5NF. 6 miles N of Stockton-on-Tees off A689.*

CARRIAGE IN THE ENTRANCE HALL, RABY CASTLE

NORTHUMBERLAND & TYNESIDE

Formidable medieval castles and ancient family halls match the dramatic scenery of this uncompromising land, where radical thinking was the norm and inventive genius came into its own.

ALNWICK CASTLE

❶ Chillingham Castle

The Edward I Room at Chillingham is where the 'Hammer of the Scots' rested in 1298 on the way to do battle with William ('Brave Heart') Wallace. The licence to crenellate granted in 1344 by Edward III is displayed here. In recent times a secret compartment was discovered, containing a cache of documents relating to the Spanish Armada and the succession of Scotland's James VI.

Chillingham was begun in the 12th century as an inward-looking border stronghold, with windows on to a courtyard, and arrow slits in its outer walls. From the reign of Elizabeth I, it received such refinements as galleries, arcading, carved stonework and mullioned windows. A Jacobean entrance and state rooms were built for the visit of James VI on his journey to take the throne of England as James I. In the 18th century Capability Brown worked on the landscape and Robert Adam's pupil John Paterson remodelled the east wing. In 1824, gardens were laid out by Sir Jeffry Wyatville. The ancient seat of the Grey family and the Earls of Tankerville was abandoned in the 1930s upon the death of the 7th Earl. It has been the subject of intensive renovation since 1981, when Kate Grey's husband, Sir Humphry Wakefield, took it on as a wreck. He took it back to bare walls and rebuilt, filling interiors with antiques, *objets d'art*, weaponry, armour and memorabilia. A sledge hanging from a ceiling recalls Sir Humphry's Antarctic expedition of 1999. Prehistoric elk horns with a 5m (16ft) span hang in the Great Hall. The Torture Chamber is gruesome. It is all wildly eccentric and fun. Wyatville's Italian garden with topiary parterre is a delight. Chillingham's wild white cattle, survivors of an ancient breed, roam the parkland.

▶ *NE66 5NJ. 5 miles SE of Wooler off A697 or B6348. Seasonal opening.*

❷ Bamburgh Castle

This dramatic seaside castle, perched high on a basalt rock outcrop, on the site of a stronghold of the ancient kings of Northumbria, was for centuries a royal domain. Bamburgh was the first castle to succumb to cannon fire in the Wars of the Roses. James I had no use for it, and gave the battle-scarred fortress to its last keeper, Claudius Forster, but in *c.*1700 Dorothy Forster inherited a bankrupt estate. Her husband, Nathaniel, Lord Crewe, Bishop of Durham, bought it, settled the debts and, on Dorothy's early death, set up a trust to manage and restore his wife's beloved castle.

Today Bamburgh appears whole and invincible thanks to rebuilding and restoration in the 18th and 19th centuries, first by Lord Crewe, and then by Lord Armstrong of Cragside (see page 162). Armstrong, the great inventor, was a distant relative of the Forsters. On learning, in 1894, that their castle was up for sale, he bought it and, at the age of 83, set about creating the 'quintessential medieval castle'. As he did at his showpiece at Rothbury, he fitted such modern conveniences as air conditioning, at the same time constructing a Great Hall with a faux hammerbeam roof. The renovations were incomplete when he died, and his great-nephew, the 2nd Lord Armstrong, took over. It remains the Armstrongs' home. A tiny pair of shoes and a dress on display belonged to Dorothy Crewe's niece, also Dorothy, who ingeniously rescued her brother Tom from imprisonment in London, after the failed Jacobite Rebellion of 1715.

▶ *NE69 7DF. On the coast at Bamburgh, 18 miles S of Berwick-upon-Tweed. Open all year (weekends only in winter).*

❸ Alnwick Castle

Shakespeare's 'hairbrained Hotspur, govern'd by a spleen', sits heroically astride his warhorse in a courtyard at 'the Windsor of the North'. Sir Henry Percy ('Harry Hotspur') took up arms against the Scots when he was just a teenager. Then in 1403 he led a rebellion against Henry IV, and met his death at Shrewsbury. His head was displayed on a pole at York's gates, as that of a later Percy, Sir Thomas, 7th Earl of Northumberland, would be in its turn, for his part in the Rising of the North (see Raby Castle, page 158).

The powerful Percys, 'a family nobler than kings', arrived with William the Conqueror. Henry Percy, 1st Baron Percy, bought Alnwick Castle in 1309 from the Bishop of Durham, and began rebuilding his palace-fortress in a style at once practical, theatrical and opulent.

After the death of Sir Thomas in 1572, the castle was abandoned, but in the latter 1700s Robert Adam made many alterations. In the 19th century, the 4th Duke of Northumberland engaged the medievalist architect Anthony Salvin to create new, palatial accommodation. The decoration of the state rooms was the work of Luigi Canina and his associate Giovanni Montiroli. Everything is on the grand scale. The library contains nearly 14,000 books. A table more than 10m (33ft) long in the Dining Room is set with family silver. The work of local craftsmen may be seen in the Drawing Room.

The carvers were trained by the Florentine Anton Leon Bulletti. Within its formidable walls, this is the comfortable but sumptuous Victorian home of Ralph Percy, 12th Duke of Northumberland, and his family. Alnwick Garden, the inspiration of the present duchess, is a separate attraction.

▶ *NE66 1NQ. 1 mile W of A1 in Alnwick town centre, 34 miles N of Newcastle upon Tyne. Seasonal daily opening of house and garden.*

❹ Cragside

William George Armstrong, Baron Armstrong of Cragside, was an environmentalist, international arms dealer, inventor, engineer and genius. He built Newcastle's Swing Bridge and designed the mechanism that operates London's Tower Bridge. When the future Edward VII invited himself and his family on a visit in August 1884, to see the achievements of a 'modern magician', he found a house that outshone Buckingham Palace.

Armstrong built Cragside as a sporting lodge, on the slopes of a rocky valley. The house he created with architect Norman Shaw, mixing gables, battlements, half-timbering and towering Tudor chimneys, is often described as 'Wagnerian' and 'fairytale'. Architectural historian Nikolaus Pevsner was impressed by its picturesque aspect, but it was not for the mansion's aesthetic qualities that this wonder of the Victorian age was most admired. It was the first house in the world to be lit by hydroelectric power. Among other mod cons were a tiled hot tub; a double-height kitchen with hydraulically powered spit and a lift to help staff to carry food and coal; hot and cold running water; central heating; an electric gong; and the first filament lightbulbs. The grounds are scarcely less astonishing, intended to evoke the Himalayas, and including one of the largest rock gardens in Europe. They are best seen when the azaleas are in bloom – and there may even be a glimpse of red squirrels.

▶ *NE65 7PX. 2 miles E of Rothbury, on B6341, 4 miles from A697. NT. Seasonal opening.*

❺ Wallington Hall

Pauline Jermyn Trevelyan must have been a dazzling hostess, entertaining the great artists, writers and thinkers of the Victorian age. It was certainly not for the fine wine that John Ruskin, the Brownings and Rossettis came here. Pauline's husband, Sir Walter Calverley Trevelyan, had the cellar under lock and key. He was a teetotal, vegetarian polymath who filled his greenhouses with rare plants, and breakfasted on foraged nettles and fungi. Before proposing marriage, he made Pauline a gift of a box of fossils. Wallington was the ancient seat of the Fenwicks. In 1684 Sir John Fenwick sold the estate to Sir William Blackett, a fellow Jacobite. Fenwick was executed for treason; Blackett kept his beliefs under his hat. He began rebuilding the old house four years later, and his grandson, Sir Walter, remodelled it in 1738, in the Palladian style, with Italian rococo plasterwork.

The property passed to the Trevelyans in 1777 and later became a northern outpost of Pre-Raphaelite society. With advice from Ruskin, in 1853, Pauline ordered the open courtyard to be transformed into a spectacular galleried central hall. The architect was John Dobson of Newcastle. Huge painted panels depict scenes from the history of Northumberland, from *The Romans Cause a Wall to be Built* through to *Iron and Coal*. These are the work of William Bell Scott, with contributions by Ruskin, Arthur Hughes and Pauline. The visitor sees many curiosities, sculptures, ceramics, a collection of dolls' houses and enchanting antique toys, and can wander in an 18th-century landscape laid out for Sir Walter in the style of a local man, Capability Brown, with lakes, woodland and parkland. Hidden in the woods is a lovely walled garden. Sir Charles Trevelyan gave the estate to the National Trust in 1937, but the family retain an apartment.

▶ *NE61 4AR. 10 miles W of Morpeth. NT. Seasonal opening of house; gardens open all year.*

❻ Belsay Hall and Castle

Ruins were all the rage when Sir Charles Monck moved out of the Jacobean wing of a 15th-century castle and into his brand new Classical villa in 1817. What could be more picturesque than a crumbling castle dominated by a massive pele tower with rounded turrets and slit windows? Monck (formerly Middleton) had been inspired by the buildings he had seen on his honeymoon in Athens to commission a Greek revival house including a two-storey Pillar Hall. He also created a romantic Quarry Garden, with ravines and rock-faces, inspired by quarries in Sicily. His grandson, Sir Arthur Middleton, planted many of the exotic species that grow there, as well as laying out the Winter Garden, Yew Garden and Magnolia Terrace. Both hall and castle stand empty today, and visitors strolling between the two makes a surreal journey from ancient Greece re-imagined to medieval England with Jacobean extension.

▶ *NE20 0DX. 8 miles SW of Morpeth. EH. Open all year.*

⑦ Seaton Delaval Hall

From his uncle, Admiral George Delaval, Captain Francis Blake Delaval inherited a half-built palace on the site of a former family pile. The admiral's architect was Sir John Vanbrugh, pioneer of the baroque style, whose penchant for drama found expression in the plays he wrote, as well as in his buildings. The house was begun in 1719 and completed over eleven years. At one time 220 labourers and tradesmen worked on the construction, but neither admiral nor architect was to live to see the project through. Captain Francis took over, meanwhile marrying Rhoda Apreece, heiress to Doddington Hall (see page 119), in August 1724.

The couple had 12 children, who ran wild. Guests stayed at their peril. They might be undressing at night, only to find the bedroom walls winched up; a bed could be lowered into a tank of cold water. Their eldest son, Sir Francis, was a ringleader, and when he inherited the estate, he enhanced the family's reputation as the 'gay Delavals' by throwing bawdy parties for his reprobate actor friends. No stranger to scandal and excess, he was always in debt. It was said that his house was 'scarred to ruin by the riotous living of that scoundrel Francis and the lust-mongers he entertains'. Seaton Delaval was unoccupied in 1822 when it was gutted by fire and left to lie derelict. The dangerous structure was shored up in 1862, but not until the 1950s did Lord and Lady Hastings return to the estate after more than a century of family absence. They lived in one of the two mighty flanking wings while the hall and the magnificent stable block were restored and collections of furniture and portraits reacquired. Described as 'a Geordie Versailles', Vanbrugh's last masterpiece was handed to the National Trust in 2009. The garden, by James Russell, laid out for Lady Hastings, contains a topiary parterre, pond and fountain.

▶ *NE26 4QR. 3 miles N of Whitley Bay off A193. NT. Open all year (closed Tuesday to Thursday).*

THE NURSERY AT WALLINGTON HALL

BRODSWORTH HALL

YORKSHIRE

From the grand to the downright palatial, these historic mansions are filled with the diverse treasures of past incumbents, intent on indulging their passions, whether for art, antiques, ecology – or cricket.

① Brodsworth Hall

The last will and testament of Peter Thellusson made legal history and put the cat among the pigeons. A Huguenot refugee and wealthy banker, he left his fortune to an as yet unborn descendant. If there were to be no great-grandson, the money was to pay off the National Debt. Peter died in 1797 and by the time Charles Thellusson came in to the inheritance in 1856, years of lawyers' wrangling had substantially reduced it. Nonetheless, he

rebuilt the old family home to persuade his wife to move, with their six children, to Yorkshire from fashionable Brighton. How could she have resisted? This lovely Italianate mansion, of pale stone, crowned with a balustrade and numerous urns, overlooked a collection of grand gardens in miniature. A tiered fountain and topiary echoed Thellusson's native Florence. There was a fern dell grotto, a wild rose dell, formal gardens, pleasure grounds with summerhouse, croquet lawn, tennis court and archery range. After that the story is a familiar one of long decline and radical rescue.

In 1990 English Heritage stepped in to repair the house, but otherwise left it untouched. Interiors are just as they were left, with their furniture, fading wallpaper, worn carpets and time-warp Victorian kitchen as well as a more intimate 'Aga kitchen' with Tupperware and Formica. There is a collection of Italian marble sculptures and the gardens continue to reassert their glories. ▶ *DN5 7XJ. 5 miles NW of Doncaster on B6474. EH. Seasonal opening of house; gardens open all year (weekends only in winter).*

❷ Nostell Priory

Young men taking the Grand Tour brought back many treasures. Sir Rowland Winn, 5th Baronet, brought back a wife. Sabine was the daughter of the Swiss Baron d'Hervart de Vevey. A portrait of the couple was painted by Hugh Douglas Hamilton upon completion of Nostell's library, to designs by Robert Adam. It shows a carved mahogany Chippendale table delivered in 1767 at a cost of £72 10s, and described by its creator as 'the best work that can be done'. Chippendale made many pieces for Nostell, but relations between the great cabinetmaker and his employer were fractious. Sir Rowland wrote to berate Chippendale for his slowness; Chippendale was constantly anxious for payment.

This Palladian treasure house was begun for the 4th Baronet in 1733 by Colonel Moyser and taken forward by James Paine with later additions by Robert Adam. The ambitious plan was for a main block with pavilions at each corner, but work stopped with the 5th Baronet's accidental death in 1785, and Nostell remains a single block, much as he left it. In 1953 it was given to the National Trust with collections that include a longcase clock with wooden mechanism made by John ('Longitude') Harrison, a doll's house so perfect that even the silver is hallmarked, and important works of art. Sabine, devastated by her husband's death, became reclusive and refused to speak to her daughter, Esther, after Esther eloped with the family baker. ▶ *WF4 1QE. 5 miles SE of Wakefield on A638. NT. Seasonal opening of house; park open all year.*

❸ Carlton Towers

It has been said of Edward Pugin that he didn't know when to stop – in his buildings, as in life. His vexatious pamphleteering found him called before the High Court, charged with libel. On his death, aged 41, from syncope of the heart brought on by overwork and overuse of the sedative chloral hydrate, he was described as 'a good hater and a firm friend – impetuous to a degree and generous to a fault'. He had designed more than 100 churches, as well as numbers of secular buildings for mainly Catholic clients.

In 1869 he remodelled Carlton Manor for Henry Stapleton, 9th Lord Beaumont. The family had endured centuries of religious persecution, and had converted to Anglicanism, but with the 18th-century Catholic revival, Beaumont re-embraced his faith. Who better, then, than the eldest son of 'God's architect', Augustus Pugin, to transform an already modified 17th-century house? The result is a mansion that embodies Beaumont's building mania and Pugin's ebullience and idiosyncratic dash. The architect clad the exterior in cement and garnished it with a mad profusion of towers, turrets, pinnacles and battlements, and a massive 18th-century clock guarded by heraldic beasts. When Pugin died in 1875, J.F. Bentley was commissioned to create the interiors, and made use of copious panelling, stained glass, carved fireplaces, stencilled and painted walls and ceilings, and more heraldic devices. The entrance hall, or 'Armoury', is a soaring, beamed space. Panelling in the Venetian Drawing Room portrays scenes from *The Merchant of Venice*. The home of Lord and Lady Gerald Fizalan Howard, Carlton Towers is offered as an events venue. ▶ *DN14 9LZ. 6 miles S of Selby on A1041.*

❹ Temple Newsam

'The Hampton Court of the North' was the birthplace of Henry Stuart, Lord Darnley, second husband of Mary, Queen of Scots. It was originally built for Thomas, Lord Darcy, in *c.*1500–20, who was executed in 1537 for his part in the Catholic Pilgrimage of Grace. Darnley, too, came to a gruesome end, slain by an unknown hand after his separation from the Scottish queen. The pair's son was king of England, James I, when Sir Arthur Ingram bought the estate and rebuilt a palatial mansion in red brick around three sides of a courtyard. It passed down by inheritance for the next 300 years, before being acquired by Leeds Corporation in 1922. The interiors blend Jacobean with neo-Jacobean and Georgian styles. The house today holds collections of family portraits, paintings, furniture, silver, ceramics and textiles of national importance. Temple Newsam encompasses 600ha (1,500 acres) of park, farmland, woods and gardens, and is famed for its Rhododendron Walk. ▶ *LS15 0AE. 4 miles E of Leeds city centre. Open all year (closed on Mondays).*

Prime locations

Stately homes are the first port of call for makers of period dramas, and where the cameras go, visitors soon follow.

In *Pride and Prejudice* Jane Austen describes Mr Darcy's stately home, Pemberley, in some detail. 'It was a large, handsome, stone building, standing well on rising ground, and backed by a ridge of high woody hills; and in front, a stream of some natural importance was swelled into greater, but without any artificial appearance ...' Viewers who watched the BBC's 1995 adaptation of the novel will picture Lyme Park in Cheshire, and recall the unforgettable 'wet-shirt scene', in which Colin Firth as Fitzwilliam Darcy emerged from the lake to become a sex symbol. The result for the National Trust was a tripling of visitor numbers at Lyme.

Chatsworth House in Derbyshire, possibly the original inspiration for Pemberley, was used for exterior scenes in the 2005 film version of *Pride and Prejudice*, while Wilton House in Wiltshire provided interiors. Harewood House in Yorkshire was another Pemberley in the ITV series *Lost in Austen*.

Britain's stately homes provide ravishing, authentic backdrops for TV and film, and advertise their charms in the process. 'The Downton effect', which has resulted in fans of the BBC's *Downton Abbey* flocking to 'the real Downton', Highclere Castle in Berkshire, is part of a wider phenomenon of 'screen tourism', worth around £1.9 billion annually to the British tourist industry.

It is not new. Castle Howard in Yorkshire became a popular destination when the BBC screened an adaptation of *Brideshead Revisited* in the 1980s. The lustre had not faded when it received a second fillip from the 2008 film version.

Tim Burton's *Alice in Wonderland* brought visitors in droves to Antony in Cornwall, and when Alnwick Castle starred as Hogwarts School of Witchcraft in the Harry Potter films, the immediate effect was a 120 per cent increase in visitors, bringing £9 million worth of tourism to Northumberland.

FILMING *MANSFIELD PARK* AT NEWBY HALL, YORKSHIRE

In a magical way, one starry stately home spreads its radiance upon others. Chatsworth did very nicely from appearing in *The Duchess*, but, as the Duke of Devonshire explained, *Downton* has been an additional boon: 'There has always been a lot of interest in historic houses ... but *Downton Abbey* is another reason for people to say, "Oh, instead of going shopping on Saturday, let's go to Chatsworth."' The interest, once sparked, is enduring. In 2005, ten years after *Pride and Prejudice*, Lyme Park pulled in 88,884 visitors, compared with 32,852 in 1994.

Celebrity attraction

The story of a real-life character in particular captures the imagination, drawing pilgrims to places associated with them. *Mrs Brown*, starring Judi Dench and Billy Connolly, was filmed at Duns Castle in Scotland's Borders, but it was to Balmoral in the Highlands, to Osborne House on the Isle of Wight, that people travelled in pursuit of Queen Victoria.

Not just stately homes but entire counties and regions become magnets for viewers alerted to their attractions by seeing them on screen. In the wake of *Braveheart*, Scotland was more than ever on the tourist map, while the shrewd marketing of the East Midlands as '*Pride and Prejudice* Country' was extraordinarily effective.

Stately-home owners are equally savvy. Holkham Hall in North Norfolk was another location for *The Duchess*. In 2009 it was able to exploit the connection by mounting an exhibition of photographs and costumes. Althorp in Northamptonshire quite reasonably jumped on the bandwagon – as former home to Georgiana, Duchess of Devonshire – with an exhibition of its own. The National Trust's Kedleston Hall in the Peak District stood in for Althorp in the movie, and Derbyshire anticipated a surge in tourism.

Cross-fertilisation of this kind is good for business – and stately homes these days have to be run as businesses. Kentwell Hall in Suffolk, to this end, offers filmmakers a unique selling point – it's own 'Tudors', better dressed, say the owners, and better equipped than regular extras. 'They are used to being Tudors and really look the part.'

Heart-warming and uplifting drama casts the most potent spell over audiences, who may be beguiled by an ideal of Britishness, by the beauties of the countryside and a half-imagined way of life.

❺ Stockeld Park

'I reached Stockeld on Saturday night ... every object round revives melancholy ideas, I long much to leave the place.' Poor William Middleton! He had inherited from his uncle, Sir William Middleton, an unfinished Palladian villa in the Vale of York. The architect was James Paine, the new house a celebration of Sir William's appointment as High Sheriff of West Yorkshire, but he would not live to see its completion in 1763. His nephew, born William Constable, took the Middleton name, and in 1782 married Clara Louisa Grace. Over the next ten years she bore him nine children, of which six survived. William enjoyed family life and country pursuits, riding to hounds and shooting game. Then Clara embarked on a passionate affair with the groom, John Rose. Despite her denials, William sent her from him. In an historic case he sued Rose for 'criminal conversation'. He was then too heartsick to stay at the blighted home.

The house passed down through Middletons until it was acquired by Robert John Foster in the 1870s. Foster built a new east wing, added a hefty portico to the north side and changed the approach. Today it is the family home of his great-grandson. For all its neoclassical inspiration, there is a sturdy quality to Stockeld. The original house is of grey-pink ashlar, under a roof of Westmorland slate. The three-storey central block is flanked by two-storey wings. The centrepiece is the Oval Hallway, with a cantilevered staircase sweeping up towards an ornamented roof dome. Stockeld doubled as Thrushcross Grange in ITV's 2009 adaptation of *Wuthering Heights*.
▶ *LS22 4AN (satnav). Wetherby. House open to special-interest groups for tours, by appointment only.*

❻ Harewood House

For 40 years this glorious treasure house was home to Mary, the Princess Royal, affectionately known as 'the Yorkshire Princess'. In 1922 she married Viscount Lascelles, and from 1929 made Harewood her residence. The palatial mansion was designed for Edwin Lascelles, heir to a sugar-plantation fortune, by John Carr of York. Its claims to stately home fame seem almost endless – opulent interiors by Robert Adam, plasterwork by Biagio Rebecca, Antonio Zucchi and Angelica Kauffman, a park landscaped by Capability Brown, furniture by Chippendale, Sèvres porcelain, and an art collection that includes works by Bellini, Titian, Veronese and El Greco, Turner watercolours, and family portraits by Gainsborough and Reynolds.

In 1843 Sir Charles Barry was employed by Lady Louisa Harewood to add an attic floor. He gave the terrace front an Italian makeover and remodelled some of Adam's rooms. Visitors entering Adam's classical Hall is confronted by his namesake – Jacob Epstein's giant sculpture of the original Adam, carved from a block of Derbyshire alabaster in 1938–9, and rescued by Lord Harewood from a Blackpool funfair in 1961. Brown's landscape includes a Himalayan garden, walled garden, parterre terrace and lakeside garden. The Bird Garden is home to species of exotic and endangered birds, from penguins in their dinner jackets to flamingos in pink froufrou.
▶ *LS17 9LQ (satnav to the main entrance); otherwise LS17 9LG. 7 miles SW of Wetherby at junction of A61 and A659. Seasonal opening.*

❼ Ripley Castle

Everywhere in the rich tapestry of English history, Inglebys seem to have been caught up in the warp and weft. This castle came to Sir Thomas Ingleby by marriage in around 1308. His son Thomas was a courtier of Edward III's, and on a hunting trip saved the king's life by spearing a wild boar – hence the boar's head on the family crest, which crops up everywhere. Another Sir William joined the Pilgrimage of Grace, the Catholic protest against Henry VIII's Reformation. His sons David and Francis were part of the failed Rising of the North against Elizabeth I. James VI of Scotland stayed at Ripley on his way to claim the throne of England as James I in 1603. Within two years his host, also Sir William, was implicated in the Gunpowder Plot, but was acquitted. 'Trooper' Jane Ingleby fought alongside her brother, Sir William Ingleby, for Charles I at Marston Moor. It is said, improbably, that she held Oliver Cromwell at gunpoint in Ripley's library.

Ripley has been home to the family for 26 generations. The main house was rebuilt in the 1780s by William Belwood. The Georgian Dining Room is hung with family portraits. The Knight's Chamber, which has oak ceiling and panelling, gave up its secret in 1964 when a priest hole was discovered by chance. The room houses arms and armour from the Civil War battlefield. Ripley village is as astonishing as the castle. It was rebuilt in the 19th century by Sir William Amcotts Ingleby, on the model of a village in Alsace Lorraine. Dying without issue, he left his estates to his cousin, because 'I don't believe that you are any longer the canting hypocrite I took you for.'
▶ *HG3 3AY. 8 miles S of Ripon on A61. Seasonal opening for guided tours only.*

⑧ Markenfield Hall

This medieval manor stands in a rural situation, surrounded by a moat, unspoiled, serene, a survivor of centuries of benign neglect. Markenfield's Great Hall dates from *c.*1280. The house was built around it on an 'L' plan by John de Markenfield, beginning in 1310. He was chancellor to the pathetic Edward II, no doubt had enemies, and was granted a licence to fortify his new home. Staunch Catholics, the family were among the leaders of the Rising of the North against Elizabeth I. Sir Thomas Markenfield and his uncle, Sir Richard Norton (see Norton Conyers, opposite), escaped execution, but died in poverty in exile. For some 200 years the manor was occupied by tenant farmers who did not ornament or update it.

In 1761 Markenfield was bought by Fletcher Norton, a future Speaker of the House of Commons. He was a descendant of Sir Richard Norton and was moved by family loyalty to recover the estate. On being knighted, he became Lord Grantley of Markenfield. However, no Grantley had lived in the house until the 1980s, when the 7th Lord Grantley began restoration and it became a family home once again. He died in 1995, and in 2001, Markenfield's chapel was the scene of a wedding ceremony for the first time since 1487, when his widow, Lady Deirdre, married writer Ian Curteis. Visitors, crossing the moat bridge, passing beneath the Tudor gatehouse and entering the courtyard, find a lived-in family home.

▶ *HG4 3AD. 3 miles S of Ripon on A61. Very limited seasonal opening.*

⑨ Newby Hall

'In all the works of Art and genius No Man ever possessed a more correct Judgement, or a more discriminating Taste.' A monument in Ripon Cathedral commemorates William Weddell, who created Newby as it is today. With an inheritance from his uncle he bought a house that had been rebuilt in the 1690s by Sir Christopher Wren for Sir Edward Blackett, in red brick with stone quoins. In 1765, Weddell set off on the Grand Tour, and on his return he set out to transform his mansion into a showcase for his 19 chests of classical sculptures, his tapestries and a portrait of himself painted by Pompeo Batoni. The redbrick mansion was altered and enlarged by John Carr of York, who added two wings to the east, remodelled the main block, and effectively turned the house around, creating an entrance on the east front. Robert Adam was engaged in 1767 to create interiors of surpassing elegance and beauty. The entrance hall, with motifs inspired by ancient Rome, has plasterwork by Joseph Rose. In the Statue Gallery niches are filled with perhaps the finest collection of Roman statuary in private ownership in Britain. In the Tapestry Room hang a set of six tapestries that Weddell ordered from the Gobelin works in Paris, depicting *The Loves of the Gods* and designed by François Boucher.

Newby's gardens were designed by the present owner's grandfather over half a century, after he noted that he had inherited 'a lovely picture but no frame'. Long double herbaceous borders flanked by yew hedges extend from the south front to the River Ure. A narrow-gauge railway runs alongside the river.

▶ *HG4 5AE (satnav); otherwise HG4 5AJ. 3 miles SE of Ripon on minor roads off B6265. Seasonal opening.*

⑩ Norton Conyers

'Three storeys high, of proportions not vast, though considerable, a gentleman's manor house, not a nobleman's seat', Norton Conyers is said to have been Charlotte Bronte's model for Thornfield Hall. It was here, apparently, that she had the idea for 'a mad woman in the attic', Mrs Rochester in *Jane Eyre*. The discovery in 2004 of a blocked-off, narrow staircase leading to a garret lends intriguing substance to the legend. Norton Conyers' attics, behind Dutch gables, would not have served to hide a priest in days of religious persecution – the pursuivants were far too dogged. The Nortons were recusant Catholics. Sir Richard Norton and his sons joined the Rising of the North in the reign of Elizabeth I. Sir Richard was forced to flee abroad (see Markenfield Hall, left) and his estate was seized.

Once a medieval house, the building was altered and extended in Tudor, Stuart and Georgian times, and has been in the Graham family since 1624. Charles I visited in 1633. Sir Richard Graham fought for his king at Marston Moor and returned home to die of his wounds, carried by his horse, at a gallop, right into the hall and up towards his bedchamber. Charles's younger son, the future James II, and his wife also visited, in 1679. The visitor can see the room and bed where that couple slept. The house is deeply atmospheric, hung with portraits, steeped in history.

▶ *HG4 5EQ. 3 miles N of Ripon on minor roads. House closed for repairs in 2012, except for pre-booked groups.*

⑪ Allerton Castle

Allerton was home to the 'Grand Old Duke of York', Prince Frederick Augustus, brother of George IV. He ordered the construction of a Temple of Victory at the top of man-made, 60m (200ft) Allerton Hill. The legions of workers he employed were said to have resembled an army of ants as they toiled up and down. The duke made his home here from 1786 to 1789, employing Henry Holland to rebuild a house begun as the ancestral home of Lord Mowbray in the 13th century. In 1805 it was bought by the 17th Baron Stourton, whose son commissioned George Martin to rebuild it once more, from 1843, in the Gothic style.

The baronial hall is one of the loftiest in England. A great feature of the main staircase is a carved rosewood elephant from the palace of the Maharajah of Mysore. A blue Venetian glass chandelier that hangs in the silk-damask-lined Drawing Room, reflected in vast rococo mirrors, is said to have an identical twin in the Doges Palace in Venice. The Gerald Arthur Rolph Foundation for Historic Preservation and Education nurtures this important building. The Temple of Victory on which the duke's 'ten thousand men' worked, can be seen from the A1.
▶ *HG5 0SE. 4 miles E of Knaresborough on A59. Close to Junction 47 of A1(M). Open for tours on Wednesdays and bank holidays in season.*

⑫ Beningbrough Hall

Big Whigs in big wigs look down from the walls of the dining room in this baroque 18th-century redbrick mansion. These are 20 of Sir Godfrey Kneller's 48 portraits of members of the Kit-Kat Club – statesmen, writers, intellectuals – painted between 1702 and 1717 and loaned to Beningbrough and the National Trust by the National Portrait Gallery. More work by Kneller can be seen in the Drawing Room. Over a door is a portrait of John Bourchier, who married Mary Bellwood, his childhood sweetheart, on his return from the Grand Tour in 1705 and commissioned William Thornton to rebuild his family house as a redbrick Queen Anne mansion for himself and his bride. Entrance is into a hallway rising over two storeys with soaring pilasters and vaulted ceiling, a work of sheer grandeur. Visitors see a canopied state bed draped with red damask, tapestries, sculpture and everywhere more paintings. The Kit-Kat Club had special toasting glasses that they would raise in honour of beautiful women. A toast, then, for Mary Bourchier, whose

portrait hangs above the door of the State Bedchamber in an ornate carved surround. A walled kitchen garden supplies produce to the Walled Garden Restaurant.
▶ *YO30 1DD. 7 miles NW of York on minor roads off A19. NT. Seasonal opening.*

⑬ Duncombe Park

When Sir Charles Duncombe bought the Helmsley estate in 1689, he acquired the spectacular ruins of Helmsley Castle and Rievaulx Abbey. This is one of the most impressive landscapes in England. At its heart is a palatial house built by William Wakefield for Sir Charles's niece and her husband, after they inherited the property in 1711. Wakefield was no doubt influenced in his design by John Vanbrugh, who was at that time at work on Castle Howard (see page 172). Service wings were added by Sir Charles Barry in 1843–6, and in 1895 the interiors were made over in French Empire style by William Young after a disastrous fire. The house is now used as a wedding and events venue.

For Thomas Duncombe III, who inherited the estate in 1746 and made the Grand Tour, the dreamy remains of Rievaulx were a 'Heaven-sent' gift as a Picturesque feature. In 1758 he laid out a terrace with a temple at each end, one a 'Tuscan' rotunda, the other rectangular, Ionic, designed for banqueting. The temples are maintained by the National Trust, which offers guided tours of the Ionic temple.
▶ *YO62 5EB. 1 mile SW of Helmsley off A170. Summer opening of park and gardens (closed on Saturdays).*

⑭ Sledmere House

Georgian elegance was restored here in the 20th century after a fire gutted the house. Sledmere was begun by Richard Sykes in the mid 1700s, but was largely the creation of Sir Christopher Sykes in the 1780s and 1790s. He was a wealthy MP for Beverley, and his wife Mary was heiress to a large fortune, so they were able to spend lavishly on their house and to expand their estate.

The catastrophic fire broke out in 1911. The First World War took up the energies of Sir Mark Sykes, 6th Baronet, an expert on the Middle East, author, MP and founder of the Wagoners Special Reserve, which recruited men from the Wold to serve their country in foreign fields. He died of influenza aged 39, in 1919, and when the 7th Baronet, Sir Richard Sykes, came of age in 1926, he ordered a complete restoration in absolute faith to the Georgian age, with ornate plasterwork, Adam-style ceilings, statuary, paintings, family portraits, swags and drapes. A tiny museum dedicated to the Wagoners is set up at the entrance to Sledmere. The park was landscaped by Capability Brown. Sir Tatton Sykes, 8th Baronet, proclaims his home 'not just an institutional showpiece but a country house fulfilling its original purpose as a magnificent jewel at the centre of a thriving rural estate'.

▶ *YO25 3XG. 8 miles NW of Driffield at junction of B1251, B1252 and B1253. Seasonal opening.*

⑮ Hovingham Hall

Thomas Worsley had a passion for horses. The entrance to his Palladian house was through a riding school flanked by stables and leading to a dismounting hall. Worsley taught George III to ride and in 1760 became his Surveyor General to the Board of Works. He made his own designs for his mansion, overlooking the fact that human and horse cannot live at quite such close quarters. Stables do not smell of roses, and they had to be moved to the courtyard. The riding school must have been really something in its day, with a Tuscan screen and loggia at either end, for spectators to watch those well-mannered beasts perform their piaffes, passages and pirouettes. The Samson Hall, where riders once dismounted, has vaults of stone supported on Doric columns.

Hovingham's art collection contains works by Van Dyck, Poussin and Boucher. Murals in the ballroom are by Sebastiano Ricci and Giovanni Cipriani. Cricket has been played on the lawn in front of the house since 1858, when the Hovingham team took on an All England XI. England won. Yorkshire cricketers Herbert Sutcliffe, Len Hutton, Freddie Trueman and Geoff Boycott have all played here. The present owner is Thomas Worsley's 'great, great, great, great, great grandson'. The Duchess of Kent was born Katharine Worsley at Hovingham in 1933.

▶ *YO62 4JX. 9 miles W of Malton on B1257. Open in June.*

SLEDMERE HOUSE

16 Castle Howard

'Nobody had informed me that I should at one view see a palace, a town, a fortified city, temples on high places, woods worthy of being each a metropolis of the Druids … the noblest lawn in the world fenced by half the horizon …' For Horace Walpole this palatial mansion was 'sublime'. Its architect, John Vanbrugh – Whig, poet, playwright, creator of the English baroque style – was a young man when he was approached by Charles Howard, 3rd Earl of Carlisle, a fellow member of the intellectual London Kit-Kat Club, to rebuild his ancient family castle as a pleasure palace in which to entertain in style. This was the first house Vanbrugh built. It took a leap of faith on Howard's part, but there is nothing tentative about Castle Howard. With the assistance of Nicholas Hawksmoor, Vanbrugh began work in 1700, liberally adorning his creation with urns, cherubs, coronets, statues, Doric and Corinthian pilasters, under a magnificent dome.

The building that Walpole saw in 1772 was not entirely to Vanbrugh's plan. After the death of Charles Howard in 1738, with the project incomplete, his son-in-law engaged Sir Thomas Robinson to build the west wing in the fashionable Palladian style. This dissonance makes some people wince, but Castle Howard is nonetheless a great spectacle, a pale gold stone masterpiece filled with antiques and art treasures, overlooking a gentle English landscape. From 1845 to 1950 it was served by its own railway. In 2011, the Howard family celebrated the 30th anniversary of the BBC's *Brideshead Revisited*, in which their stately home played a starring role. It was, however, an impostor. For the 'real' Brideshead, the visitor must go to Worcestershire (see Madresfield Court, page 140).

▶ YO60 7DA. *6 miles SW of Malton on minor roads off A64. Seasonal opening.*

17 Burton Agnes Hall

Robert Smythson was, according to his tombstone, 'architector and survayor' of 'diverse and most worthy houses of great account'. Burton Agnes is one of them. It was begun in the last years of the Golden Age of the reign of Elizabeth I, in pinkish-red brick, with stone dressings, its bowed and bay projections displaying Smythson's characteristic use of symmetry and light. No great drive or avenue approaches it. The visitor mounts steps from the village and passes under a three-storey Tudor gatehouse to find this gem.

Burton Agnes has been in the same family since 1598, when it was built for Sir Henry Griffith. It has passed down through the male and female lines, to Griffiths, Boyntons and Cunliffe-Listers. Much of the original carving and plasterwork survives. In the Great Hall the screen is carved with biblical, allegorical and mythological figures; the alabaster chimneypiece depicts the Wise and Foolish Virgins – the foolish

ones clearly have a far better time. In the King's Room a canopied bed is still draped with its original blue damask hangings. The Long Gallery runs the length of the house on the third floor with views to Bridlington Bay. Palladian windows at each end were a Georgian addition. Works by Cezanne, Corot, Gauguin, Matisse, Renoir and Pissarro are displayed alongside recent commissions, such as a Kaffe Fassett tapestry, furniture by John Makepiece and a glass sculpture by Colin Reid. Pictures by Gainsborough and Reynolds hang in the Georgian dining room. A walled garden contains more than 4,000 species of plant. There are herbaceous borders, a jungle garden, woodland walks and a maze.

▶ *YO25 4NB. 7 miles NE of Driffield on A614. Seasonal daily opening.*

⓲ Burton Constable Hall

William Constable was an amateur geologist, botanist and zoologist, an avid collector, patron of the arts, bon vivant and martyr to gout. He made three Grand Tours in the late 18th century, pocketing shells and fossils, buying art. The family seat of the Constables, Lords Paramount of the Seignory of Holderness, appears at first to be a typically fine redbrick Elizabethan mansion, but, above all, it is William's influence that pervades the house.

There have been Constables here since the 12th century, recusant Catholics who somehow managed to keep their heads and hang on to their estate. The house stands in an isolated situation amid Capability Brown parkland. It received its Elizabethan façade in around 1560. In the Georgian period an attic floor was added, along with two bays, topped with domes, and a central door and frontispiece crowned with the Constable coat of arms. The interiors are mostly 18th century. The visitor steps into the Great Hall, remodelled for William Constable by Timothy Lightoler in 1763 in neo-Jacobean style. Hercules and Demosthenes, in niches, flank the fireplace. A painting of William and his sister Winifred shows them in the garb of ancient Rome. The dining room is a celebration of Bacchus, god of wine. The Ballroom was designed by James Wyatt, and features furniture by Thomas Chippendale. In the upstairs Long Gallery, under a Victorian neo-Jacobean moulded ceiling, are 13 elm and mahogany bookcases, commissioned by William's father, Cuthbert, to accommodate his library. Visitors see William's 'Cabinet of Curiosities', his scientific implements, ammonites, rocks and minerals. There are 30 treasure-filled rooms to explore, revealing endless surprises. The house and collections are run by a trust and Leeds City Council, but the family still live in one wing.

▶ *HU11 4LN. 9 miles NE of Hull off B1238. Seasonal opening.*

CASTLE HOWARD

Wales

From Marcher fortresses to rambling manors caught
in time, the houses of Wales offer a glimpse of the
grand life, and of the world below stairs. Fantasy
is never far away, with castles built by aristocrats
who let their imaginations run riot.

KEY

1 Main entry
County boundary
Motorway
Principal A road

Holyhead

Anglesey

Rhyl

Llandudno

Bangor

1 2

3

A55

Caernarfon

Mold

A470

Betws-y-Coed

A494

A5

Wrexham

Snowdonia
National
Park

Porthmadog

4

A487

A499

Llangollen

5

6

Bala

A494

Dolgellau

A458

Welshpool

10

NORTH and MID WALES
176-183

Machynlleth

A483

Newtown

Aberystwyth

A44

LLangurig

A470

8

Cambrian
Mountains

Llandrindod
Wells

A44

A487

A485

A483

Builth
Wells

Cardigan

A470

A438

Fishguard

Llandovery

Black
Mountains

A 40

9 Brecon

SOUTH WALES
184-187

Pembrokeshire Coast
National Park

Brecon
Beacons
National Park

7

A479

Carmarthen

3 Llandeilo

Haverfordwest

A40

A48

Abergavenny
Monmouth

A4076

Milford
Haven

A477

A465

Merthyr
Tydfil

A449

Chepstow

Tenby

Llanelli

A470

A4042

M48

Neath

Newport

Swansea

Port
Talbot

2

5

Bridgend

M4

Cardiff

1

4

NORTH & MID WALES

Castles and halls with their roots set firmly in the past stand amid a blaze of colour from spring to autumn. Imaginative gardens, a tribute to the skill of their creators, thrive in this spectacular landscape.

❶ Plas Newydd, Anglesey

Henry Paget, 5th Marquis of Anglesey, squandered millions on bejewelled costumes, pink poodles and a car that emitted patchouli-scented exhaust fumes. Known as 'Toppy' and 'the dancing marquis', for his impromptu, sinuous, suggestive snake dance, Paget converted the chapel at Plas Newydd into the 150 seat Gaiety Theatre. He cast himself in the lead role of Oscar Wilde's *An Ideal Husband*, but for his wife he was far from ideal. His marriage to his cousin Lily was not consummated, and ended in November 1900, by which time he had run up vast debts. Henry died aged 30 and was succeeded by his cousin, Charles Paget, 6th Marquis.

The house that Charles inherited is breathtakingly situated on the shores of the Menai Strait with views of Snowdonia. It was built by James Wyatt in the 1790s, blending the Classical style with Wyatt's trademark Gothic.

The new marquis sold the furniture and the family's other ancestral homes to pay off creditors. Since 1976 Plas Newydd has been owned by the National Trust, although the 7th Marquis retains rooms. The Trust presents it with its 1930s interior and invites visitors to explore the life lived by Charles Paget, his wife, Marjorie, and their six children – days of leisure and pleasure spent swimming, playing tennis, flying kites and making home movies. A unique feature here is Rex Whistler's largest painting on canvas, measuring 18 x 3.7m (58 x 12ft), an Italianate coastal landscape, executed in 1936–7. Whistler included himself in the work, as Romeo, gazing up at Juliet, a likeness of Lady Caroline, the Marquis's daughter, socialite and actress, with whom he had fallen in love. The spring garden, summer terrace and Australasian arboretum complement the idyllic setting.

▶ *LL61 6DQ. 3 miles SW of Menai Bridge on A4080. NT. Seasonal opening.*

THE COOK'S SITTING ROOM, PENRHYN CASTLE

❷ Penrhyn Castle, Gwynned

The term 'mock castle' does not do justice to what has been described as an 'outstanding instance of Norman revival' – grand, picturesque, audacious. Penrhyn began life as a fortified manor for Ednyfed Fychan. Ioan ap Gruffued obtained a licence to crenellate in 1438, founded a stone castle and added a tower house. The edifice was rebuilt in the 1780s by Samuel Wyatt, in Gothic style. Thomas Hopper, a favourite of George IV's, transformed it in 1820–40 for George Hay Dawkins-Pennant, changing it beyond recognition, but keeping an original spiral staircase and vaulted basement. The interiors are rich but restrained, reflecting Norman tastes, and among specially designed pieces of furniture is a 1 tonne slate bed built for Queen Victoria when she came to stay in 1859. There are 150 rooms, with some fine carving and plasterwork, and an art collection that includes paintings by Rembrandt, Gainsborough and Canaletto. Kitchens and servants' quarters are presented as they were in the late 19th century. The stable block houses a model railway and dolls' museum. Within the surrounding grounds and park there is a Victorian walled garden in which tropical plants flourish.
▶ *LL57 4HN. 1 mile E of Bangor off A5. NT. Seasonal opening (closed on Tuesdays).*

❸ Bodnant Garden, Conwy

Henry Davis Pochin, a Victorian entrepreneur, created the 55m (180ft) laburnum arch at Bodnant – and invented a way to produce coloured soap. He bought the Bodnant estate in 1875, and transformed the 18th-century house into a romantic, wisteria-draped mansion. It rises dreamily out of the trees and looks down upon terraced acres. Pochin's grandson, Henry McLaren, 2nd Lord Aberconwy, spent 50 years developing the garden at Bodnant. Five generations have tended and added to it. Plants from all over the world have been grown here from seed. From daffodil time to the blaze of autumn, Bodnant is glorious, its pleasures enhanced by the backdrop of Snowdonia. There are sweeping lawns, ponds, shrubs and borders. The Hiraethlyn stream skitters and glitters in the shade of the Dell with its wild garden and 200-year-old trees. The tallest coastal Giant Redwood in the UK soars heavenward. At the heart of the garden is 'The Poem', the family mausoleum, truly a place to rest in peace.
▶ *LL28 5RE. 7 miles S of Llandudno Junction off A470. NT. Seasonal opening.*

❹ Plas Brondanw Gardens, Gwynned

'Nothing, just then, could possibly have been more ecstatically welcomed by me ... The guardianship of a rambling old Carolean Plas set in a wildly romantic little estate among the Welsh mountains, that had been held by my family for over four centuries, was well calculated to inflame me.' Clough Williams-Ellis was recalling the day in 1908 when his father, the Reverend John Ellis, unexpectedly handed him ownership of this house and estate. After the First World War, Clough and his new wife, Amabel Strachey, made Brondanw their family home, and Clough set about restoring house and gardens.

He is best known for his Italianate model village, Portmeirion, but the garden he created is perhaps a greater achievement. This was truly a labour of love, which continued until his death, aged 95. 'It was for Brondanw's sake that I worked and stinted,' he recalled, 'for its sake that I chiefly hoped to prosper.' He had a singular gift for landscape design – and Snowdonia was a gift to him. Vistas open up towards the soaring peaks. Dramatic and romantic prospects come into view. Inspiration was drawn from Italy, with stone walls, trees and avenues. The garden is divided into a series of 'rooms', each surrounded by topiary. The visitor to this transcendently beautiful place may be reminded of Dorothy Frances Gurney's words, 'One is nearer God's heart in a garden/Than anywhere else on earth.'
▶ *LL48 6SW. 5 miles NE of Porthmadog at junction of A4085 and B4410. Open all year.*

❺ Chirk Castle, Wrexham

A formidable Marcher fortress on the estuary of the River Ceiriog, built in the reign of Edward I, is today a magnificent stately home. In 1595, the castle was bought by Thomas Myddelton for £5,000. His son, also Thomas, was a Sergeant-Major-General in the Civil War, and in 1643 his castle was seized by Royalists in his absence. Thus, on December 21, 1644, he found himself attacking his own stronghold. His heart cannot have been in it, for on Christmas Day Prince Rupert of the Rhine wrote that he had beaten Myddelton off. In 1659 Sir Thomas joined Charles Booth's 'Cheshire Rising' against Richard Cromwell, and his castle was slighted. Upon the Restoration of the Monarchy the castle curtain wall and five semi-circular towers were rebuilt, and a new stone range was added, including the first-floor Long Gallery, with an arcaded walkway overlooking the courtyard.

This is the last of Edward's border castles – built to subdue and overawe the Welsh – still lived in today. Visitors see the Myddeltons' grand 18th-century state apartments, the servants' hall, laundry and dungeons. The gardens, landscaped by William Eames (also spelt Emes) from 1764, are Chirk's great glory, with sculpted yews, herbaceous borders, shrub and rock gardens. The terrace affords views over the plains of Cheshire and Shropshire. The parkland is approached through ornate wrought-iron gates made in 1719 to present a grand entrance to the castle forecourt. They are by the Davies brothers, Robert and John, of Wrexham – whose work architectural historian Nikolaus Pevsner described as 'miraculous' – and incorporate the Myddelton coat of arms, complete with 'bloody hand'.
▶ *LL14 5AF. 8 miles S of Wrexham on A5. NT. Seasonal opening of castle and gardens; park open all year.*

❻ Erddig Hall, Wrexham

'A family who never threw anything away', the Yorkes lived here for seven generations and their home is a place of endless fascination. When Philip S. Yorke handed the estate to the 'National Distrust' in 1973, he stipulated that everything must be kept in place.

Erddig was begun as a nine-bay, redbrick house by Thomas Webb in the 1680s. John Meller, Master of the Chancery, bought it in 1718 and enlarged it. On his death in 1733, it passed to his nephew Simon Yorke. Meller's furniture and possessions remain in the house to this day. Simon's son Philip, author of *The Royal Tribes of Wales* (1799), further remodelled the building, and created a 'Tribes Room' in the basement with painted coats of arms over the fireplace. From the age of five he had 'chused chiefly to dine on vegetables', and many of the Yorkes were vegetarian. They had a passion for antiquities, resisted modern conveniences, and retained a unique series of paintings and verse portraits of their servants.

In the Music Room, visitors see a Gothic organ, a Swiss musical box, a Regency harp-lute – a small instrument suitable for ladies to play – and a portrait of 'Hanging Judge Jeffries' together with one of his brother Thomas. Family portraits include one of Philip by Gainsborough. There is Chinese wallpaper in the State Bedroom. The grand New Kitchen, with a lovely Venetian window, further reveals the employers' unusual regard for their staff. A laundry, bakehouse, stables, sawmill, smithy and joinery, ancient cars and bicycles provide further diversions. The park

was landscaped by William Eames in 1768–9. In the large walled garden are ancient varieties of fruit trees, and, appropriately, the national collection of ivies.
▶ *LL13 0YT. 2 miles S of Wrexham town centre. NT. Open all year.*

❼ Treberfyd House, Powys

A fine example of Victorian Gothic architecture, between the Black Mountains and the Brecon Beacons, has been home to the Raikes family since it was built. Robert Raikes was heir to a banking fortune. He could have lived the high life but chose to retreat to this small village and build a house, church and school. While at university he had been impressed by the Tractarian, or Oxford, Movement, and he was on a mission to bring High Anglican worship to the Methodist Welsh. John Loughborough Pearson was his designer, a disciple of 'God's architect' Augustus Pugin, and his trio of buildings have been described as 'Tractarian Utopia'.

The house, featuring battlements, pointy gables, tall chimneys, mullioned windows and gargoyles, overlooks 4.5ha (11 acres) of garden laid out by W.A. Nesfield, with lawns, herbaceous borders and woodland. The interior retains such features as carved stone fireplaces, oak staircases and stained-glass windows. A portrait of Charles II was given to a loyal Raikes ancestor after the Restoration. Visitors see a typical Victorian house with school room, scullery, nursery, billiards room and rear service stairs. There are pieces of Gothic oak furniture designed by Loughborough, and a secret passageway. Outside, surviving parts of Nesfield's design include the Long Walk, from the croquet lawn to a walled kitchen garden, then back to the house. The North American Sequoias and Cedar of Lebanon he planted are in their glory. Tours are conducted by the family.
▶ *LD3 7PX. 7 miles SE of Brecon on minor roads off A40. Seasonal opening for guided tours, and at other times by appointment.*

❽ Abbey-Cwm-Hir Hall, Powys

Paul and Victoria Humpherston promise visitors 'tours of enchantment' at 'The Abbey in the Long Valley', and they do not disappoint. A triumph of the Victorian Gothic revival, Abbey-Cwm-Hir was built in 1834 by Thomas Wilson, a London lawyer, poet, art collector and connoisseur. Around it he created gardens and pleasure grounds overlooking the ruins of a dissolved Cistercian abbey, final resting place of Llewellyn the Last. Sadly, Wilson

THE LIBRARY, ERDDIG HALL

Bathing in the spotlight

Bathroom arrangements exert an endless fascination, from Tudor privies to Edwardian luxury via the odd power shower.

Sir John Harrison, anxious for the favour of his godmother Elizabeth I, designed for her a 'better ajax', a 'privie in perfection' – England's first flushing lavatory. Harrison's design of 1595 shows fish swimming in a 'cesterne', a 'little washer', 'wast pipe', 'seate boord', 'stoole pot', 'stopple', 'current' and 'sluce'. In his instructions for its use he exhorts: '... the vault into which it falles: always remember that at noone and at night, emptie it, and leave it halfe a foote deepe in fayre water. And this being well done, and orderly kept, your worst privie may be as sweet as your best chamber.'

The Roman invaders brought their high standards of cleanliness to Britain, but those ideas didn't catch on. The history of English hygiene is an unedifying one. In medieval times great houses might have privies or 'garderobes', but they emptied into pits or drains via shafts that soon became foul. By the time of Elizabeth I's reign the 'close stool' had been introduced. This was a box containing a removable receptacle to be emptied by a servant. However, the queen deplored the stench from these contraptions – hence Harrison's invention, but his water closets did not solve the problem of the stink of cess pits, often situated beneath castle floors. Before the introduction of the 'S' bend, they would not have smelt at all sweet. Earth closets were preferred. Not until 1775 did Alexander Cummings obtain a patent for a flushing toilet with a water trap in the sewer pipe.

A bigger splash

William Cavendish, 1st Duke of Devonshire, had a rare 'bathing room' built at Chatsworth in Derbyshire. Celia Fiennes, on her travels by side-saddle, reported seeing it in 1697, relating that 'the bath is one entire marble all white finely veined with blue and is made smooth ... it was as deep as one's middle on the outside and you went down steps into the bath big enough for two people; at the upper end are two cocks to let in one hot the other cold water ... the windows are all private glass'.

Cavendish was way ahead of his time. A ball in the Georgian era may have been a glittering affair, but even high society was not big on washing. The seductive fluttering of fans had as much to do with dispersing smells as keeping cool. Washing became more popular in the Regency period. The Prince Regent had an en-suite bathroom installed at Brighton Pavilion in Sussex; this was the first house in the country to have running water, piped from the beach. Sea bathing also came into vogue and bathing machines were introduced. At Chatsworth, meanwhile, the 'Bachelor Duke', the 6th Duke of Devonshire, updated the facilities, with plunge pools lined with the marble from the 1st Duke's bathing room. However, it was more usual to step into a hip bath, filled by servants from cans of hot water, although cold and draughty mansions were not conducive to stripping off.

Hot and cold

In the Victorian era, hot and cold running water were available and modest provisions of bathrooms were made, but hip baths and the bedroom washstand with china jug and bowl remained the convention. When the eccentric family at Erddig in Wrexham introduced a bamboo-effect tin shower, it was novel enough to be the subject of a *Punch* cartoon in 1851. Captioned 'Domestic Sanitary Regulations', it portrayed children swathed in towels, cold and reluctant, lining up to be sluiced down as a servant filled the overhead receptacle. There is a similar shower in the bathhouse at Wimpole Hall in Cambridgeshire. These are primitive affairs compared with the power shower installed at Kinloch Castle on the Isle of Rum in the 1890s.

Turkish baths were a Victorian craze. The Prince of Wales frequented the hamam on Jermyn Street. Lord Armstrong, the 'modern magician' at Cragside in Northumberland, had one built for him by Norman Shaw, complete with bath suite, a room for cooling and a plunge pool with a shower. The prince used it when he came to visit this extraordinary house.

Bathrooms became more common from the 1920s. Over decades, the erratic plumbing in the English country house became something of a joke. In his song 'The Stately Homes of England' Noel Coward wrote 'the pipes that supply the bathroom burst/And the lavatory makes you fear the worst'. However, their dimensions are often sublime, since bathrooms occupied spaces formerly put to other use. In *Brideshead Revisited*, his fictional evocation of Madresfield Court in Worcestershire, Evelyn Waugh writes of a bathroom that had once been a dressing room, in which watercolours were dimmed by steam and towels, on the back of an armchair, were warmed by the fire. 'I often think of that bathroom ... and contrast it with the uniform, clinical, little chambers, glittering with chromium-plate and looking-glass, which pass for luxury in the modern world.'

THE SHOWER, ERDDIG

overspent on his creation, a business venture failed, and he sailed for Australia, where he prospered and became Mayor of Adelaide.

In 1869, the Philips family doubled the size of Wilson's house, making it a dwelling of 52 rooms, including a snooker room with a stained-glass ceiling. Stained glass is also to be found over the main staircase. The snooker room explores the theme of Arthurian legend; bathrooms are themed to trains, castles and the 1930s; bedrooms to schooldays, the seaside and transport. There are rococo ceilings, Gothic windows, bell pulls and shutters, marble fireplaces, clocks, lamps, books, mirrors, paintings and statuary. The entrance hall has a dazzling mosaic tiled floor. The south-facing gardens contain a lake and waterfall, specimen trees brought from Regent's Park, and a walled garden incorporating some of the stones from the original abbey. This has been a prodigious rescue operation by the Humpherstons, who bought the Hall in 1997 and set about a ten-year programme to restore the building and the ravaged, weed-choked gardens. The setting is glorious. Tours are conducted by family and friends.

▶ *LD1 6PH. 9 miles N of Llandrindod Wells on minor roads off A483. Open all year for guided tours, booking advised.*

9 Abercamlais, Powys

For 400 years home to generations of parsons and squires, this originally medieval house was rebuilt in the 1720s in the Georgian style, rare in Wales. It is the westerly of two family mansions that sit side by side in parkland on the River Usk, at the northern edge of the

Brecon Beacons National Park. The interiors have fine period furniture and panelling. An octagonal dovecote serves as a bridge over the Camlais stream. It used to house a privy. A 17th-century stone bridge also spans the river. Mature beech and oak woods protect against prevailing winds. Private tours of the house are offered and there are delightful woodland and riverside walks.

▶ *LD3 8EY. 7 miles W of Brecon on A40. Open in summer, by appointment.*

10 Powis Castle and Gardens, Powys

The seat of the Earl of Powys dominates a rocky ridge, surrounded by terraces, baroque gardens, parkland and a deer park. 'The Red Castle' (not to be confused with Castell Coch, see page 186) has frequently played host to kings and queens since the reign of Charles II. Prince Charles has lodged here when visiting the Royal Welsh Show, and is reported to consider it one of the most beautiful castles in the country.

The original castle of 'Pole' was a stronghold of a dynasty of Welsh princes until 1266. It was remodelled as a grand country mansion in the reign of Elizabeth I. In the Civil War, Piercy, Lord Powys, declared for the king, fortified the building and took personal command.

His stronghold came under siege by Sir Thomas Myddelton, who had his own problems at Chirk (see page 177), and Powys was afterwards slighted to prevent further military use.

The red sandstone edifice that has grown up around the medieval stone keep has been preserved by continuous occupation over centuries by generations of Herberts and Clives. The Clive Museum exhibits artefacts collected in the 18th century by Edward Clive, eldest son of Clive of India, who married Lady Henrietta Herbert, daughter of Lord Powys, in 1784. Her portrait, by Reynolds, is on display, as is Kneller's Charles II. The Long Gallery is lined with baroque marble sculpture. Visitors see rich panelling, tapestries and paintings. The gardens emulate French and Italian styles, with terraces, statuary, balustrades and clipped yews.

▶ *SY21 8RF. 1 mile S of Welshpool off A458. NT. Seasonal opening of castle, museum and gardens.*

POWIS CASTLE

SOUTH WALES

Near ruins transformed into Gothic fantasies, a medieval manor turned into a pre-First World War home, two can-do visionaries and an eccentric viscount – delving into the past in these old houses is richly rewarding.

❶ Cardiff Castle

John Patrick Crichton-Stuart, 3rd Marquis of Bute, was a keen medievalist and rich beyond the dreams of avarice. The Butes had helped to transform Cardiff into 'the coal metropolis of the world'. In 1865 the 3rd Marquis also began to transform its crumbling castle, unleashing William Burges upon it. The result was Burges's most important work, a creation of unbelievable lavishness. Not an inch is unornamented; the visitor's head spins.

Burges was an eccentric and childlike character, overindulgent, flamboyant. He smoked opium, wore fancy dress, and was in thrall to the values of a utopian medieval England. He also had a sense of humour. Everywhere his high spirits find expression in the sumptuously decorated interiors, with gildings, carvings and allegorical murals. In Lord Bute's bedroom, biblical scenes explore the life of John the Evangelist, under a mirrored ceiling. The Winter Smoking Room in the Clock Tower is adorned with figures of ladies and gentlemen hunting and skating. At the top of the tower, in the double-height Summer Smoking Room, couples court beneath a starry vaulted ceiling and above a zodiac tiled floor.

Burges's fascination with Moorish design is in evidence in the spectacular Arab Room. 'The most dazzling exponent of the High Victorian dream' was overseeing works at Cardiff when he caught a chill. He returned to London, half paralysed, to die. A Latin inscription on a marble overmantel succinctly translates as: 'John, Marquis of Bute built this in 1881. William Burges designed it.'

A short walk from castle and city centre are Bute Park, mature parkland by the River Taff, Sophia Gardens and Pontcanna fields.

▶ *CF10 3RB (satnav). Castle Street, Cardiff city centre. Open all year.*

3RD MARQUIS OF BUTE'S BEDROOM, CARDIFF CASTLE

❷ Castell Coch, Cardiff

Here is another Bute-Burges extravaganza, the 'Red Castle', smaller than Cardiff, but more romantically situated, its fairytale round towers rising above the trees. Work was begun in 1875 on transforming this 13th-century stronghold, although Cardiff Castle was far from complete. Lady Bute's domed and circular bedchamber is a tour de force, painted with monkeys, birds and pomegranates. Her spectacular medieval bed is adorned with crystal balls. In the Dining Hall, murals portray the fate of early Christian martyrs.

The double-height octagonal Drawing Room has decorations exploring the themes of nature's fecundity and the fragility of life. Butterflies and birds cavort under a rib-vaulted roof. A fireplace by Thomas Nicholls portrays the Three Fates and the Thread of Life. The thread of Burges's life was cut when he was just 53, as Bute's would be at the same age in 1900. The energy, vision and ambition of these two Victorian obsessives almost defy comprehension. How much they achieved in such a short span!

▶ *CF15 7JS. Signposted off A470 Merthyr Tydfil road (M4, Junction 32). CADW. Open all year.*

FAIRYTALE ROUND TOWERS RISE ABOVE THE TREES
CASTELL COCH

❸ Dinefwr Park and Newton House, Carmarthenshire

'Nature has been truly bountiful,' exclaimed Lancelot Brown, as he surveyed a scene of water meadows, gentle hills and a medieval castle rising above venerable trees. The great landscaper, usually so quick to see the 'capabilities' of a place, could suggest only small improvements to an 18th-century park created by George Rice and his wife, Cecil. Dinefwr is the ancient seat of the Lords Rhys, rulers of the medieval kingdom of Deheuberth, from whom the Lords Dynevor are descended. Their castle is a ruin but stands as a symbol of Welsh pride and defiance.

Newton House, a 15th-century manor house at the site, was seized by Henry VII, and rebuilt in the 1660s by Edward Rice and his brother Walter. In the 1850s it was given a fashionable Gothic facelift and acquired a fountain garden. The late Richard Rhys, 9th Lord Dynevor, inherited the baronial pile in 1962 along with accumulated death duties. The house was sold in 1974, passed through various hands and was in a state of decay in 1990 when it was acquired by the National Trust, which already owned the park. Newton House is now offered as 'a hands-on experience' and presented as it would have been before the First World War. The park, with waymarked walks, is grazed by fallow deer and an ancient herd of wild white cattle brought over by the Romans. Some of the trees are 700 years old.
▶ *SA19 6RT. 1 mile W of Llandeilo off A40. NT. Open all year.*

❹ Fonmon Castle, Vale of Glamorgan

'We cannot longer have this country ruled from a small castle in Wales.' In the eleven years of the Commonwealth, from 1649, Colonel Philip Jones of Fonmon, an ancestor of the present owner, Sir Brooke Boothby, was Oliver Cromwell's right-hand man. As his influence increased, one English MP was heard to lament that Colonel Jones was running England from his seat in the Vale of Glamorgan.

The castle's history stretches back into the hazy mists of Norman England, and the building is still lived in today. It has, of course, been much altered and extended. In the 18th century Robert Jones hired Thomas Paty of Bristol to modernise it, creating a library/salon that ran the width of the first floor. Gilded mirrors were hung and rococo plasterwork created by Thomas Stocking to a design by Thomas Johnson. Light flooded in

through new sash windows. The old watchtower in the grounds was restored as a folly tower. When improvements were complete, Jones erected a sundial on the south tower to celebrate. He was a man who liked to celebrate, enjoying London's social life to the full, and investing in racehorses. As a consequence, parts of the estate had to be sold to pay his debts.

Visitors see Georgian interiors on a relatively homely scale, family portraits and the 17th-century kitchen, the ceiling of which is supported by massive oak beams. The gardens have been created from the castle's outer defences.
▶ *CF62 3ZN. 5 miles W of Barry on B4265. Limited seasonal opening.*

❺ Tredegar House and Gardens, Newport

The Morgans, Lords Tredegar, were, said the Duke of Bedford, 'the oddest family I have ever met'. Evan Frederic Morgan, 2nd Viscount Tredegar (1893–1949), was a poet and Privy Chamberlain of Sword and Cape to Popes Benedict XV and Pius XI – and at Tredegar he kept a menagerie that included a boxing kangaroo, honey bear and baboons. The house parties he held here were attended by his fellow occultist Aleister Crowley, H.G. Wells, Aldous Huxley and Augustus John.

Tredegar was the Morgans' family seat for 500 years. In 1664–72, William Morgan rebuilt an earlier stone house in red brick, on a palatial scale, with an enfilade of state rooms, for himself and his heiress wife and distant cousin, Blanche Morgan. The choice of brick made a statement about the family's wealth and ambition. The baronetcy died out in 1962 with the death of the childless 6th Baron. The house had been sold in 1951 and the contents dispersed, but the visitor would not know it. From 1974 Tredegar was cared for by Newport Council and a charity. It is now managed by the National Trust, and presented with period furniture, some original to the house and reacquired. The baroque interiors display superb carving. Ornate iron gates were an 18th-century addition. In February 2012 the Gilt Room was used as a film set for the BBC's *Upstairs Downstairs*. There are formal gardens and a park. At 22, Captain Godfrey Morgan survived the Charge of the Light Brigade at Balaclava. His horse, Sir Briggs, also survived, and lived on here to the age of 28. There is a monument to him in the Cedar Garden, where he was buried with full military honours.
▶ *NP10 8YW. 2 miles SW of Newport city centre close to Junction 28 of M4. NT. Seasonal opening.*

wales

Upstairs, downstairs, in my lady's chamber

Great country houses now thrown open to public gaze reveal a way of life that was the norm for many not so long ago.

So that a rich élite should live in conspicuous luxury, legions of servants had to be engaged. Labour was cheap, and men and women were not only willing to toil for a small wage, but even felt privileged to attend the nobility. In 1901 a scullery maid might earn just £12 a year, but she was provided with bed and board and a uniform, when the alternative might have been the workhouse.

Life below stairs was rigidly hierarchical. An 'army' of servants had its officer class, including the housekeeper and ladies' maids, and its lower ranks, all under the command of the generalissimo, the butler. His employers would address him by his surname but he was 'Mr' to the staff, as the housekeeper was 'Mrs', whether married or not.

An endless round of drudgery was the lot of the lowest-paid, some as young as 12 years. They were largely unseen upstairs, and must never be heard. The scullery maid would be up before dawn to heat the range and light fires, while the hall boy emptied chamber pots and polished boots. They would be kept busy until 10pm, seven days a week. Frivolity was strictly forbidden and dismissal without a 'character' was a terrible fear. They used back stairs, and should they meet their employers by chance they would contrive to disappear face-first into the wall. They had to know their place – but in an uncertain world, just having a place gave a measure of security.

In 1901 a butler typically earned £60 (£3,662) a year. It was his responsibility to hire and fire male staff, to take charge of the wine cellar, to announce visitors, to supervise footmen, to open the front door and to close the house up in the evening. The housekeeper, on an annual £45 (£2,746), was in charge of female staff; she kept the larder stocked and, with the cook or chef and the lady of the house, devised menus. A lady's maid, for her annual £32 (£1,953), waited on her mistress hand and foot, dressed her, brushed her hair, laced her corsets and helped her to make the *de rigueur* five or six changes of clothing a day.

Party time

The rich, at the close of the Victorian era and dawn of the Edwardian 'Golden Age', were a decadent and effete class. They lived it up as if they sensed that there was no tomorrow. Especially at their celebrated house parties, they ate for England, starting with breakfast. On offer would be porridge, eggs, bacon, ham, kedgeree, devilled kidneys, game, pressed meats, fresh fruit, scones and more.

It required a military-style operation to cope with an influx of guests. When the Prince of Wales, the future Edward VII, stayed at Penrhyn Castle in Gwynedd in 1894, he was one of 35 guests, all with their personal servants. He was notoriously greedy, insisting upon lobster salad for his tea. Caviar, truffles, snipe, ptarmigan would all be set before him and he seldom ate fewer than 12 courses. Over four days at Penrhyn, more than 1,150 meals were served, including 89 dishes for the prince and other principal guests. Of course, all that gluttony came at a price and such excesses took their toll. The king went six times to Marienbad to 'take the cure'.

All in it together

Two conflicting pictures emerge. The first is of a highly privileged, self-indulgent, snobbish few exploiting a subservient majority. The other, rosier view is of camaraderie – a family atmosphere – below stairs, servants sufficiently nourished and a mutual respect between classes. Neither is entirely true or false. What intrigues us today is the contrast between two symbiotic groups. Those who served below stairs are as much a part of a stately home's story as those whose portraits stare out from drawing-room walls. The National Trust offers insights into the nether world of servants at Charlecote Park in Warwickshire, Felbrigg Hall in Norfolk, Ickworth House in Suffolk, Petworth House in Sussex, Lanhydrock House in Cornwall, and many more.

A question to ponder is how much happier the moneyed employers really were than their servants. In his 1970 book *The Edwardians*, J.B. Priestley suggested that, far from being idle, the rich were enslaved. 'No matter how much money they may have, very few people can face empty days, months, years. If they have no useful work, then they invent useless work. If they have no ordinary duties and responsibilities, then collectively and very solemnly they make up duties and responsibilities ... so fashion and the social round are called in to act as ferocious taskmasters ... Toiling away at pleasure, these drones and butterflies might as well be worker ants.'

PENRHYN CASTLE , BRUSHING ROOM

Scotland

In every restored mansion, refurbished castle and renovated laird's house, the country's turbulent past lies waiting to be discovered. Stirring tales abound, enhanced by architectural prowess and glorious art treasures on show.

Durness

Thurso

Wick

Stornoway

Lewis

NORTH HIGHLANDS AND ISLANDS
214-215

Lairg

4

A99

Ullapool

A835

A9

2 Skye

Portree

Kyle of Lochalsh

3

A87

A87

A887

Loch Ness

Newtonmore

A86

A9

16 Elgin

17 Nairn

Inverness

A96

15 Fraserburgh

13

14

12 Peterhead

A96

A90

18

A95

Cairngorms National Park

Braemar **19**

11 Aberdeen

8 **9**

A93

A82

Mull

1

Mallaig

A830

Fort William

A82

A9

2

Pitlochry

CENTRAL AND NORTHEAST
202-213

7 A90

3

10 Forfar

A92

Oban

A85

Crianlarich

Loch Lomond & The Trossachs National Park

A82

A84 A9

A91

5

6 Perth

Dundee

St Andrews

M90

11

A816

Loch Lomond

A811

4 Stirling

Kirkcaldy

Lochgilphead

Dumbarton

12 **10** Edinburgh

A1

9

8

A78

Glasgow

A737

4

M8

FIFE AND SOUTHEAST
196-201

6 **7**

5

East Kilbride

A70

A702

3 **4** Coldstream

6

Irvine

Kilmarnock

A70

Peebles

1

5

Jedburgh

A68

Ayr **2**

A76

A74

M74

A701

2 Hawick

A7

1

3

Moffat

SOUTHWEST
192-195

A701

A7

Dumfries

Stranraer

A75

A75

SOUTHWEST SCOTLAND

Strategically located, defensive fortresses of past centuries have evolved into elaborate showcases for art and culture, while one Victorian creation majors on faux medieval, astrology and the occult.

CULZEAN CASTLE

❶ Culzean Castle
South Ayrshire

'Brandy for the Parson, 'Baccy for the Clerk./Laces for a lady, letters for a spy,/ And watch the wall my darling, while the Gentlemen go by!' If the Kennedy clan were not smugglers, they must certainly have 'watched the wall' as contraband was stashed in caves beneath their castle in the 1700s. Let us just say that they did well from the wines and spirits business.

Culzean was begun in 1569 as a tower house. By the 1600s it had become a comfortable family home with terraces and pleasure gardens. When Thomas Kennedy, 9th Earl of Cassillis, returned from the Grand Tour in 1750 with an art collection, he ordered improvements, and in the 1770s his brother David, 10th Earl, called in Robert Adam to create a spectacular stately home. 'Cullane' is one of the finest surviving examples of Adam's castle style, standing in a man-made landscape designed to exploit the drama of its clifftop situation. Adam's circular Saloon affords panoramic views, 46m (150ft) above the roiling Firth of Clyde. The cantilevered Oval Staircase is a masterpiece of grace and ingenuity. In the Armoury the display of weaponry, amassed by the flamboyant 12th Earl, is second only to Windsor Castle's. A 1920s lift conveys guests to the second-floor Eisenhower Apartment, offered to America's 34th president in recognition of his role as Supreme Commander of the Allied Forces in Europe in the Second World War, and now run as small, country-house-style hotel.

▶ *KA19 8LE. On A719, 12 miles S of Ayr. NTS. Seasonal daily opening.*

❷ Dumfries House
East Ayrshire

"Tis certainly a great undertaking, perhaps more bold than wise, but necessity has no law!' William Crichton Dalrymple, 5th Earl of Dumfries, was contemplating the building of a house for himself and his wife by John and Robert Adam. This mansion has been described as 'a perfect 18th-century time capsule'. Its interiors and contents have been little changed in 250 years. The house the Adam brothers built between 1754 and 1759 underwent some grand though sensitive remodelling from 1897 by the Arts and Crafts architect Robert Weir Schultz. The owner, Patrick Crichton-Stuart, 3rd Marquis of Bute, worked with Weir Schultz to create the Pewter Corridor, which provided a colourful link between the side pavilions and the first floor of the main block. It was painted grey in 1956 for the Dowager Marchioness Lady Eileen, to create a 'purer' space, but has been returned to its former gilded radiance. The corridor gave access to the cedar-panelled Tapestry Room, where four Gobelin tapestries portrayed scenes from Greek mythology. The Family Bedroom contains a superb carved mahogany Chippendale four-poster. In the Blue Drawing Room there are Chippendale armchairs, sofas and a rosewood bookcase. By 2007 racing driver Johnny Dumfries, 7th Marquis of Bute, despaired of holding it all together. The house was to be auctioned, its treasures dispersed. Some pieces were on their way to Christie's when the Prince of Wales stepped in with a plan to save Dumfries House for the nation. ''Tis certainly a great undertaking, but necessity knows no law.'

▶ *KA18 2LN (satnav). 14 miles E of Ayr on A70. Open all year (weekends only in winter).*

❸ Drumlanrig Castle
Dumfries & Galloway

Throughout this ravishing pink sandstone palace can be seen the motif of a winged heart. According to the tale, in 1329 the dying Robert Bruce asked that his embalmed heart be carried on a crusade. James Douglas travelled to Spain wearing about his neck Bruce's heart in a silver and enamel casket. Lured into a trap by the Moors, he took the casket and flung it into the enemy's midst, crying, 'Forward, brave heart, as ever thou were wont to do, and Douglas will follow thee and die!' The family motto remains to this day 'Forward'.

Drumlanrig was built by William Douglas, 3rd Earl of Queensberry, Lord High Treasurer of Scotland, upon being created 1st Duke by Charles II in 1684. He was so appalled at the cost that his pleasure in it was ruined. He sealed the accounts in a packet with an awful warning: 'the de'il pike out the een [eyes] of any who should open it.' Yet he had his money's worth. Daniel Defoe related in the 1720s: 'The gallery may well be call'd a gallery of beauties, itself a beauty. And being fill'd from end to end … with the family-pieces of the duke's ancestors, most of them at full length, and in their robes of state, or of office, as their history directed.' A room in which Bonnie Prince Charlie slept, the gardens and a bicycle museum are among Drumlanrig's charms. The home of the Duke and Duchess of Buccleuch and Queensberry is also home to the renowned Buccleuch Art Collection, which includes such masterpieces as Rembrandt's *Old Woman Reading*.

▶ *DG3 4AG. 15 miles N of Dumfries on A76. Seasonal opening.*

SCOTLAND

❹ Pollok House, Glasgow

In this Georgian mansion, modernised in 1900, hang works by El Greco, Goya and Blake. This was the ancestral home of the Maxwell family for more than 700 years, although the present house dates from around 1750. It exhibits one of the finest collections in the UK of Spanish art from the Golden Age of 1500–1700. The house is set within a country park, 15 minutes' drive from the city centre. Here, also, in a 1970s gallery, is the collection brought together by shipping magnate Sir William Burrell – more than 8,000 objects and art works, from the French Impressionists to Chinese and Islamic art.

In 1966 Mrs Anne Maxwell Macdonald granted the house and estate to Glasgow Corporation, stipulating that the park must remain public. This was quite a gift. In 2007 it was named best park in Britain, and in 2008 best in Europe. The house is now presented by the National Trust for Scotland as a 'lived-in' Edwardian country home of around 1930. In its heyday Pollok had 48 staff to serve three family members. The Edwardian Kitchen Restaurant is a popular attraction.

▶ *G43 1AT. 4 miles SW of Glasgow city centre in Pollok Park. NTS. Open all year.*

❺ Mount Stuart, Argyll & Bute

As light relief from creating Cardiff Castle (see page 184), the 3rd Marquis of Bute found time to build Xanadu on an island in the Firth of Clyde. This redbrick extravaganza is one of the finest Gothic revival domestic buildings in the British Isles. It was designed by Sir Robert Rowland Anderson, to the marquis's vision, in 1879, and was unfinished at the time of Bute's death in 1900. The Marble Hall soars to 25m (80ft) – just higher than the nave of Canterbury Cathedral. The look is ecclesiastical, the theme occult, with stained-glass windows depicting signs of the zodiac, and vaulted ceilings exploring astrology and astronomy. The marquis's fascination with mysticism finds expression, also, in the Horoscope Room, dedicated to the cosmos. The ceiling shows the alignment of planets on the date of his birth, September 12, 1847. With typical Virgo attention to detail, he left no surface of his mansion unembellished. Flanking marble arches in the Drawing Room are intricately carved; the ceiling is adorned with heraldic shields.

Mount Stuart was a back-to-the-future country house, a celebration of the medieval, equipped with all mod cons. It was among the most technologically advanced houses of its age, the first home in Scotland to have electric lighting, and possibly the first in the world to have a heated indoor swimming pool. Central heating, a telephone system and Victorian passenger lift are still in use. The 'policies', or pleasure grounds, have wild-flower meadows and woodlands. A series of pools and cascades replicate the Via Dolorosa where Christ took his last steps *en route* to crucifixion. The path stretches from the pebbly West Coast shoreline to Calvary pond.

▶ *PA20 9LR. 5 miles S of Rothesay on E coast of Isle of Bute. Seasonal daily opening.*

❻ Brodick Castle, North Ayrshire

In the reign of Queen Victoria this red sandstone castle, the ancient seat of the Hamiltons, put its turbulent past behind it and became a genteel family home. It stands overlooking Brodick Bay against the looming backdrop of rugged Goatfell mountain, but its island situation, once strategic, is now purely scenic. The castle, scene of clan warfare, was attacked by Henry VIII in the 'Rough Wooing', and suffered religious paroxysms before being seized by Roundheads. In more peaceful times it was used mainly as a sporting estate.

Then in 1843, William, later 11th Duke of Hamilton, married Princess Marie of Baden. A year later, his mother, Susan Euphemia Beckford (see Lennoxlove House, page 199), inherited a fortune from her father, William Beckford, an outrageous and eccentric art collector and author. At one time the richest commoner in England, Beckford was unfairly dismissed by William Hazlitt as 'an industrious *bijoutier* … an enthusiastic collector of expensive trifles', and, justifiably, by Byron as 'the great Apostle of Paederasty'. Now that sufficient funds were available, James Gillespie Graham was called in to remodel the castle, adding the massive southwest tower.

In 1895 the property passed to Lady Mary Louise Hamilton. The home she created with her husband, the 6th Duke of Montrose, from 1906, is what visitors see. Silver, paintings and porcelain are survivors of the 'bijoutier's' and Hamilton collections. More than 80 stags' heads look down upon the hall and stairway. The Woodland Garden is a fine sight when the rhododendrons are out. The Gulf Stream allows exotic plants to flourish. The country park extends from sea to mountaintop. Wild-flowers bloom. Highland cattle graze. Brooks come from haunts of coot and heron and bicker down the valley.

▶ *KA27 8HY. 1 mile N of Brodick on E coast of Isle of Arran. NTS. Seasonal daily opening of castle; park open all year.*

VAULTED CEILINGS, DARK SHADOWS, GOTHIC DRAMA
THE POOL, MOUNT STUART

SCOTLAND

FIFE & SOUTHEAST SCOTLAND

The hand of Sir Walter Scott rests lightly on the land that inspired him, the house he designed, those he visited. Relics of the past, displayed with sensitivity, evoke the romance at the heart of his work.

1 Traquair House, Borders

Two carved stone bears holding the Stuart family coat of arms at the end of the avenue to Traquair flank gates that remain forever closed. The Stuarts were recusant Catholics. A secret top-floor chamber where Mass was once said, and a hidden escape route for a priest, recall years of religious persecution. John Stuart, 4th Laird of Traquair, was Captain of the Queen's Bodyguard in the employ of Mary, Queen of Scots. A cradle in which she rocked her son, the future James VI (James I of England), is still here. Charles, 5th Earl, remodelled the interiors of the house in the Scottish Renaissance style of which the High Drawing Room and Library are fine examples. He also installed the Bear Gates in 1738. One story goes that, following a visit from Bonnie Prince Charlie in 1745 and his defeat at Culloden in 1746, the earl vowed they would stay closed until a Stuart king was crowned in London.

Traquair was home to the Stuarts from 1491, passing to a cousin, Henry Maxwell, in 1875. A quaint, turreted, fortified mansion in the Scottish baronial style, it was built on the site of a hunting lodge used by Scottish kings, and was completed in 1695 by James Smith of Edinburgh, who added side wings and two ogee-roofed pavilions overlooking the gardens. When John Brown made an engraving of Traquair in 1862 he found 'everything subdued to settled desolation … a gaunt old house …' and yet 'it looks the Earl's house still, and has a dignity of its own'. Walter Scott took Traquair, with its 'steep roofs … narrow gables … corner turrets … its rampant bears', as his model for Tully-Veolan in *Waverley*. Scotland's oldest inhabited house is home to the family of Catherine, 21st Lady Traquair, and also houses a brewery.

▶ *EH44 6PW. 2 miles S of Innerleithen on B709. Seasonal opening.*

TRAQUAIR HOUSE

➋ Bowhill House, Borders

'When summer smiled on Sweet Bowhill, and July's eve with balmy breath, waved the bluebells on Newark Heath, the aged Harper's Soul awoke.' So the Borders home of the Duke of Buccleuch and Queensberry was celebrated by Sir Walter Scott in the 'Lay of the Last Minstrel'. Legend tells how an ancestor of the Scott family seized a cornered roebuck after it turned on the king's hounds while they were hunting in a ravine ('cleuch') and as reward the family was granted ownership of Ettrick Forest, which surrounds the house.

The present mansion is, at its core, a fairly modest 18th-century building, once used as an occasional summer house. In the 19th century it was extended and transformed into a villa with a gallery hall. Sir Walter Scott, a friend, wrote of 'junketing' at Bowhill, of musical entertainments and the 4th Duke's preparations for a cattle show. The original manuscript of 'The Lay' is displayed in the study. A significant part of the Buccleuch art collection is here, including works by Canaletto, Raeburn, Reynolds and Gainsborough, as well as silverware, Sèvres and Meissen china and porcelain, tapestries and French furniture.

James Scott, 1st Duke of Monmouth, 1st Duke of 'Bucloo', was the eldest illegitimate son of Charles II by Lucy Walter. He was beheaded in 1685 after the Monmouth Rebellion, when he sought to depose his uncle, James II. His execution shirt and saddle are among relics, along with letters from Queen Victoria to the Duchess of Buccleuch, her Mistress of the Robes. A Victorian game larder serves as a 72-seat theatre. Romantic woodland, loch and riverside walks are there to be enjoyed.
▶ *TD7 5ET. 3 miles W of Selkirk on A708. Limited seasonal opening.*

➌ Mellerstain House, Borders

One respected architect began this splendid house; his famous son completed it more than 40 years later. Robert Baillie, a Covenanter, was executed for high treason in Edinburgh on Christmas Eve 1684. His son George fled abroad and served in the Prince of Orange's Horse Guards. In Holland he fell in love with Grisell Hume, the daughter of a fellow exile. After the prince took the English throne as William III in 1689, the family estates were returned and George and Grisell married. In 1725 a new family home was begun here, in place of an 'auld melancholic hous'. The architect was William Adam, father of John and Robert. He drew up plans for a Palladian mansion with

central block and flanking wings. The wings were completed and the parkland was laid out, but, following George's death in 1738, work stopped. The family lived in the East Wing; servants and horses in the West.

In 1759 the estate passed to Baillie's grandson, also George, who in 1770 called in Robert Adam to complete what his father had begun. This is an early example of Adam's castle style. The interiors are rich in plasterwork and radiant colours. The gardens were designed by Reginald Blomfeld in 1910 and are entered from an 18th-century courtyard. One of Scotland's finest stately homes is lived in today by the 13th Earl of Haddington and his family. It is open to day visitors and is offered as a wedding and funeral venue, with a natural burial ground in Hundy Mundy Wood.
▶ *TD3 6LG. 7 miles NW of Kelso on A6089. Limited seasonal opening.*

➍ Floors Castle, Borders

When William Playfair was commissioned to remodel a ducal country residence, he really went to town. The original mansion was built for the 1st Duke of Roxburghe by William Adam. 'Flurs' stands on a terrace overlooking the River Tweed, with a distant prospect of the Cheviots, and is a castle in appearance only. Adam extended and altered an existing tower house to create a symmetrical, plain Georgian country residence, in accordance with the 1st Duke's wishes. Between 1837 and 1847, Playfair was asked to revamp the building for the 6th Duke, and gave it the full Gothic works. The headgear is incredible – so many battlemented parapets, pinnacles, pepper-pot turrets, towers, cupolas and water spouts. He also redesigned many of the interiors, to which successive duchesses applied their tastes. In 1903 the 8th Duke married Mary ('May') Goelet, an American heiress, who brought to Floors her own art collection and a series of 17th-century tapestries depicting *The Triumph of the Gods*.

There is, in every sense, a wealth of things to see at the home of the 10th Duke. A sitting room was the work of Robert Adam. The Bird Room contains a congregation, a volery, a sedge, a siege, a muster, a veritable murder of stuffed birds. There is a woodland garden, a 19th-century walled garden and a Millennium garden. Produce from the kitchen garden and estate is served in café and restaurants. The parkland, said Sir Walter Scott, was 'a kingdom for Oberon and Titania to dwell in'.
▶ *TD5 7SF. 1 mile W of Kelso town centre off A6089. Seasonal opening.*

❺ Abbotsford House, Borders

This fantastical baronial mansion was created by Sir Walter Scott – his 'Conundrum Castle'. Towers, turrets, crow-stepped and pointy gables, Gothic windows, chimneys and pinnacles make for a composition at once preposterous and pleasing. Dark oak panelling, stained glass, armour and weaponry set the tone within. In the entrance hall is a clock that once belonged to Marie Antoinette. The library contains 7,000 books; in Scott's study there are 2,000 more, annotated by the author. Here is his writing desk and 'Robroyston chair', made from timber from the house in which William Wallace was run to earth. Gothicism was Scott's stock in trade and made him an international bestseller. The *Waverley* novels, wrote Kenneth Clark, 'spread Gothic sentiment to every class of reader'. Scott scratched out more than 20 novels as well as poetry, short stories and essays. He kept a diary and was a prolific letter-writer, yet he still found time to plan Abbotsford's interiors almost down to the last tassel. 'The Chinese wallpaper in the drawing room is most beautiful,' he related. 'I should like the mirror handsome and the frame plain; the colour of the hangings is green with rich Chinese figures.' The wallpaper is indeed beautiful.

Abbotsford was the first house in Scotland to have gas, which was installed in 1823. In the drawing room hangs a gas lustre chandelier and a portrait of a young Sir Walter with his dogs Camp and Percy by Sir Henry Raeburn. A silver urn was a gift from Lord Byron. In the entrance court is a fountain that 'once belonged to the Cross of Edinburgh, which flowed with wine at the coronation of our kings and other joyous occasions'. The river Tweed runs romantically by.
▶ *TD6 9BQ. 2 miles W of Melrose off B6360. Visitor centre featuring exhibition on Sir Walter Scott open all year. House open following restoration in 2013.*

ABBOTSFORD HOUSE

❻ Manderston, Borders

From the world's only silver staircase to teak stalls and marble fittings in the stables, Manderston is an essay on opulence. In 1893, Sir James Miller married the Hon. Eveline Curzon, daughter of Lord Scarsdale and sister of the Viceroy of India. Miller was known as 'Lucky Jim'. His elder brother, William, was not so lucky – he choked to death on a cherry stone at Eton – and James came into a baronetcy and a fortune built on hemp and herrings. 'Money simply doesn't matter,' he assured architect John Kinross when he appointed him in 1901 to rebuild a relatively restrained 18th-century residence as a country house that would shout of wealth and status. A grand entrance was created by the addition of an Ionic portico, with a coat of arms above the door. Quantities of plaster, marble and alabaster, antiques and art treasures were shipped in. Stuccodores went to work on ceilings and friezes. New money even bought 'ancestors' – a set of portraits in the dining-room were brought in to impart a sense of family history. The cantilevered marble staircase was inspired by Madame de Pompadour's at Petit

Trianon in Versailles. Before the Great War it would take three men three weeks to dismantle, polish and put together the silver-plated balustrade; today it is buffed up by volunteers.
▶ *TD11 3PP. 2 miles E of Duns on A6105. Limited seasonal opening.*

❼ Paxton House, Borders

Patrick Home dreamed of carrying his lady love, Sophie de Brandt, across the imposing threshold of the home he built for her on the River Tweed. She was a lady-in-waiting to Queen Elizabeth Christina of Prussia. He met her at the court of Frederick the Great, after he was sent to study in Leipzig. He was 22, she 18. Sophie's tiny white gloves are in a frame in the Morning Room here, but the star-crossed lovers were thwarted by Fate and never married. Patrick sold the shell of a Palladian masterpiece to his nephew, Ninian Home.

The architect was John Adam, assisted by James, brothers of the supremely talented Robert, who was later commissioned by Ninian to create some of the interiors. In the early 1800s, Edinburgh architect Robert Reid added a library and picture gallery. Visitors see original stucco work and wallpaper, furniture by Thomas Chippendale and William Trotter, paintings by Reynolds and Raeburn, books, costumes and antiques collected by Patrick Home on the Grand Tour. Paxton House is managed by a trust and presented as a lived-in home. In the gallery are more than 70 paintings from the late 18th and 19th centuries, on loan from the National Galleries of Scotland.
▶ *TD15 1SZ. 5 miles W of Berwick-upon-Tweed at junction of B6460 and B6461. Seasonal daily opening. Group visits all year by arrangement.*

❽ Lennoxlove House, East Lothian

The 14th Duke of Hamilton was an MP, pugilist, pilot and Lord Steward of the Royal Household. His family seat, 17th-century Hamilton Palace, was demolished in 1921, after it was literally undermined for coal. In 1946 he bought this ancient house – originally four storey Lethington Tower, begun in the 14th century – as a repository for family treasures. A cabinet, veneered in tortoiseshell and ebony, kept in the Stewart Room, is thought to have been a gift to Frances Stewart, Duchess of Richmond and Lennox from Charles II. 'La Belle Stuart' may have been the king's mistress. Her marriage was childless, and on her death she left £50,000 to

SCOTLAND

her nephew Lord Blantyre, stipulating that he must buy a house and name it 'Lennox's love to Blantyre'. Her trustees bought Lethington on his behalf and he shortened its name to Lennoxlove.

Among the treasures transferred here from Hamilton Palace is a Pleyel piano, which can be seen in the Blue Room. A later beauty, Susan Euphemia Beckford, brought to her marriage to the 10th Duke of Hamilton a fortune and the fabulous art collection of her outrageous father, William (see Brodick Castle, page 194). It was he who gave her the piano. Chopin performed on it and it is said to play itself at dead of night. Also to be seen here is the death mask of Mary, Queen of Scots – 'not dead,' the observer thinks, 'but only sleeping' – and her sapphire ring, bequeathed to the family upon her execution. Many fine portraits bring history alive.

▶ *EH41 4NZ. 1 mile S of Haddington off A1. Limited seasonal opening for guided tours.*

❾ Gosford House, East Lothian

Francis Wemyss Charteris built this house to serve as a counterpoint to Edinburgh Castle, to hold parties, and to be 'closer to the golf'. Local courses include Muirfield, Gullane and Craigielaw. He styled himself 7th Earl of Wemyss ('Weems'), despite the attainder of his elder brother David, Lord Elcho, for his part in the 1745 Jacobite Rising, which excluded him from the peerage. Gosford was one of Robert Adam's last commissions; he died eight years before its completion in 1880. It is a very grand neoclassical mansion. Perhaps its greatest glory is the Marble Hall in the south wing, which was completed in 1891 by William Young for the 10th Earl. Rising to a height of three storeys, it has a double staircase ascending to a surrounding picture gallery. Standing in parkland on the south of the Firth of Forth, Gosford is offered as an events venue, thus fulfilling the 7th Earl's purposes.

▶ *EH32 0PY. 8 miles SW of North Berwick on A198. Limited seasonal opening.*

❿ Dalmeny House, Edinburgh

Archibald Primrose, 5th Earl of Rosebery, married Hannah de Rothschild, owned three Derby winners and was briefly prime minister (1894–5). He was a Liberal Imperialist of whom it was said: 'He is subjective, personal, a harp responsive to every breeze that blows … He is a creature of moods and moments, and spiritually he often dies young.' Physically, he lived to 82, passing away in 1929 to the sounds of the *Eton Boating Song.*

Dalmeny has been home to the Primrose family, Earls of Rosebery, for 300 years. It contains two important collections – 18th-century French furniture and Sèvres porcelain were passed down from the Rothschilds, while Napoleonic portraits and memorabilia, and paintings from the 16th to the 19th century were acquired by Archibald, who was a connoisseur of art. His portrait, by Millais, hangs in the hall with those of Hannah and the present earl and his family. Five Spanish tapestries portraying scenes from childhood were designed by Franciso Goya for Spanish royal palaces.

In a room devoted to Napoleon is the throne on which he sat as First Consul, his shaving stand from the palace of Compiègne, and the collapsible campaign chair of his nemesis, the Duke of Wellington. Among more than 20 portraits and busts in the dining room are works by Raeburn, Reynolds, Romney and Gainsborough. This ornate Gothic revival mansion is surrounded by a wooded park, with views across the Firth of Forth. It was designed by William Wilkins, and completed in 1817. Interiors are Regency. It remains a family home and can be seen by guided tour. Visitors are greeted by a fine bronze statue of a racehorse.

▶ *EH30 9TQ. 3 miles E of South Queensferry off B924. Limited seasonal opening for guided tours.*

⓫ Falkland Palace, Fife

James IV and James V of Scotland transformed a former castle into this beautiful Renaissance Palace. The castle had come to the Crown in the 14th century. James IV (1488–1513) was a cultured, educated patron of the arts who engaged a keeper of the castle to tame the overgrown garden and park. He ordered the building of a new palace complex, which James V, in his turn, remodelled, employing craftsmen from France and Italy. He also installed a court for real tennis – Scotland's oldest, which can still be seen today. The Stuarts used Falkland as a retreat, where they hunted native deer and wild boar imported from France. Here James V died in December 1542, having heard that at Linlithgow his wife, Mary of Guise, had given birth to a daughter. So it was that, at the age of seven days, Mary became Queen of Scots.

Following her return from exile in France in 1561, already a widow, Mary was a frequent visitor to the palace. After the Union of the Crowns, her son James VI (James I of England), Charles I and Charles II all visited Falkland. In the Civil War Cromwell's men set the palace on fire and it fell into ruin. John Crichton-Stuart, 3rd Marquis of Bute, began restoration in 1887. Visitors see panelling, tapestries and period

furniture. The painted ceiling in the Dressing Room off the Keeper's Bedroom depicts the Bute coat of arms; its four-poster perhaps belonged to James VI. The Chapel Royal survives from the reign of James V. The Bake House gives a flavour of life below stairs. Herbaceous borders brim with flowers. The orchard still grows in its original site and affords a striking view of the palace.

▶ KY15 7BU. On A912, 10 miles SW of Cupar. NTS. Seasonal daily opening.

⑫ Hopetoun House, West Lothian

No British monarch had crossed the border into Scotland for 170 years, until George IV paid a state visit in 1822. On his last day he came to the palatial home of the 4th Earl of Hopetoun, and arrived wearing Highland dress, which had been banned from 1745 to 1782, after the second Jacobite Rebellion. Sir Walter Scott, on a mission to promote the romantic image of Scotland, stage-managed the tour. The king ate a modest lunch of turtle soup with three glasses of wine, then adjourned to the Yellow Drawing Room, where he knighted the Scottish portraitist Henry Raeburn, and Captain Adam Ferguson, Keeper of the Regalia in Scotland. The 4th Earl was Captain General of the Royal Company of Archers, which served as bodyguards to His Majesty. Its members meet every summer at Hopetoun to shoot for the Hopetoun Royal Commemoration Prize.

'Scotland's finest stately home' was built for Charles Hope, 1st Earl of Hopetoun, by Sir William Bruce in 1699–1707, but it owes its beautiful façade to William Adam. In 1721, Adam added colonnades, flanking pavilions and grand state apartments. Upon his death in 1748, his sons, John, James and Robert, supervised the completion of the elegant, carved and gilded, Georgian interiors. These have changed little in 300 years and contain period furniture, important paintings, tapestries and antiques. Amid extensive grounds, the Sea Walk Trail has views over the deer park, and Hope's Walk is a riot of colour at rhododendron time.

▶ EH30 9SL. 3 miles W of South Queensferry off A904. Seasonal daily opening.

CENTRAL & NORTHEAST SCOTLAND

Fairytale transformations, landscaped parks and peerless gardens belie the troubled past of this region so beloved of Victoria and Albert, but at least one castle still bears witness to a fierce spirit of defiance.

❶ Inveraray Castle, Argyll & Bute

The Duke of Argyll is head of the legendarily fierce Clan Campbell. At Inveraray, those warriors did not lay down their weapons – they put them on show. The castle, on the shores of Loch Fyne, was inspired by the work of John Vanbrugh and begun for the 2nd Duke in 1746 to designs by Roger Morris and William Adam. After they both died, John and Robert Adam took over. Forty-three years in the building, it combines elements of baroque, Palladian and Gothic styles. The Armoury Hall soars to 21m (69ft) and has the highest ceiling in Scotland. The walls are adorned with fearsome pikes, dirks, swords and axes. In the first-floor Clan Room, a family tree traces Campbell lineage back to Colin the Great in 1477. A map shows the property possessed by the dynasty at the height of its powers.

For all this, the abiding impression is of elegance, with decorative painting, plasterwork and gilding, chandeliers, Oriental and European porcelain, Beauvais tapestries and family portraits by Kneller, Hoppner and Gainsborough. A collection of costumes worn by family members through the ages includes Coronation robes and the wedding dress designed by Bruce Oldfield for the current duchess. Visitors might look into the Saloon to see the grand piano on which Lerner and Loewe composed songs for *My Fair Lady*, then retire to the tearoom for Earl Grey and buttered scones. Wouldn't that be luverly?
▶ *PA32 8XE. 1 mile N of Inveraray town centre off A819. Seasonal opening.*

❷ Blair Castle, Perth & Kinross

Blair Castle and the earldom of Atholl were granted to John Stewart by his half brother, James II of Scotland, in 1457. In 1530, the 3rd Earl ordered the building of a Great Hall over a series of vaulted rooms to the south of the tower. Mary, Queen of Scots stayed in 1564 and joined a hunt in which 360 deer and five wolves were slaughtered. There was further carnage in 1652 when the castle was besieged by

Cromwell's forces, and in 1689, when it was occupied by Jacobites. In more peaceful times Prince Albert chose Blair as the ideal place for Queen Victoria to convalesce after the birth of their fourth child, Alfred, in 1844. In her journal, Victoria described 'a large plain white building, surrounded by high hills'. The Georgian stately home had been developed in phases from the original 13th-century Cumming's Tower. From the 1860s the castle was made over for the 7th Duke of Atholl in the Scottish baronial style, with crenellations, turrets and a ballroom.

Prince Albert had less success at hunting than Mary. As Victoria sat sketching, a herd of deer were driven down, but 'most provokingly two men were walking on the road ... and then the herd all ran back up again ... My poor Albert had not fired one shot.' The stuffed stag and displays of weaponry that greet visitors set the tone for the interiors. Tapestries belonged to Charles I. Every May bank holiday weekend a gathering of the Atholl Highlanders, Blair Castle's private army, is held here, with a parade and Highland Games.
▶ *PH18 5TL. 8 miles NW of Pitlochry on A9. Open all year (weekends only in winter).*

❸ Dunninald, Angus

This mansion, completed in 1824, is the third dwelling on the site since the Middle Ages. It was built for Peter Arkley by James Gillespie Graham, a specialist in the Scottish baronial style, on the footings of a late 16th-century manor. Graham designed the Glenfinnan Monument, erected in 1815 to commemorate the Jacobites who fell in the uprising of 1745. He planned something pretty monumental for Dunninald, but Arkley scaled down his plans, and had just a year to enjoy his sturdy Gothic mansion before his death in 1825.

The gardens are glorious. The Wild Garden was planned on a grid pattern in the early 1700s around a beech avenue. The Walled Garden dates from *c.*1740 and was extended a century later with stone from the demolished second house.
▶ *DD10 9TD. 2 miles S of Montrose on minor roads off A92. Open for a month in summer.*

❹ Stirling Castle, Stirling

A monumental survivor of centuries of siege and seizure, this magnificent edifice stands on volcanic rock and looms above the plain, dominating its surroundings. Stirling is more than just a castle – it symbolises Scottish pride and independence. The principal buildings date from the 15th and 16th centuries, but its history stretches back to the 1100s. It was occupied by Edward I on his invasion in 1296. Between 1490 and 1600 Stirling took shape under the Stuart kings. James IV spent a fortune remodelling it, including the forework gatehouse and the largest medieval banqueting hall ever built in Scotland. James V was crowned at Stirling; he and Mary of Guise created the centrepiece Renaissance palace.

Upon James's death in 1542, his daughter succeeded him at just seven days old. She was crowned Mary, Queen of Scots at Stirling on September 9, 1543. Her son James was baptised here in 1566, and brought up as James VI after Mary's forced abdication in 1567. In 1594 he built the Chapel Royal for the baptism of his son, Henry (who predeceased him). With the Union of the Crowns, the king departed for London as James I of England.

A £12 million programme of restoration enables visitors to see six apartments returned to their Renaissance splendour of the mid 1700s. Four hundred oak trees went into the Great Hall's hammerbeam roof.

▶ *FK8 1EJ. Access Stirling from Junction 10 of M9. Castle in city centre. HS. Open all year.*

STIRLING CASTLE

⑤ Drummond Castle Gardens, Perth & Kinross

'Is this Alice in Wonderland's garden?' asked a wide-eyed young visitor on seeing Drummond. A good question! It is certainly a wonder. The seat of the 28th Baron Willoughby de Eresby, Drummond Castle stands on a rocky ridge, overlooking Scotland's most important formal gardens, among the finest in Europe. The castle comprises a tower house and baronial mansion, both rebuilt in Victorian times and not open to the public. The gardens were laid out in the 1630s. Their appearance is of the courtly 17th-century Scottish Renaissance, although they were restructured in Victorian times and again in the 20th century. Terraces step down, with fabulous topiary and blazing copper beech, a parterre in the form of the St Andrew's Cross, peacocks, a sundial carved by Charles I's master mason, box hedges and geometric plantings. As the rose says in *Alice Through the Looking Glass*: 'It's the fresh air that does it … wonderfully fine air it is, out here.'

▶ *PH7 4HZ. 3 miles S of Crieff off A822. Seasonal daily opening.*

⑥ Scone Palace, Perth & Kinross

Edward I, 'the hammer of the Scots', removed the Stone of Scone to Westminster in 1296 as spoils of war. When Victoria and Albert visited Scone in September 1842, the queen recorded: 'We walked out, and saw the mound on which the ancient Scotch kings were always crowned; also the old arch with James VI's arms, and the old cross, which is very interesting.' The royal couple were guests of Lord Mansfield and the Dowager Lady Mansfield at 'this fine-looking house of reddish stone'. It stands on the site of the lost Augustinian Scone Abbey, and was rebuilt in 1803, from a 16th-century palace, in the late-Georgian Gothic style, complete with castellation. The 'mound' shown to the royal couple is Moot Hill, once known as Caislean Credi, 'Hill of Credulity'. Since the first king of Scotland, Kenneth McAlpin, brought the sacred 'Stone of Destiny' to Scone in 843, most Scottish kings were crowned here. Charles II was the last, in 1651, nine years before he returned from exile to take the throne of England. Moot Hill has a tiny Presbyterian chapel upon it, and a replica of the famous stone, now returned to Scotland and displayed in Edinburgh Castle.

The Mansfields have been great collectors from the time of the 1st Earl, and the palace brims with artworks and treasures. In 1803,

DRUMMOND CASTLE GARDENS

when the current house was built, the village of 'Skoon' was demolished and rebuilt 2 miles away, so the grounds could be landscaped. Remains of the village include a graveyard, the old market cross, on which Victoria remarked, and a 16th-century arch that was once the grand entrance to the 'City of Scone'.

▶ *PH2 6BD. 2 miles N of Perth off A93.*
Seasonal daily opening of palace; grounds open all year.

➐ Edzell Castle and Garden, Angus

A unique Renaissance garden laid out in 1604 by David Lindsay, Lord Edzell, at this red-stone castle, was designed, not just to please the eye but to appeal to other senses and to stimulate the mind. The enclosing walls are adorned with carved panels portraying the Seven Cardinal Virtues, the Seven Liberal Arts and the Seven Planetary Deities. Scented flowers, in the Lindsay colours of blue and white, spill from recesses. There are nesting holes for songbirds. Geometric flowerbeds are bordered by miniature box hedging. The patterns of fleur de lys, Scottish thistle and English rose are exquisite. A gabled two-storey pavilion remains in fair condition, with vaulted cellars and an angled turret.

Edzell was home to the Lindsays from 1358. They built the castle in the 16th century, and David contrived this place of peace in which to contemplate eternal verities. The castle is a noble ruin and visitors can contemplate the mixed fortunes of a 'lichtsome' (carefree) family, fallen on hard times, who lived up to their motto, 'Endure forte' (endure with strength), and whose garden indeed endures – thanks to 1930s re-creation.

▶ *DD9 7UE. 6 miles N of Brechin on minor road off B966. HS. Open all year.*

➑ Crathes Castle, Aberdeenshire

This 16th-century tower house rises over six floors, clad in roughcast pink render, with turrets, battlements and crow-stepped gables. It was built for the Burnetts of Leys in the latter 1500s and was their home for 350 years; the clock is a Victorian addition. The interiors are not huge but the High Hall and Long Gallery border on the spectacular. There are some superb painted ceilings, an enormous four-poster in the Laird's Bedroom, panelling and tapestries. In the High Hall, with its superb carved oak ceiling, hangs the Horn of Leys, a decoratively carved ivory horn presented to Alexander de Burnard in 1323 by Robert the Bruce as a badge of office when he was appointed Royal Forester of Drum.

SCOTLAND

Crathes is also famous for its gardens. The castle is surrounded by banks of 300-year-old yew hedges, clipped into fantastical shapes. Tunnels through the trees lead to the Fountain Garden and the Rose Garden. These 20th-century Arts and Crafts creations, and the abundant herbaceous borders and terraces, have earned 'Crath-iss' the nickname 'the Sissinghurst of Scotland'. There are peaceful woodland walks in the 240ha (600 acres) estate.
▶ *AB31 5QJ. 3 miles E of Banchory on A93. NTS. Open all year.*

❾ Drum Castle, Aberdeenshire

'Gude Sir Alexander Irvine the much renounit Laird of Drum' fought hand to hand with 'Red Hector of the Battles' at Harlaw in fierce combat that left both dead. Red Hector was chief of the MacLeans of Duart in Mull. In 1411, the valiant Alexander, 3rd Laird, led the fighting men of Aberdeenshire, with his cousin the Earl of Mar, to meet the wild invaders from the Hebrides.

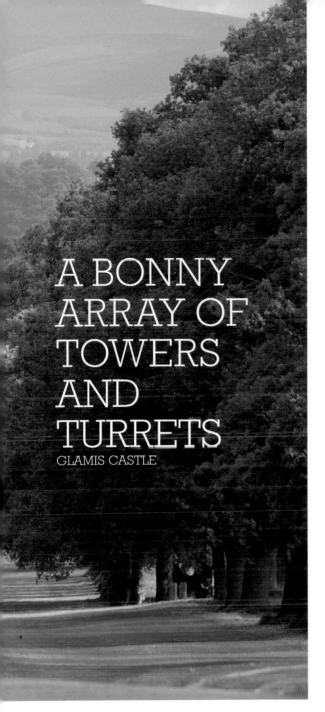

A BONNY ARRAY OF TOWERS AND TURRETS

GLAMIS CASTLE

Drum Castle was granted to William Irvine in 1323 for his loyal service, and it remained in the family's possession for more than 650 years. For Clan Keith the Irvines were the neighbours from hell, engaging in a long-running and bloody feud. Their castle was a 13th-century square tower, one of the oldest in Scotland, built to be impregnable, as it would need to be. In 1619 the 9th Laird, another Alexander, built a Jacobean mansion on to the castle, to which a rear extension was added in 1876. The result, viewed from the west, is a quaint mix of styles – hulking square tower, turrets, gables, dormers. Visitors can explore the grand rooms of the 17th-century mansion and see Victorian interiors and the beautiful library with more than 3,000 books, sensing everywhere the continuity of a home occupied by the same family for centuries. From the battlements views extend over the ancient oak woods of Drum. The gardens date from the late 18th century and include a garden of historic roses and an arboretum.

▶ *AB31 5EY. 12 miles SW of Aberdeen on A93. NTS. Seasonal opening of castle; gardens open all year.*

⑩ Glamis Castle, Angus

The medieval fortress of Shakespeare's *Macbeth* is today more reminiscent of a sublime French château, but set against the backdrop of the Angus Hills. Elizabeth Bowes-Lyon, future wife of George VI and from 1952 the nation's beloved Queen Mother, was ninth of the ten children of Lord and Lady Glamis. She spent a happy childhood here and retained an abiding love for Scotland. In 1904 her father inherited the earldom of Strathmore and Kinghorne, and with it the castle. 'Glahms' has been in the family since 1372, with one hiatus. It was seized for a time by James V, who held court here between 1538 and 1542. In 1543, following his death, it was returned, and in 1606, Patrick Lyon, 9th Lord Glamis, ordered extensive rebuilding, probably by William Schaw, Master of Works to James VI.

During the Commonwealth the castle was garrisoned for Parliament, and when Patrick Lyon, 3rd Earl, recovered it, he found it wrecked. Thorough restoration, completed in 1689, transformed it into a fairytale palace with towers and turrets. Visitors entering through the Queen Mother Memorial Gates approaches it up a mile-long drive. Glamis remains the family's ancestral home, full of portraits, antiques and rich furnishings. The lofty vaulted Drawing Room was once the Great Hall. The Dining Room table is set for a banquet. The grounds include an Italianate garden, pinetum and walled garden.

▶ *DD8 1RJ. On A928, 12 miles N of Dundee. Seasonal daily opening.*

⑪ Castle Fraser, Aberdeenshire

A towering, turreted granite edifice with balustrades and gables, Castle Fraser looks deeply romantic, but romance was to be denied Lady Elyza Fraser. Surrounded by woodland, this baronial mansion looms six storeys, with a viewing platform at the top of a round tower.

CAIRNESS HOUSE

Built on a 'Z' plan, it is largely the work of master masons Thomas Leiper, James Leiper and John Bell in the 16th and 17th centuries. Classical style improvements were ordered in the late 1700s by the lady laird, Elyza, with the installation of sash windows. She also had the grounds landscaped. Between 1820 and 1830 the interiors were remodelled for Lady Elyza's nephew Charles Fraser, by John Smith and William Burn. The Great Hall has a fine fireplace, family portraits and the 'Laird's lug' – a concealed room from which the laird could eavesdrop on visitors' conversations. The Trophy Room is filled with antlers, stags' heads and stuffed falcons. The Worked Room was the preserve of Lady Elyza.

As a young woman she conceived a passion for her uncle, the Laird of Udny, and was sent abroad to avoid scandal. She never married, dying, aged 80, in 1814. Her portrait hangs over the fireplace and most of the needlework was executed by her and her companion, Mary Bristow. Elyza was bedridden for the last years of her life and when nephew Charles moved in he found many empty picture frames. There is no knowing how much was plundered, but Castle Fraser still contains a wealth of pictures and antiques, and has the feel of a family home.

▶ *AB51 7LD. 16 miles NW of Aberdeen on minor roads off A944. NTS. Seasonal opening.*

⑫ Fyvie Castle, Aberdeenshire

Both Edward I and Robert the Bruce stayed at this baronial fortress in the turbulent 13th century. Although it was the property of the Scottish kings, Edward meant to lord it over the British Isles. The castle passed through different hands – not always consensually – before Sir Alexander Seton, later Earl of Dunfermline and Chancellor of Scotland, bought it in 1596 and set about enlarging the building, embellishing it with bartizans, crow-stepped gables, sculpted dormers and ornamental finials of huntsmen and musicians.

The castle was confiscated by William III from the Jacobite 4th Earl, who died in exile in 1694, and it remained Crown property until it was bought by William Gordon, 2nd Earl of Aberdeen. His son built the Gordon Tower and laid out the landscape, planting trees and creating the lake and gardens. Alexander Forbes-Leith, later Lord Leith of Fyvie, a steel magnate who made his fortune in Chicago, bought the castle in 1889 and added another tower (it is said that each of the five great families who owned Fyvie built a tower). Leith commissioned some magnificent interiors, including the Gallery and Drawing Room, approaching Thomas Agnew art dealers in London to advise on creating an art collection worthy of his historic residence. In 1984, Sir Andrew Forbes-Leith, Laird of Fyvie, sold the property to the National Trust for Scotland. A place of curses, ghosts and legends, Fyvie is nonetheless presented as a richly furnished and comfortable family home. The gallery, with barrel-vaulted ceiling, is hung with tapestries and has a pipe organ. There are suits of armour and paintings by Reynolds, Gainsborough, Turner, Millais and Raeburn.

▶ *AB53 8JS. 8 miles S of Turriff on A947. NTS. Seasonal opening.*

⑬ Cairness House, Aberdeenshire

'The crowning achievement' of James Playfair's life was also one of his last. In the 1790s, he designed this neoclassical mansion for Charles Gordon. Neither Playfair nor Gordon lived to see it completed, and Sir John Soane finished the job. Playfair essentially transformed a smaller mansion designed by Robert Burn a decade earlier, adding flanking wings and a rear semicircle, creating a ground plan of a C and an H. Symbolic details hint at an association with Freemasonry. The exterior is quite restrained but once inside, all heaven breaks loose. Some of the rooms are themed as temples – the Drawing Room is the Temple of Apollo, the Dining Room the Temple of Bacchus. Hieroglyphs in the Egyptian Room convey a coded message, suggesting that it was intended for meetings of 'The Brotherhood'. Gordon's heir, Major-General Thomas Gordon, 2nd Laird, growing up in a Greek-revival fantasy, developed a passion for Greece. He was a friend of Lord Byron's and lent his support throughout the Greek War of Independence in the 1820s.

The interiors at Cairness are on a homely scale but glorious. Visitors are stunned – not least to know that the mansion served as a farmhouse after 1945, before being turned over to bedsits. In 1994 it was rescued by architect and historian Philip Miller and his wife Patricia, an interior designer. In 2000 it was sold to Khalil Hafiz Khairallah, a journalist of Lebanese descent, and the Spanish artist Julio Soriano-Ruiz. They set about further restoration, which entailed replacing or repairing 180 windows and removing and recasting 51 iron chimneypots. In 2009 they scooped the prize for best restored country house at the Georgian Group Architectural Awards.

▶ *AB43 8XP. 7 miles SE of Fraserburgh off B9033. Tours by appointment.*

Plant hunters – root and branch heroes

Majestic trees and colourful flowers from far away flourish in northern climes thanks to a bunch of intrepid explorers, intent on botanic discovery.

Nowhere in the world are there more glorious rhododendron gardens than in Scotland. Visitors can see them at Scone Palace, Dunvegan Castle and Benmore. Then what of the magnificent Douglas Firs planted by William Sawrey Gilpin in the forested grounds around romantic Bowhill? And how sweet are the primulas at Brodick Castle! However, although Scotland may be plant paradise now, it wasn't always so. Such abundance and variety is found here largely due to Scottish botanist explorers, who introduced more plants into the west than all the plant hunters of other European nations put together. At least half of non-native plants in British gardens were discovered by Scots.

Risky business

Plant hunting was once the work of ships' doctors of modest ambition, who collected medicinal plants, but fascination with beautiful and exotic blooms, strange fruit and mighty trees eclipsed interest in medicinal herbs. After the John Tradescants, father and son, set to work in the 1600s, plant hunters would embark on perilous voyages, and spend years travelling in far countries, over hostile terrain, passionately, obsessively searching for new species. They faced appalling danger and risked death in pursuit of the perfect orchid or azalea, lupin or lily.

When the craze for chinoiserie took hold in the 18th century, and the magical land of Cathay held such mystique, wealthy sponsors sent 'flower missionaries' to bring home exotic oriental blooms.

One of the bravest and most driven of the collectors was David Douglas (b. 1798), who had worked as a gardener's boy for the Earl of Mansfield at Scone Palace. He was the first European to climb the Northern Rockies, and covered 10,000 miles in pursuit of all things that grow. He brought home penstemon and mimulus, or monkey flower, and the

noble fir tree that bears his name. He suffered many a mishap, had his botanical booty stolen, lost cuttings in a whirlpool when his boat capsized, and was killed at just 34, not by knife-wielding warriors (whom he sloughed off) but by wild cattle in Hawaii.

Another of the greats was Victorian plant hunter George Forrest (b. 1873), whose seven oriental voyages produced the world's largest collection of Chinese plants outside China itself, to be seen at Edinburgh's Royal Botanical Gardens. Forrest introduced 50 plant species, including rhododendrons, primulas, camellia, anemone, jasmine, clematis, daphne and acer. Despite the trauma of seeing his helpers massacred and evading pursuit for days over mountainous country, with the loss of thousands of specimens, he did not return home but resumed his collecting. *Rhododendron forrestii* is named for him.

BENMORE GARDENS

At Brodick Castle, the restoration of the garden that took place in the early 1900s included plantings of species collected by Forrest.

Archibald Menzies (b. 1754) was being dined by the viceroy in Chile and picked out of his dessert some nuts he did not recognise. Back on board ship he planted them, the seedlings survived and one was replanted at Kew, where it grew into that great stately home favourite *Araucaria auricana* – the monkey puzzle tree.

Francis Masson (b. 1741) tangled with escaped convicts on Table Mountain, survived capture by pirates, lost everything in a hurricane, and was imprisoned by French expeditionary forces on Grenada. He introduced the flamboyant *Strelitzia regina*, the Bird of Paradise flower, from South Africa. *Encephalartos altensteinii*, a cycad that he

brought back in 1775, is still growing at Kew – the oldest known pot plant in the world. Cycads are known as 'living fossils', unchanged for millennia.

Visitors to Cawdor Castle can take a half-hour walk to the dower house of Auchindoune and a garden inspired by a journey into Tibet's Tsangpo Gorges. In the 1920s, explorer and collector Frank Kingdon Ward and Jack Cawdor, 5th Earl of Cawdor, sought the legendary Tsangpo waterfall. Failing to find it they wrote *The Riddle of the Tsangpo Gorges*, from which the Royal Geographical Society concluded that the falls were 'a religious myth'. Lord Cawdor did, however, bring back to the Highlands a collection of rare Tibetan plants. Rather than risk them to the castle garden, where the head gardener, nicknamed 'Death Ray', might have rooted them out, he planted them here in the garden of his uncle, Ian Campbell.

⑭ Delgatie Castle, Aberdeenshire

Over tea and home-made scones served on dainty vintage china, visitors can contemplate the long and bloody history of Delgatie. Begun in around 1049, this was the home of the Hay family for 650 years. After Robert the Bruce's spectacular victory against the English at Bannockburn in 1314, the castle was taken from the Earl of Buchan. Mary, Queen of Scots stayed here in 1562 after the Battle of Corrachie put down the powerful Gordons (her bedchamber can be viewed). In the 16th century, Delgatie was rebuilt with stronger fortifications to withstand siege engines. Sir William Hay fought for Charles I and was hanged in 1650. Once the monarchy was restored, he was exhumed and given a grand state funeral. In 1743 a chapel and dovecote were added on the west wing and servants' quarters and kitchen on the east.

In the 20th century the building was almost lost to dry rot, the roof was falling in and Delgatie was fast sinking into ruin. It was rescued by the late Captain John Hay and is today managed by trustees. It is a plain building, not a palace, not even, to the popular perception, a castle, but it is rich in associations. Some of its painted ceilings are among the finest in Scotland, including fascinating depictions of strange animals with human faces – probably those of 18th-century inhabitants. A turnpike stair of 97 treads spirals up over eight floors.

▶ *AB53 5TD. 3 miles E of Turriff on minor roads. Open all year.*

⑮ Duff House, Aberdeenshire

In 1735 William Duff of Braco, Earl of Fife, commissioned William Adam to build a grand baroque mansion in parkland – and then refused to live in it. Architect and patron fell out over costs, and Adam successfully sued Duff, who would never afterwards even look on Adam's creation. Duff House stands in lush parkland, bounded by river and coast. It took five years to build, but the interiors were not completed for a century. The National Galleries of Scotland have an admirable policy of loaning important works to suitable stately homes, and so significant masterpieces are on display here during spring and summer. However, some paintings and furnishings, and a 4,000-volume library, the property of the Erskines of Torrie, are housed here permanently. The library was bequeathed by Magdalene Erskine for the promotion of the study of fine arts.

James Duff, 2nd Earl, had the grounds laid out and built the picturesque Bridge of Alvah and Gothic Mausoleum. There is also a Temple of Venus, and, in the Wrack woods, a pets cemetery. The gates that once marked the entrance to the estate are still in operation – at Banff Castle in the town high street.

▶ *AB45 3SX. Just S of Banff town centre. HS. Open all year.*

⑯ Brodie Castle, Moray

Ninian, 25th Brodie of Brodie, was a great character, who entertained the visiting public at his ancestral home with saucy limericks and patter. Theatrical in real life, he was part actor by profession, and a showman. Before his death in March 2003, aged 90, he delighted in conducting tours of this property, of which he had such deep knowledge.

A 16th-century Z-plan castle on this site was torched in 1645 by the Catholic Lewis Gordon of Clan Gordon, 3rd Marquis of Huntly, in revenge, after Alexander Brodie signed the Presbyterians' Covenant. In 1824 William Burn transformed the building into the striking pale-pink fortified mansion of today, in the baronial style, with towers, turrets and stepped gables and a secret passageway. Brodie is known for its elegant interiors, its intricate ceilings, an important art collection – and the bitter feud that ensued between Ninian and his grandchildren when he sold the castle to the National Trust in 1978. The three siblings' lawsuit collapsed and Brodie remains a Trust property.

Spring is the best time to come. Ninian's father, Major Ian, the 24th Brodie of Brodie, was a distinguished daffodil breeder. He created the National Collection and named 185 varieties. Some 110 of these grow here, including 'Fortune's Bowl', 'Loch Maree', 'Copper Bowl' and 'Ben Avon'. The hunt is on for the lost cultivars.

▶ *IV36 2TE. 4 miles W of Forres on A96. NTS. Seasonal opening of house; grounds open all year.*

⑰ Cawdor Castle, Highland

The most romantic and beautiful of the Highland castles was built around a holly tree. According to legend, the Thane of Cawdor set a donkey free to roam, laden with panniers of gold. Wherever the donkey chose to rest for the night, the Thane resolved, he would build his castle. The donkey lay down by the holly, which was thus at the prickly heart of the new stronghold. Radiocarbon measurement dates the long-dead tree to 1372. The story may, of course, be untrue, as was Shakespeare's suggestion that Macbeth was 'Thane of Cawdor'. 'I wish the bard had never written his damned play!' the exasperated 5th Earl once said. Macbeth died in 1057, having taken the throne of his cousin Duncan I, whom he killed in battle or (in Shakespeare's telling) murdered. The castle was not begun until the 1300s. A building licence was granted to William, Thane of Cawdor, in 1454, but some parts of the castle stonework have been dated to around 1380, when the holly would have grown. The iron yett (gate) was brought here in 1455 when the Thane was instructed to dismantle Lochindorb Castle and helped himself to a souvenir.

The ancestral home of the Dowager Duchess of Cawdor has evolved over centuries; 17th-century additions are in the Scottish vernacular style. It is hung with portraits and tapestries. The Great Hall, which dates from the 16th century, has a minstrels' gallery, and has been much remodelled. There are three glorious gardens, the Walled Garden, laid out in c.1600, the Flower Garden, created a century later, and the Wild Garden, begun in the 1960s between the castle and the Cawdor Burn.
▶ *IV12 5RD. 6 miles SW of Nairn on B9090. Seasonal daily opening.*

⑱ Ballindalloch Castle, Moray

As a donkey decreed where Cawdor (above) should be built, so a mysterious voice decided the location of Ballindalloch.
According to legend, the laird began his castle on a more defensive site, but whatever he built by day was dismantled overnight. In the end he heard a voice tell him, 'Build in the cow-haughs, and you will meet no interruptions.' He did as he was bidden and had no further difficulties.

The 16th-century 'Pearl of the North', one of Scotland's most beautiful castles, stands in the Spey Valley between the rivers Spey and Avon. It has been home to the Macpherson-Grants since 1546 and is one of the few Scottish castles in continuous private ownership. The original Z-plan castle has been much altered and extended over centuries. In 1770, General James Grant – for some time governor of Florida – added two new wings, the one to the north designed to house his French chef. Grant's military career in America, although distinguished, was not without controversy. He was an MP and had a fondness for the gaming table. In 1794 George Canning described him as 'a great fat laughing old man ... a sort of Falstaff' who, 'if not witty himself ... is the cause of wit in others – and affords infinite

room for all sorts of bad jokes, which are lavished on him unsparingly'. One such was a spoof letter offering him the governorship of Corsica – he almost accepted.

In the mid 19th century Ballindalloch had a fairytale makeover – castellation, gabled dormers, stair turrets with conical roofs and decorative detailing. Internally, the castle was transformed into a comfortable Victorian country house. The Walled Garden was redesigned in 1996 to mark the castle's 450th anniversary. A spring skitters and tumbles through the 1930s Rock Garden.
▶ *AB37 9AX. 18 miles NE of Grantown-on-Spey on A95. Seasonal daily opening.*

⑲ Braemar Castle, Aberdeenshire

'September 12, 1850. We lunched early, and then went at half-past two o'clock ... to the Gathering at the Castle of Braemar ... There were the usual games of "putting the stone", "throwing the hammer" and "caber"'. When Queen Victoria and Prince Albert chose to buy and develop Balmoral Castle, Deeside became 'Royal Deeside', and the Gothic Revival style took a hold. The royal couple regularly attended the famous Highland Gathering, and took tea with the Farquharsons in their drawing room at Braemar Castle.

The ancient seat of the Erskines, Earls of Mar, has survived through troubled times. John Erskine, 6th Earl of Mar, known as 'Bobbin Jock' for switching allegiance, raised the standard for the House of Stuart, signalling the start of the 1715 Jacobite Rebellion. Following defeat in battle that September, he fled to France, his lands were forfeit, his title extinguished. By 1730 Braemar had been returned to his son Thomas, but not until 1824 was the noble Mar title restored to John Francis Erskine. Meanwhile, the castle was leased to the government and turned into military quarters, with star-shaped curtain wall, by John Adam. It was garrisoned until 1831, when it was redone as a family home by James Farquharson, 10th Laird, and its turrets and curtain wall were crenellated. Its rugged exterior belies luxurious interiors. In the 1950s Mrs Frances Farquharson of Invercauld decorated many of the rooms in shades of pink and yellow, and so many people asked to come and have a look at her charming creation that, in the early 1960s, the castle was opened to the public. Since February 2007 it has been managed by the charity Braemar Community Ltd and maintained by volunteers.
▶ *AB35 5XR. On A93 16 miles W of Ballater. Limited seasonal opening.*

NORTH HIGHLANDS & ISLANDS

In these isolated outposts, where the unexpected lies just around the corner and the skirl of pipes hangs on the wind, legendary tales seem believable. Under the gaze of once-living animals, eeriness prevails.

❶ Kinloch Castle, Highland

Sir George Bullough spent weeks of excess in the stalking season, in his red sandstone mock castle on the wild, remote island of Rum. George's father, John, a self-made millionaire, bought the island in 1888, having previously leased the shooting rights. Sir George shipped in stone quarried in Dumfriesshire along with 100 masons and craftsmen clad in kilts of Rum tweed. The two-storey building, completed in 1902, has towers and battlements and was equipped with everything that a playboy could desire, including heated ponds for turtles and alligators. Birds of paradise flaunted their plumage in the aviary. A German-built Orchestrion simulated the music of a 40-piece orchestra. The house had its own hydro-electric power supply, central heating, air-conditioning and an ingenious power shower. Stags' heads stare glassily out from the walls of the galleried main hall, its floors strewn with lion-skin rugs. Sir George and Lady Monica threw lavish house parties. The 'castle' employed 100 domestic and estate workers, gardeners and under-gardeners. The music stopped in 1914 when the male staff were called up to fight. In 1957 the widowed Lady Bullough sold the island, but maintained the family mausoleum in which she and Sir George are buried. The property houses a bistro, bar and hostel, but its future is uncertain. Rum is run as a nature reserve.
▶ *PH43 4RR. On E coast of Isle of Rùm. Ferry from Mallaig.*

❷ Dunvegan Castle, Highland

'Hold Fast' is the family motto of Clan MacLeod, and their ancient stronghold has held fast to its sheer basalt crag above the sea for 800 years. Seen against a backdrop of mountains, under a lowering sky, its massive towers and battlements inspire awe. In Victorian times Dunvegan underwent 'romantic restoration'. Defensive battlements were added to the roofline and pepper-pot towers, but behind the façade a series of genuinely historic buildings remains.

This is a place steeped in legend. A faded scrap of ancient fabric hanging in the drawing room, known as the 'Fairy Flag of Dunvegan', is a most prized possession. The fabric is silk from the Middle East and dates from between the 4th and 7th centuries. It may have been a holy relic, but the MacLeods prefer the story that it was woven by fairies as a gift to protect the clan from disaster. The MacCrimmons were hereditary pipers to the MacLeods for 13 generations, and every year Dunvegan becomes a place of pilgrimage for pipers, when it holds a recital in honour of the 'Chanter' upon which the Fairy Lady promised the first MacCrimmon that he would play the finest music in the world. The terrain of Skye is wild and barren, and yet in the castle gardens rhododendrons thrive among cultivated woodlands, glades, pools, burns and cascades.
▶ *IV55 8WF. On NW coast of Isle of Skye, 22 miles NW of Portree on A850. Seasonal daily opening.*

❸ Eilean Donan Castle, Highland

The situation of this castle, on an island where three sea lochs meet, is at once defensive and powerfully evocative.
The stronghold of the MacRaes appears to be as old as the surrounding hills, and yet it is a 20th-century re-creation. The first fortified castle was built here in the 13th century, added to and reduced in phases until 1719 when it was blown to pieces with its own gunpowder stores. It lay in ruins until John MacRae-Gilstrap rebuilt it as a private home between 1912 and 1932. His clerk of the works, Farquar MacRae, made no reference to records, but was guided by a dream in which he saw the precise layout of halls, passages, turrets, towers and battlements. The accuracy of his vision was confirmed by plans later discovered in a vault in Edinburgh. Visitors tour the home of an Edwardian millionaire. MacRae tartan is rolled out as carpets and runners. In the Great Hall a stag's head above a fireplace is adorned with coats of arms.
▶ *IV40 8DX. 10 miles E of Kyle of Lochalsh on A87. Seasonal daily opening.*

❹ Dunrobin Castle, Highland

Surely this was where Cinderella lost her glass slipper as she ran home at the chimes of midnight. Home to the Earls and Dukes of Sutherland since the 13th century, Dunrobin was given a Disney makeover by Sir Charles Barry from 1845. The château-style castle stands on a terrace, looking towards the sea across gardens inspired by Versailles. A fire in 1915 destroyed many of Barry's interiors and those seen today are mainly the work of Sir Robert Lorimer. A superabundance of treasures includes mahogany furniture by Chippendale, portraits by Kneller, Hoppner and Ramsay, a fine Tintoretto, tapestries commissioned for a visit from Queen Victoria, a spectacular drawing room and a library of more than 10,000 books. If visitors, ascending the gravity-defying staircase, are unsettled by the array of stags' heads, they should brace themselves for the museum. Built as a summerhouse for the 18th Earl in 1762, it is animal Valhalla, hall of the slain. Heads of animals line the walls from floor to ceiling – trophies bagged by the 5th Duke and his wife on their big-game-hunting safaris.
▶ *KW10 6SF. 2 miles N of Golspie on A9. Seasonal daily opening.*

EILEAN DONAN CASTLE

Index

Page numbers in **bold** refer to main entries. Page numbers in *italic* refer to pictures.

Acknowledgements

Front cover Getty Images/Epics (Chatsworth, Derbyshire); **Back cover** National Trust Images/John Hammond (Saltram, Devon); **1** National Trust Images/John Millar (Baddesley Clinton, Warwickshire); **2–3** National Trust Images/Bill Batten (Osterley Park, Middlesex); **6–7** National Trust Images/Arnhel de Serra (Petworth House, West Sussex); **8–9** National Trust Images/David Sellman (Dunster Castle, Somerset); **11** National Trust Images/John Millar; **12** National Trust Images/Andreas von Einsiedel; **15** www.arcaid.co.uk/Florian Monheim/Bildarchiv-Monheim; **17** Courtesy of Powderham Castle and the Earl and Countess of Devon; **18** National Trust Images/Nadia Mackenzie; **20–21** Country Life Picture Library/John Critchley; **23** Carole Drake; **24** Getty Images/Carole Drake; **26–27** National Trust Images/Steve Stephens; **28–29** John Parker (Herstmonceux Castle, Sussex); **30–31** John Parker; **32–33** Alamy Images/Jeff Gilbert; **34** National Trust Images/John Millar; **36–37** Alamy Images/Maurice Savage; **38–39** National Trust Images/James Dobson; **41** National Trust Images/Andrew Butler; **43** National Trust Images/Andreas von Einsiedel; **46–47** National Trust Images/Jonathan Buckley; **49** Country Life Picture Library/Paul Barker; **51** John Parker; **52–53** Getty Images/Paul Felix; **55** National Trust Images/John Hammond; **56** Angelo Hornak; **58** Getty Images/VisitBritain/Joanna Henderson; **60, 63** National Trust Images/Andreas von Einsiedel; **64–65** Angelo Hornak; **67** National Trust Images/Ian Shaw; **68** National Trust Images/Andrew Butler; **72–73** Getty Images/Duncan Davis (Hampton Court, Surrey); **74–75** Getty Images; **76** www.arcaid.co.uk/Christopher Simon Sykes/Interior Archive; **78** English Heritage; **81** Angelo Hornak; **82** National Trust Images/John Hammond; **86–87** National Trust Images/Robert Morris (Ickworth, Suffolk) **89** National Trust Images/Dennis Gilbert; **91** John Parker; **92–93** Holkham Estate; **94** National Trust Images/Mark Fiennes; **96–97** Corbis/Harpur Garden Library; **98–99** National Trust Images/Martin Charles; **100–101** Country Life Picture Library/Will Pryce (Owlpen Manor, Gloucestershire); **102–103** Devonshire Collection, Chatsworth. Reproduced by permission of the Chatsworth Settlement Trustees; **104** National Trust Images/Nadia Mackenzie; **106** National Trust Images /Andreas von Einsiedel; **111** John Parker; **112** Getty Images/Latitudestock; **115** Country Life Picture Library/Tim Imrie-Tait; **116–117** The Interior Archive/Christopher Simon Sykes; **118–119** National Trust Images/Andreas von Einsiedel; **120** National Trust Images/John Millar; **122** Country Life Picture Library /Paul Barker; **124–125** Getty Images/Dave Porter Peterborough UK; **126–127** National Trust Images/James Mortimer; **130–131** National Trust Images/John Hammond; **132** Collections/Quintin Wright; **135** National Trust Images/Robert Morris; **136–137** National Trust Images/John Millar; **139** National Trust Images/Nadia Mackenzie; **140** National Trust Images/John Hammond; **142–143** National Trust Images/Robert Morris (Lyme Park, Cheshire); **144** National Trust Images/Derek Croucher; **146** National Trust Images/Nadia Mackenzie; **148** Collections/Robin Weaver; **152–153** National Trust Images/Geoffrey Frosh; **154** National Trust Images/John Hammond; **156–157** National Trust Images/Don Bishop (Bamburgh Castle, Northumberland); **159** Collections/Quintin Wright; **160** Getty Images/VisitBritain/Pawel Libera; **163** National Trust Images/Andreas von Einsiedel; **164** www.arcaid.co.uk/Nigel Corrie/English Heritage; **166–167** Newby Hall; **171** Collections/Roger Scruton; **172–173** Getty Images/Richard Watson; **174–175** National Trust Images/David Noton (Newton House, Carmarthenshire); **176, 179, 181** National Trust Images/Andreas von Einsiedel; **182–183** National Trust Images/Stephen Robson; **184–185** John Parker; **186** Crown copyright (2012) Visit Wales; **189** National Trust Images/Arnhel de Serra; **190–191** Getty Images/VisitBritain/Britain on View (Eilean Donan Castle, Highland); **192** National Trust for Scotland; **195** www.arcaid.co.uk /Lucinda Lambton; **196** Country Life Picture Library/Simon Jauncey; **198–199** Getty Images/Michelle Kelley Photography; **201** Collections/Michael Jenner; **203** Collections/Dennis Barnes; **204–205** Getty Images/Craig Roberts; **206–207** Getty Images/VisitBritain/Rod Edwards; **208** Country Life Picture Library/Simon Jauncey; **210–211** Royal Botanic Garden Edinburgh; **214–215** Getty Images/Ben Cranke.

Every effort has been made to find and credit the copyright holders of images in this book. We will be pleased to rectify any errors or omissions in future editions. Email us at gbeditorial@readersdigest.co.uk

Contributors

Project Editor Jo Bourne
Art Editor Julie Bennett
Designers Martin Bennett and Sailesh Patel
Sub-editor Marion Paull
Cartographic Consultant Alison Ewington
Picture Editor Caroline Wood
Proofreader Barry Gage
Indexer Marie Lorimer
Maps Map Graphics Limited

Writer Rose Shepherd

FOR VIVAT DIRECT
Editorial Director Julian Browne
Art Director Anne-Marie Bulat
Managing Editor Nina Hathway
Trade Books Editor Penny Craig
Picture Resource Manager Eleanor Ashfield
Pre-press Account Manager Dean Russell
Product Production Manager Claudette Bramble
Production Controller Jan Bucil

Origination by FMG
Printing and binding Arvato Iberia, Portugal

Front cover Chatsworth, Derbyshire
Back cover Saltram, Devon

The Most Amazing Stately Homes in Britain is published
in 2012 in the United Kingdom by Vivat Direct Limited
(t/a Reader's Digest), 157 Edgware Road, London W2 2HR

The Most Amazing Stately Homes in Britain is owned
under licence from the Reader's Digest Association, Inc.
All rights reserved.

We are committed both to the quality of our products and
the service we provide to our customers. We value your
comments, so please do contact us on **0871 351 1000** or
via our website at **www.readersdigest.co.uk**

If you have any comments or suggestions about the content
of our books, email us at **gbeditorial@readersdigest.co.uk**

ISBN 978 1 78020 138 2
Book Code 400-610 UP0000-1